Managing Criminal Justice Organizations

Managing Criminal Justice Organizations

An Introduction to Theory and Practice

2nd Edition

Richard R.E. Kania
Richards P. Davis

Routledge
Taylor & Francis Group

LONDON AND NEW YORK

First published 2012 by Anderson Publishing

Published 2015 by Routledge
2 Park Square, Milton Park, Abingdon, Oxon OX14 4RN

and by Routledge
711 Third Avenue, New York, NY 10017, USA

Routlege is an imprint of the Taylor & Francis Group, an informa business

Acquiring Editor: Pam Chester
Development Editor: Ellen S. Boyne
Project Manager: Gretchen Otto
Designer: Joanne Blank

Notices
No responsibility is assumed by the publisher for any injury and/or damage to
persons or property as a matter of products liability, negligence or otherwise,
or from any use of operation of any methods, products, instructions or ideas
contained in the material herein.

Practitioners and researchers must always rely on their own experience and
knowledge in evaluating and using any information, methods, compounds, or
experiments described herein. In using such information or methods they should
be mindful of their own safety and the safety of others, including parties for
whom they have a professional responsibility.

Product or corporate names may be trademarks or registered trademarks, and
are used only for identification and explanation without intent to infringe.

Library of Congress Cataloging-in-Publication Data
Kania, Richard.
   Managing criminal justice organizations : An introduction to theory and practice / Richard R.E. Kania,
Richards P. Davis.
      p. cm.
   Rev. ed. of: Managing criminal justice organizations : An introduction to theory and practice / Richard R.E.
Kania. Newark, NJ : LexisNexis Matthew Bender, c2008.
   Includes index.
   1. Criminal justice, Administration of. I. Davis, Richards P. II. Title.
   HV7419.K36 2012
   364.068–dc23   2011027582

British Library Cataloguing-in-Publication Data
A catalogue record for this book is available from the British Library

ISBN 978-1-4377-3489-8 (pbk)

Printed and bound in the United States if America by Edwards Brothers Malloy on sustainably sourced paper

Dedication

This edition of our book became possible because of the support and encouragement extended to me by my faculty colleagues in Criminal Justice at Jacksonville State University, especially my co-author Richards P. Davis and contributor Randal L. Wood, and our department secretary Mrs. Sue Gardner. My thanks to Jauneth Skinner whose original art works do much to improve our book. I also wish to thank Michael C. Braswell for inviting me to submit the original manuscript to Anderson and to the Anderson, Lexis-Nexis, Michie, and Elsevier production teams for their help in bringing the current project to its conclusion.

RREK

I would like to thank Richard Kania for inviting me to contribute to this edition. I also appreciate the support of the faculty and staff of the Criminal Justice Department, especially Sue Gardner. Finally, I would like to thank my wife, Lea, and my kids, Drake, Jordan, Noah, and Tara for their patience and support.

RPD

Contents

About the Authors

Richard R. E. Kania

Richard R. E. Kania joined Jacksonville State University (JSU) of Alabama in December 2005 to be the department head of Criminal Justice. Prior to that, he had been at the University of North Carolina (UNC) at Pembroke since 1999, leading their Department of Sociology and Criminal Justice. From 1982 to 1999, he rose to full professor and headed the Department of Justice and Policy Studies at Guilford College in Greensboro, North Carolina. He also has taught at UNC–Charlotte and for the Southern Police Institute of the University of Louisville. Kania was a Senior Fulbright Professor for the Central European University in Warsaw, Poland, while on sabbatical in 1997–1998. In 2004–2005, he was awarded his second Fulbright Fellowship to teach at the Belarusian State University in Minsk, in the Republic of Belarus.

Kania originally majored in anthropology at Florida State University, where he earned his BA with Honors in 1968. He continued his studies of anthropology at the University of Virginia, earning an MA there in 1974, and wrote his MA thesis on conflict resolution and the law ways of the Hopi of Arizona. In between earning his BA and MA degrees, he served in the Army in Berlin and in Vietnam. He also was a city police officer in Virginia, and that experience led him to "change his major" midway through his doctoral studies and redirected him into a teaching career in criminal justice.

He has published extensively, with articles in more than 20 scholarly journals and a number of book chapters. He has authored one previous book, co-edited another, and has edited one journal special issue and several major government and research reports. His articles have been published in Poland, Belarus, Russia, and Romania. He is the recipient of several awards and grants and has held various offices in professional and public service organizations.

Kania has had managerial experience in the U.S. Army, working in operations, personnel, intelligence, contracting, facilities, and logistics assignments. He commanded an army engineer company in combat in Vietnam and served on the Army Staff in the Pentagon, rising to the rank of lieutenant colonel in the Army Reserve. His civilian managerial experience was as a criminal justice and public safety regional planner and as the academic department head for three colleges.

Richards P. Davis

Richards P. Davis is a Professor of Criminal Justice at Jacksonville State University and the Director of the Criminal Justice Graduate Studies program. He was hired by the JSU Department of Political Science and Public Administration in 2000, where he taught in the Master of Public Administration program as well as Political Science and Criminal Justice at the undergraduate level. He moved to the Department of Criminal Justice full time in 2002. Prior to Jacksonville State he was on the faculty of Dalton State College in Dalton, Georgia, where he taught numerous courses in Political Science and Criminal Justice from 1993 to 2000.

Davis received his BA degree, with honors, from the University of Georgia in 1989. He received an MA in 1992 and his PhD in 1995, both from the University of Alabama. He has authored several published works and has served as a textbook revision author. He has also made multiple professional conference presentations. He is designated as an International Crime Prevention Specialist by the International Society of Crime Prevention Practitioners and is a member of the advisory board for the United States Designing Out Crime Association. He also holds advanced certification in Crime Prevention Through Environmental Design (CPTED), and has worked with crime prevention practitioners and police officers from all over the United States and the United Kingdom in his crime-prevention activities.

1 :::

An Introduction to Criminal Justice Management

A textbook on criminal justice management should begin by answering some basic questions about what management is and why studying it is important. Often the words **administration, organization,** and **management** are used as if they were synonymous, and they certainly do have overlapping meanings. Other related key terms important in this discussion are **supervision, agency, functionaries (officers, officials, administrators, and agents)** and **bureaucracy**. This imprecision in our language will result in some disagreement and confusion about these terms that we and others are and should be using. Different authors have used them in different ways. So we will begin by discussing these concepts.

Management is the art of overseeing, controlling, and exercising authority over the workforce of an agency and the organizational activities needed to guide it to accomplish a purpose or function. The *management* of an organization is the leadership team of the organization, and is comprised of the chief executive, department or division heads, middle-level managers, and their support staffs. A *manager* is an official who has authority, managerial, and supervisory functions.

Administration is the art of attending to an organizational activity or function—being in charge of some aspects supporting the conduct and exercise of that function and of the individuals assigned to achieve it. The *administration* is the leadership team of the organization, comprised of administrators and their support staffs. An *administrator* is an official who has authority and administrative and supervisory functions.

Organization is the art of planning, arranging, and structuring human activities and agencies, and also the condition of being organized. An *organization* is a work group united for some purpose or function; it includes managers, administrators, first-line supervisors, support staff, and the functionaries of the organization. **Functionaries** are the **administrators; officials** and **officers** are those who do the actual work of the agency. The term **agent** also is used to refer to those who are engaged by the organization to support its work; it includes those under contract to do tasks for the organization as well as employees of the organization. *Organizing* is the task of applying systematic structure and order to a human enterprise such as a governmental bureaucracy. Dean Champion has introduced the concept of "**units of analysis**" to the discussion of organizations (2003, pp. 10–14), by which he means the individuals of an agency, the small

1

BOX 1.1 A ROSE BY ANY OTHER NAME? MANAGEMENT OR ADMINISTRATION

In general, courses and textbooks in business curricula prefer the term *management* (Drucker, 1954, 1980, 1985, 1990; Fiedler & Chemers, 1974; Hersey & Blanchard, 1982; Massie, 1987; Roethlisberger, 1941; Roethlisberger & Dixon, 1939; Sisk & Williams, 1981; Taylor, 1911), while courses and textbooks in government and political science have preferred *administration,* as in "public administration" (Berkley, 1981; Mosher, 1975; Nigro & Nigro, 1973; Stahl, 1971). Many authors in criminal justice follow the preference for the term *public administration* (Carlson & Garrett, 1999; Champion, 2003; Peak, 2006; Phillips & Roberts, 2000; Souryal, 1995; Swanson & Territo, 1983; Wilson & McLaren, 1977). Exceptions abound though, as many criminal justice authors prefer the term *management* (Buchholz, 1990; Chase & Reveal, 1983; Cohn & Ward, Forsyth, 2004; 1980; Greene, 1982; Lynch, 1986; Lynch & Lynch, 2005; McDonald, 2002; Roberg, Kuykendall, & Novak, 2002; Thibault, Lynch, & McBride, 2001; U.S. Bureau of Prisons, 1973; Whisenand, 1981; Whisenand & Ferguson, 1978) and some criminal justice authors use both terms comfortably (Allen & Sawhney, 2010; Klofas, Stojkovic, & Kalinich, 1990). There are no hard-and-fast rules to settle this nomenclature question.

---

interpersonal work groups (the **teams**), and the formal organization as a whole (the **agency**).

A **bureaucracy** is a specific type of organization managed by officials selected and appointed on the basis of their objective preparation, talents, and merits. A **bureaucrat** is an official or functionary within such a bureaucracy.

Because *management* is the term more commonly associated with business, it carries additional connotations of greater initiative, more innovation, and more entrepreneurial efforts. *Administration,* the term in greater favor among political scientists, carries with it an implication of subservience to political institutions, the legislature, courts, and the elected chief executive transferring initiative and innovation to those branches of government and leaving administration to carry out the policies those three branches establish. As we will discover in Chapter 3, there is room for innovation, entrepreneurship, and initiative within the senior levels of the bureaucracy. It is for this reason that we prefer to focus on management. Yet it should be clear that the differences of administration and management are subtle and reflect the approach of the author choosing to write about them.

Dean Champion (2003) writes:

For our purposes, the administration of justice, or justice administration, is the description and elaboration of the structural, functional, and managerial processes involved in the coordination of activities related to determining the incidence of criminal conduct, the detection and apprehension of alleged criminals, an assessment of the credibility of evidence against the accused, a formal judgment about that conduct, and how that conduct is punished. (p. 5)

While all that is true, the main focus of this book is the *managing* of criminal justice organizations. What we will study has less to do with the traditional approaches to the study of criminal justice, crime, or criminological theory than it does with business administration or public administration, but this management aspect is critical to understanding the proper running (both managing and administering) of criminal justice agencies in their efforts to reduce and ameliorate crime. As Kenneth Peak (2006) uses and explains it, the concept of "administration" includes both management and supervision. His view is that it also involves the processes whereby workers are organized to achieve organizational objectives. Peak sees management as part of administration. In this book, we will reverse that. Peak and several others place administrators at the top of the organizational hierarchy, managers in the middle, and supervisors at the working level. It might be just as well to place managers on top, administrators next, and agree that first-line supervisors rank third in the administration–management team of an organization.

We do agree that all are involved in the organization of the workforce, and we also agree that there are basic, sound principles of organization in play that effective supervisors, administrators, and managers will use in the running of their agencies. So this book is about criminal justice *organization, administration,* and *management,* viewed from the perspective of a criminal justice *manager.* Managers use principles of administrative science to manage. Like Peak, we include within management the concept of *supervision,* even though it might be better seen as an aspect of leadership, to be discussed in Chapter 4, which is devoted to that topic.

As this discussion has suggested, the study of administration, organization, and management is complicated by popular misunderstandings of the key terms. It is not uncommon to find even bright, well-informed students who confuse management with administration and mix both with organization. It is easy to limit the conceptualization of *organization* to only its "corporate-entity" meaning, a synonym for *agency* (e.g., *the* organization, as in the FBI), thereby ignoring its process meaning (e.g., organization), that is, the process of arranging and structuring cooperative human effort. Indeed, there are scholars who use these words with such indiscrimination that the distinctions are blurred. The study of *organization* is not the study of *organizations,* but the science of how organizations are best organized, that is, structured and arranged. Champion (2003) tells us what a criminal justice organization is: "Any criminal justice organization is a predetermined arrangement of persons whose interrelated tasks and specialties enable the total aggregate to achieve goals" (p. 7). He also warns us that the agencies have diverse goals, implicitly, and sometimes conflicting goals (p. 6). Part of the task of the manager is sorting all of this out.

Management, as to be used in this book, is not just the study of the management teams of organizations, but is also the study of the art of managing, including both skills in organization and in administration. **Administration** here is more than just the administrative personnel component of the agency; it is the science and art of the administrative process by which the agency is operated.

BOX 1.2 FIVE FRIENDS, FIVE MANAGERS

So who, then, is a criminal justice manager? Let me introduce you to five young criminal justice managers who recently came together for their 10th anniversary class reunion. Each had majored in criminal justice at the university, and each has followed a different path in his or her career. Each is working in a different city, and they have not seen much of each other over the past decade. Over dinner, they recount their careers for each other and for you. Each has enjoyed the "fast track" in his or her career, and each is now a criminal justice manager. None is yet the chief executive officer of their agency, but each of them has the ambition to be.

Paul was a fair athlete, playing in both team and individual sports at the university. He was hired by the police department in Vollmer City right after graduation, stayed in uniform, and recently was promoted to lieutenant in the patrol division. He still plays golf and tennis when he can find the time. His department sent him to the FBI National Academy in Quantico, Virginia, last year.

Carol Anne always had a talent for writing and was also quite sophisticated in the use of computers. She was hired as a deputy clerk of court after taking some additional paralegal courses and is now the chief clerk of the lower, misdemeanor court for Vanderbilt County. She also is writing a novel based on some of the interesting and unusual cases that have passed through her court.

Jerry minored in psychology and went into juvenile justice. After working as an intake counselor for the juvenile court and completing a master's degree in counseling, he now runs one of the residential juvenile shelters for delinquent youths in his city. He was in a rock band while at the university and sponsors a similar group of amateur musicians among the teens assigned to his juvenile home. He feels that encouraging their musical talents will help them turn their lives around, give them career options, and enhance their social skills, and he observes that their playing entertains the other young men in their residence.

Cory went into federal corrections after graduation, leaving the state to work in a federal correctional unit. He completed an MPA part-time, online while working for the "feds." He moved back home 4 years ago to take a supervisory position in the state correctional system, where he now is the deputy warden of a medium-security custodial unit, the Alexander Maconochie Correctional Center. He had enjoyed gourmet cooking while at the university and worked in an upscale restaurant while a student, but an assignment placing him in charge of the prison kitchen at the federal correctional institution spoiled his love for cooking for several years. He reports rediscovering the fun of gourmet cooking only recently, now that running a kitchen is not a major part of his state job.

Diane went to law school right after graduation, passed the bar, took a position as an assistant district attorney, and now is the chief deputy DA in charge of a team of junior deputy DAs dealing with high-priority and career-criminal felony prosecutions for her district. She was politically active at the university, held office in student government, and admits to her dream of becoming the district attorney some years from now when her current boss retires.

As they compare notes about their careers, families, and life experiences to date, they find that each of their positions involves them in many of the same responsibilities: leading, organizing, making decisions, evaluating individual subordinates and entire work teams, taking part in staffing actions, training subordinates, allocating resources, and reporting on their and their units' activities. They remember a criminal justice management class at the university where they learned Luther Gulick's (1937) "POSDCORB," the mnemonic acronym standing for planning, organizing, staffing, directing, coordinating, reporting, and budgeting, and they discuss how it applies to their work as middle managers now.

They also see some aspects of their work that POSDCORB does not fit quite as well. For example, while each is involved in budgeting to some degree, their duties involve other allocation functions related to agency budgets but not directly involving financial transactions. Paul explains that he must assign police patrol officers to various duties, making sure each is provided the equipment necessary to do their jobs. Jerry agrees, noting that running a juvenile detention facility involves all manner of decisions and resource allocation duties indirectly bearing on agency finances and budgets. Cory observes that it is much the same in his correctional unit, especially so when he was managing the federal prison kitchen. Moreover, each is involved in agencies that operate "24/7" (24 hours a day, 7 days a week), so that time also is a major factor in their resource allocation decisions.

All five agree that Gulick's formulation did not really cover training, but that too is a major responsibility for each of them. Diane points out that each new junior assistant DA knows sufficient law right out of law school, but most do not have enough experience with practical procedures to prepare and present a case in court. She explains that she pairs a newly hired assistant with a more experienced litigator. Paul says that's much like the FTOs (field training officers) his police department assigns, and Carol Anne joins their chorus. All agree that they are held responsible for any training shortcoming of their subordinates, and they must be attentive to their training needs.

Each of them has seen his or her job change. Initially each of them was "doing" criminal justice, but now each of them manages others who are doing criminal justice. Each now has an executive position in his or her agency, and each hopes someday to become the chief executive of that or a similar agency. Each one is a manager.

Rethinking Luther Gulick's POSDCORB

In 1937 Luther Gulick's contribution to management science, **POSDCORB,** first appeared to help us reflect on the questions he asked: "What is the work of a chief executive? What does he do?" His answer was the mnemonic acronym POSDCORB, the abbreviation for planning, organizing, staffing, directing, coordinating, reporting, and budgeting.

The mnemonic acronym POSDCORB and what it stands for has become common in managerial terminology. Most public administration and management principles texts make at least a passing reference to it. Many textbooks and managerial guides have been written with chapters to correspond to the content, if not also the precise order of planning, organizing, staffing, directing, coordinating, reporting, and budgeting. Many more cover these same topics in slightly different words, as they attempt to answer the questions posed by Luther Gulick.

These questions remain before us today as we study the role of the criminal justice manager anew, not unanswered, but ever in need of refinements to address the changes in the public service workplace. In the 1937 article in which he answers his

BOX 1.3 LUTHER HALSEY GULICK—A PIONEER OF PUBLIC ADMINISTRATION

Luther Halsey Gulick (1892–1992) was and is a major figure in the development of the study of public administration in the United States. Gulick was an American author and early expert on public administration. He earned his doctorate at Columbia University in 1920 and upon completion of his studies, he joined the New York Bureau of Municipal Research (renamed in 1921 as the Institute of Public Administration). He taught at Columbia for several years and then returned to the Institute of Public Administration to be its director. He was a prolific author. He wrote ***The Metropolitan Problem and American Ideas*** (1966) soon after he retired, but his most famous contribution to managerial sciences was the 1937 article that contributed the term "POSDCORB" to the managerial vocabulary (Fitch, 1996). Both his grandfather, a missionary (1828–1891), and an uncle (1865–1918), a famous physician and physical fitness advocate, bear the same name, as does his son, L. H. Gulick, Jr.

FIGURE 1.1 Luther Halsey Gulick. *Portrait by Jauneth Skinner ©2011. All rights reserved to the artist.*

own questions with POSDCORB, Gulick was writing for his own times. This mnemonic device has been with us ever since, but the times and environment of the public service workplace have changed greatly. We ought to take the time to reflect upon what his ideas have brought to management in the past six decades, and even question whether the same answer would be given today. POSDCORB is used less frequently today, and other answers are now being given to Gulick's questions.

Do almost three-quarters of a century of subsequent management experience confirm his answer to his own questions? Certainly, to some extent we can answer "yes," but some consideration of contemporary public administration and commercial management writings suggests that his topics have not fared quite as well as one might initially suppose. The seven-item list has not proven to be exhaustive, as the contemporary emphasis on evaluation shows.

In Gulick's day, the more authoritarian, scientific management–based Theory X managerial style was in vogue but was not yet spoken of as such. Although Gulick was aware of the early human relations studies, his was an approach to management solidly based in the scientific management principles advocated by the likes of Frederick Taylor (1911/1967). Today, a modified Theory Y systems approach is the recommended managerial style in most managerial texts and guidebooks. Theory X presupposes that a worker naturally will avoid work and needs to be closely supervised. Theory Y presupposes that a worker has the capacity to be self-motivated. Thus, the "directing" function Gulick championed has been overtaken by events and the trend toward more democratic management. Theory X and Theory Y approaches to managerial leadership will be explained in more detail in Chapter 4.

We are also aware that the order used by Gulick, placing budgeting as the final item, as if an afterthought, ought to be improved upon. Experience has shown that budgeting should not be viewed as a separate activity following the others, but should be an integral part of resource allocation, planning, and decision-making. As a key managerial task, it should come up early and often in the astute manager's actions.

LODESTAR versus POSDCORB

Indeed, were Gulick to address his questions to us today, we would not reply with his POSDCORB, but with LODESTAR. LODESTAR stands for leading, organizing, deciding, evaluating, staffing, training, allocating, and reporting. Not only is the acronym easier to say and recall, it also fits the current social and organizational climate better. Its metaphorical value is also worthy of note. The job of the ideal, more democratic manager today is not "directing," so much as serving as a guide to the organization, to point the way, just as the "Lodestar" or "North Star" served as the guide to ancient mariners and travelers. In this book, it is the source of the organization and sequencing of the chapters that follow.

LODESTAR, as a new mnemonic acronym and a metaphor for the task of the manager, represents eight managerial functions, some of which Gulick considered, others that are related to his suggestions, and a few new ones that more recent experiences suggest. Even those that are taken from Gulick's original thoughts are recast somewhat to stress the different perspectives and priorities of the present day.

Leading This has to come first among the managerial functions. Although the concept is similar to Gulick's fourth and fifth terms, directing and coordinating, we now can argue that it should take clear precedence over Gulick's priorities of planning, organizing, and staffing. The volume of literature on this topic is an impressive testimonial to this belief. Leadership is the intangible attribute that sets the successful manager apart from his or her also-ran competitors. In recent years, we have discovered that it is not the particular style of leadership that is the critical factor, but the attribute itself that makes one person a leader and leaves others behind as mere supervisors or officeholders (Feldman & Khademian, 2001: 339, 341–342). An impressive list of top management scholars have examined leadership. Gulick himself does precisely that in his 1937 essay. Mary Parker Follett (1926; Graham, 1995), Chester Barnard (1938), Peter F. Drucker (1964, 1967), Douglas McGregor (1960), Theodore Caplow (1983), Fred Fiedler and Martin Chemers (1974), and Warren Bennis (1966, 1973) are among the many who have stood out in offering answers to the question, "What are the best ways to lead an organization?" What is troubling is the discovery that the answers are not always in agreement.

Organizing No fault can be placed on the emphasis that Gulick gave to sound organizational skills. However, had this article been written in the heyday of Theory Y (human relations) management, its placement might have fallen farther back. The excesses of the human needs emphasis at the expense of efficiency and occasionally even organizational objectives have been set right, but only recently. We again see the wisdom of organizing the workplace intelligently. From human relations, we have learned that such organization must consider human factors and not be the cold, impersonal human engineering originally implied by the founding father of American scientific management, Frederick Taylor (1911/1967). We have been warned by James March and Herbert Simon (1958) that some of the basic principles of organization operate in opposition to one another. This represents a further challenge to the astute manager, for the axioms of organization are sound and need to be applied, as in Gulick's day, with the temperance of leadership.

Deciding This is not the "D" of Gulick's POSDCORB. His "D" stood for "directing." The modern criminal justice manager is not the authoritarian director that once was the norm. The workplace does not operate as it did in 1937. Managers must be more constrained in making their decisions. The ideal criminal justice manager must be deliberative, combining coordinating, planning, budgeting, and decision-making into a single synthetic process. Here we will just call it all "deciding" or "decision-making," but we must recognize that much more is involved. What we seek to describe is not a unilateral process in the contemporary workplace. The Theory Y advocates have made a sound case for group input, MBO (management by objectives), the Delphi Method, rapping, workshops, task forces, and other group-input activities rather than unilateral managerial decision-making. The modern criminal justice manager "directs" at one's own risk. One rarely even "decides" anything without significant input from coworkers, support staff, and subordinates, especially the planners and budgetary analysts on a work team. Collectively, they come to answers via a deliberative process. The wise manager is one who knows when and how to assemble the judgments of others; to weigh the suggestions and opinions of subordinates, peers, and superiors; to factor in budgetary considerations; and to plan ahead, developing tactics and grand strategies within the organizational system. In short, the modern manager uses the processes of deliberation before coming to the work team's decision.

Evaluating Once people have been organized, they have to be converted into an effective team to get the agency's mission accomplished. The criminal justice manager who can put one's people to work on a good idea and can convert it into a successful project remains as rare today as in Gulick's time. This was what he meant by including "coordinating" in POSDCORB, but there is much more to it than just coordinating. With so much of criminal justice work done out of sight of the manager, the modern criminal justice executive needs to develop the means to see how the work is going, who is effective, and who is having problems. This is the role of evaluation, both of individuals and of the entire work team. Having a positive effect on an organization requires the leadership and organizational skills already cited, but evaluation is needed to see that the desired effect is being achieved.

There has been a great deal written in recent years about evaluation. Evaluation conveys the meaning of attaching a value to something and should be viewed as a positive aspect of management. However, evaluation has taken on a somewhat negative connotation in the context of the personnel evaluation, the periodic review that often is associated with unfavorable personnel actions. Evaluation should be understood to contain the concept of "appraising," which retains some of the positive tone of its root, "praising." The modern criminal justice manager has to know how to evaluate and appraise in an upbeat manner. The evaluative responsibility cannot be ignored, but even negative evaluations can be given in a positive, rewarding manner. Even when they contain negative assessments and call for correction of present behavior or performance, appraisals can be positive instructional tools. The effective appraisal should be given in the "I'm OK, you're OK" approach that Thomas Harris (1967) advocated in his book of the same name. The manager needs to present himself or herself as being helpful and advisory, and the evaluation itself needs to be positive in tone, even when identifying areas of weakness where improvement is needed. The evaluated worker should emerge from the appraisal process with his or her sense of self-worth still intact, aware that specific improvements are needed and guided in how to make these improvements.

The modern manager must develop the evaluative techniques that permit him or her to criticize the defects of the work without undermining the self-confidence of the individual or group undertaking the work. Once the flaws, failures, and malfunctions of the organization are recognized, then there must be planned change. Thus, out of the evaluation function will arise organizational development efforts, as the manager seeks to implement a deliberate change strategy to improve organization effectiveness.

Staffing As one of Gulick's original seven concepts, staffing has remained as important as ever, and may even be more important in this era of affirmative action, equal opportunity, equality of and for women, comparable pay for comparable work, veterans' preference, and so on. When Gulick wrote of staffing, he was thinking of it in the original, limited sense of matching the right person to the right job, arranging for the perfect fit of a prospective employee's skills to job requirements. This is no longer adequate today; staffing involves far more that that. Especially in the public service sector, the manager has been obliged to accept social responsibilities toward the whole community and cannot consider only what will be best for the organization. Programs initiated in the 1970s, such as CETA (Comprehensive Employment and Training Act) and the Job Corps, have given rise to demands that the contemporary manager actively seek employees who do not conform to the ideal type of employment prospect. Also gone are the artificial restrictions that closed the doors to the employment and assignment of women and minorities to responsible positions within organizations. The manager can do, in these areas, what no manager could do in Gulick's day: place a qualified woman or minority member in a key staff position. The available talent pool has more than doubled by the lifting of these old, restrictive social encumbrances.

Training The greater the demands of the modern workplace, the less likely it will be that the manager will find new staff fully qualified to assume the responsibilities of the workplace at the time they are hired. In-service training programs are more of a management responsibility and concern than they were in the early days of scientific management, when Frederick Taylor (1911/1967) spoke of training the workman in the unique requirement of a particular workplace. Increasing levels of education as a precondition to entry into public service careers have not been enough to overcome the demands of the new, high-tech public service workplace. Moreover, training is not simply an entry-level activity in public service careers. Mid-level and executive-level training programs are part of the contemporary career pathways a public service manager must follow for one's self and for one's subordinates.

Allocating Assigning people to tasks and budgeting funds, time, and resources to support those tasks are part of the allocation functions of the public service manager. Gulick's "budgeting" is expanded, because more than funds are allocated by a manager. Time, space, facilities, labor, resources, and funds are all involved in the allocation processes. Implementation planning or "action planning" as advocated in MBO manuals is important to this allocation process. Such methods as PERT (program, evaluation, and review technique) and critical path network analysis come into play as the modern manager integrates these resources into the work product.

Reporting Reporting is one of the original seven responsibilities carried over from POSDCORB. But like some of the other answers retained from Gulick's original response to his own questions, this one has been modified and expanded. Reporting now involves far superior data storage and transmission means. There was no photocopier, computer, microfiche file, word processor, or any of the other superior aids to reporting that we now have available to us. CompStat and other computer-aided tools have improved upon reporting functions (Kania, 2004; Magers, 2004; Walsh & Vito, 2004).

Written reports and records are only a small part of the communications process. There is far more to reporting than what Gulick understood in his day. We often are told that this is the age of communication, the era of the Internet and the World Wide Web. Thus, we must see that reporting is an aspect of both communicating and of public accountability. The manager who can communicate effectively both within the organization and between the organization and the general public will be more likely to succeed than the less effective communicator, even if one's work quality is no better.

Reporting also involves the whole range of public relations activities, conveying one's message to the general public. The anguish some government officials and political figures have felt in giving news interviews is a self-fulfilling prophecy. By showing their discomfort, they convey the negative messages they seek to avoid. Those who have mastered communication skills are able to promote their organizations and themselves. Think of the success of Ronald Reagan's "Teflon coating" or the "aw shucks" appeal of Bill Clinton when they made and admitted mistakes, and the inability of negative press and opposing party smears to stick and hurt their popular appeal. Why did such attacks cripple the presidencies of Lyndon Johnson and Richard Nixon and yet leave Reagan and Clinton unmarred? Reagan and Clinton certainly were superior presidential communicators, always able to convey their points of view, even in the face of criticism.

Reporting is also the essence of accountability, another key concept and responsibility in the work of the public service manager. How should the political elites, who control the scarce resources a public service manager will use, function if their subordinate managers are ineffective in passing along their requirements? How is the public to know if a public service organization is successful if the management withholds that news or is evasive in keeping the public informed of its activities?

Managing in the public sector differs in numerous ways from managing private, commercial organizations. While the two have much in common, there are distinctions that you should know (see Box 1.4).

The LODESTAR functions need to be collectively used within the general concepts of American public service. These are the abstract values that our criminal justice agencies were created to serve. They are the ***principles of public management*** that should guide the criminal justice manager in the conduct of his or her duties and responsibilities (see Box 1.5). They underlie the ethics of criminal justice professions.

As others have before him, Kenneth Peak makes a good point that the criminal justice system is more of a "nonsystem" than a system because of its internal divisions that often are in competition with one another (Peak, 2006): police try to convict criminals; the courts try to acquit some while agreeing to send some to corrections facilities; and the corrections system tries to process out its referrals. The bureaucratic ideal of uniform and consistent treatment is defeated by both intentional and unintentional biases in the system. Alternatives to the formal process are actually institutionalized, again in violation of bureaucratic simplicity. Some suspects are tried; others are diverted out of the system. Some convicted people are probated; others are incarcerated. Some incarcerated people are paroled; others are held for the full term. On top of it all, the system is horribly backlogged and understaffed. So it is not the efficient "system" that it aspires to be (see Box 1.6).

The system operates under competing and conflicting mandates. Herbert Packer (1968) once explained this tension as the competition of the *due process* and *crime control* models (p. 153). There are widely differing perspectives governing policy, ranging

---

BOX 1.4 PUBLIC versus PRIVATE MANAGEMENT

1. Criminal justice agencies must act for the "public good." But that is ill-defined. They must deal with a broad-based clientele (the community at large), and not customers and investors whose interests are more specific and much more limited.
2. Criminal justice managers have a responsibility to guard public funds and resources. They are restricted by state regulations and requirements like "low bid" contract requirements, which private-sector managers do not need to contend with.
3. Public employees are not typically "at will" employees. They have civil service protections that do not apply in private-sector employment. This makes discipline a much more formal process for criminal justice managers.
4. Criminal justice managers must take into account that most rewards for public servants are more intrinsic, as stated in the text. Public managers have far less control over things such as pay and benefits and therefore must be more creative in how they motivate employees.
5. Politics and political influence are a daily part of criminal justice management.
6. While both may be providing the public with services, often the services provided by the public agencies are not those actually sought out or wanted by all of their clientele. After all, who among us actually wants a parking ticket or speeding citation?
7. Measuring performance is often difficult. This is true for agencies and individual employees. There is no "profit" or other bottom-line measurement in public service by which to measure success.

BOX 1.5 PRINCIPLES OF PUBLIC MANAGEMENT

1. In the "Jeffersonian Ideal," a manager is a "public servant" who works for the people as a whole; as such, a manager in criminal justice serves, rather than rules, the people.
2. Managers in criminal justice are selected to represent the people collectively, rather than to satisfy individual, private interests.
3. Criminal justice managers must balance competing mandates: for abstract justice, due process of law, professionalism, competence, fairness, equality, consistency, and crime control.
4. Managers in the public service seek to make their agencies productive, efficient, and effective within the lawful limits of their constitutional authority.
5. The actual tasks of management and labor (the routine administration of a criminal justice agency) are substantially different. Criminal justice managers make agency policy and oversee its implementation. Public administration implements and administers the policies of criminal justice management.
6. In a democratic society, senior criminal justice policymakers are held accountable to the public, usually through the elective process, and therefore they should either be elected or politically appointed by elected officials.
7. Political loyalty should be one of the essential criteria for selecting people for senior management positions (the policymakers) in criminal justice.
8. Objective merit should be the essential criterion for selecting people for appointive criminal justice middle-level management positions.

BOX 1.6 THE KEY ASPECTS OF PROFESSIONALISM

Dean Champion (2003), drawing upon the ideas of Max Weber, identified five aspects of professionalism:

1. a defined body of knowledge,
2. a code of ethics,
3. ongoing education,
4. uniform standards in selection, education, training and performance, and
5. a service or career orientation.

---

from consensus views to conflict views. Due process is not very efficient and requires that wrongdoers whom we cannot prove are guilty beyond a reasonable doubt must go free. Paying some people to convict offenders and others to help them beat conviction (public defenders and appointed counsel) seems internally conflicted, and certainly does not suggest efficiency. Yet criminal justice managers (or administrators) are expected to make intelligent public policy amid all of these conflicting expectations, values, and standards.

Private versus Public Management

By choosing management over administration as the preferred focus of this book, it is important to recognize that there are differences in the managerial principles of private, commercial management. Peak makes the point that the "rewards" of work in the private sector are mostly extrinsic (external), and further, mostly are material. For employees of the public service sector, the "rewards" are more intrinsic and internal. People entering public service careers are told, "you'll never get rich in public service," and my own life experiences confirm that. Yet a public service career can be very rewarding in the satisfaction that doing a good job can provide. Criminal justice practitioners and managers make this a better world by making it safer for us all, and by identifying and punishing the guilty and helping the weak, victimized, and injured.

Just what constitutes doing a good job is hard to determine, however. In the commercial private sector, it is measured by the financial bottom line, income, sales, profits, and so on. There are no comparable measures available to those in the public service sector. Moreover, it is important to note that people in public service also seek material rewards for their efforts, just as people in commercial private enterprise also enjoy intrinsic rewards. A task of the supervisor, administrator, and manager in public service is facilitating the receipt of these intrinsic rewards.

Characteristics of individuals include personal demographic features (sex, age, race, nationality, education, experience, marital status, etc.) as well as less precise evaluations of motivations, talents, and "professionalism."

The **agency** is the formal structure of the work group and often is too large to be an interpersonal association. The chief of police of a major city, the DA of a large urban prosecutorial office, the chief judge in a big city, the warden of a large state prison, and other leaders of large units do not know and do not interact at a personal level with their subordinates. In many cases, they will not even know all of their employees' names or jobs. Indeed, it was this attribute of the large organization that gave rise to the principles of administration, organization, and management that will be taught with this text.

One of the points to stress is the role of policy-making in the work of criminal justice management (Champion, 2003 pp. 16–17). Much of criminal justice policy is made by the legislature, but laws often are vague or provide only general guidelines. Executives in police, court, and corrections agencies apply those guidelines in practical ways. They are making secondary policy, that is, "implementation policy." They also advise and counsel legislators on what policies to make. At that point they are involved in formulating primary policy.

Summary

When Luther Gulick asked "What is the work of a chief executive? What does he do?" and answered his own question with POSDCORB, he expressed the classical views of the role of the manager in the public sector, thinking derived from the scientific management school. The past half century has shown us some of the inadequacies of this approach to management and has given rise to newer perspectives. LODESTAR is just one possible expression of these newer ideas. It is not a radical departure from the wisdom of Gulick, but a statement of the gradual refinement, adaptation, and evolution of those ideas through decades of public management. It places more emphasis on the "people" aspects of management (e.g., their selection, training, and appraisals), reflecting the human relations emphasis that arose in management theory at about the time POSDCORB was being proposed. It is time to retire POSDCORB to the role of a historical footnote, perhaps to be replaced by LODESTAR, or some other mnemonic device that better sums up the views of this time in the history of ideas.

LEARNING OBJECTIVES

Upon finishing this chapter, you should be able to do the following:

1. Discuss the meanings of the key terms "management," "administration," and "organization" as used in criminal justice.
2. Distinguish between each of these term-pairs:
   - administration versus the administration
   - management versus the management
   - organization versus the organization
3. Identify the eight principles of public management, and explain the values each of these principles reflects.
4. Contrast public versus private management.
5. Explain how both LODESTAR and POSDCORB answer Luther Gulick's question, "What is the work of the chief executive?"

IMPORTANT TERMS AND NAMES

- *agent*
- *agency*
- *administration*
- *administrator*
- *bureaucracy*
- *bureaucrat*
- *functionaries*
- *LODESTAR*
- *management*
- *officer*
- *official*
- *POSDCORB*
- *professionalism*
- *team*

References and Supplemental Sources

Allen, J. M., & Sawhney, R. (2010). *Administration and management in criminal justice: A service quality approach*. Thousand Oaks, CA: Sage.

Barnard, C. (1938/[1968]). *The functions of the executive*. Cambridge, MA: Harvard University Press.

Bennis, W. (1966). *Changing organizations*. New York: McGraw-Hill.

Bennis, W. (1973). *Beyond bureaucracy*. New York: McGraw-Hill.

Berkley, G. E. (1981). *The craft of public administration* (3rd ed.). Boston: Allyn & Bacon.

Buchholz, R. A. (1990). *Essentials of public policy for management* (2nd ed.). Englewood Cliffs, NJ: Prentice Hall.

Caplow, T. (1983). *Managing an organization* (2nd ed.). New York: Holt, Rinehart and Winston.

Carlson, P. M., & Garrett, J. S. (1999). *Prison and jail administration*. Gaithersburg, MD: Aspen.

Champion, D. J. (2003). *Administration of criminal justice*. Upper Saddle River, NJ: Prentice Hall.

Chase, G., & Reveal, E. C. (1983). *How to manage in the public sector*. Reading, MA: Addison-Wesley.

Cohn, A. W., & Ward, B. (1980). *Improving management in criminal justice*. Beverly Hills, CA: Sage.

Drucker, P. F. (1954/[1984]). *The practice of management*. New York: HarperCollins, HarperBusiness.

Drucker, P. F. (1964/[1993]). *Managing for results*. New York: HarperCollins, HarperBusiness.

Drucker, P. F. (1967). *The effective executive*. New York: Harper & Row.

Drucker, P. F. (1980). *Managing in turbulent times*. New York: Harper & Row.

Drucker, P. F. (1985). *Management: Tasks, responsibilities, practices, abridged and revised edition*. New York: Harper Colophon.

Drucker, P. F. (1990). *Managing the non-profit organization*. New York: HarperCollins, HarperBusiness.

Feldman, M. S., & Khademian, A. M. (2001). Principles for public management practice: From dichotomies to interdependence. *Governance, 14*(3), 339–361.

Fiedler, F. E., & Chemers, M. M. (1974). *Leadership and effective management*. Glenview, IL: Scott, Foresman.

Fitch, L. C. (1996). *Making democracy work: The life and letters of Luther Gulick, 1892-1993*. Berkeley, CA: University of California Press.

Follett, M. P. (1926). *Scientific foundations of business administration*. Baltimore: Williams & Wilkins.

Forsyth, R. (2004). M-A-N-A-G-E-M-E-N-T defined—Subordinates' expectations. *FBI Law Enforcement Bulletin, 73*(3), 23–27.

Graham, P. (Ed.). (1995). *Mary Parker Follett: Prophet of management*. Cambridge, MA: Harvard Business School Press.

Greene, J. R. (1982). *Managing police work: Issues and analysis*. Beverly Hills, CA: Sage.

Gulick, L. H. (1937). Notes on the theory of organization. In Gulick, L., & Urwich, L. (Eds.), *Papers on the science of administration*. New York: Institute of Public Administration.

Gulick, L. H. (1966). *The metropolitan problem and American ideas*. New York: Knopf.

Harris, T. A. (1967). *I'm OK, You're OK: A practical guide to transactional analysis*. New York: Harper & Row.

Hersey, P., & Blanchard, K. (1982). *Management of organization behavior: Utilizing human resources* (4th ed.). Englewood Cliffs, NJ: Prentice Hall.

Kania, R. R. E. (2004). A brief history of a venerable paradigm in policing. *Journal of Contemporary Criminal Justice, 20*(1), 80–83.

Klofas, J., Stojkovic, S., & Kalinich, D. (1990). *Criminal justice organizations: Administration and management*. Pacific Grove, CA: Brooks/Cole.

Lynch, R. G. (1986). *The police manager: Professional leadership skills* (3rd ed.). New York: Random House.

Lynch, R. G., & Lynch, S. (2005). *The police manager* (6th ed.). Newark, NJ: LexisNexis Matthew Bender.

Magers, J. S. (2004). CompStat: A new paradigm for policing or a repudiation of community policing. *Journal of Contemporary Criminal Justice, 20*(1), 70–79.

March, J. G., & Simon, H. A. (1958). *Organizations*. New York: Wiley.

Massie, J. L. (1987). *Essentials of management* (4th ed.). Englewood Cliffs, NJ: Prentice Hall.

McDonald, P. P. (2002). *Managing police operations: Implementing the New York Control Model—CompStat*. Belmont, CA: Wadsworth.

McGregor, D. (1960). *The human side of enterprise*. New York: McGraw-Hill.

Mosher, F. C. (Ed.). (1975). *American public administration: Past, present, future*. Tuscaloosa: University of Alabama Press.

Nigro, F. A., & Nigro, L. G. (1973). *Modern public administration* (3rd ed.). New York: Harper & Row.

Packer, H. (1968). *The limits of the criminal sanction*. Stanford, Ca.: Stanford University Press.

Peak, K. J. (2006). *Justice administration: Police, courts, and corrections management* (5th ed.). Upper Saddle River, NJ: Pearson/Prentice Hall.

Phillips, R. L., & Roberts, J. W. (2000). *A quick reference to correctional administration*. Gaithersburg, MD: Aspen.

Roberg, R. R., Kuykendall, J., & Novak, K. (2002). *Police management* (3rd ed.). Los Angeles: Roxbury.

Roethlisberger, F. J. (1941). *Management and morale*. Cambridge, MA: Harvard University Press.

Roethlisberger, F. J., & Dixon, W. J. (1939). *Management and the worker*. Cambridge, MA: Harvard University Press.

Sisk, H. L., & Williams, J. C. (1981). *Management and organization* (4th ed.). Cincinnati: South-Western.

Souryal, S. S. (1995). *Police organization and administration* (2nd ed.). Cincinnati: Anderson.

Stahl, O. G. (1971). *Public personnel administration* (6th ed.). New York: Harper & Row.

Swanson, C. R., & Territo, L. (1983). *Police administration.* New York: Macmillan.

Taylor, F. W. (1911/1967). *The principles of scientific management.* New York: Norton Library, Harper & Row.

Thibault, E. A., Lynch, L. M., & McBride, R. B. (2001). *Proactive police management* (5th ed.). Upper Saddle River, NJ: Prentice Hall.

U.S. Bureau of Prisons, *Jail management: Administration of jail operations.* Washington, DC: Government Printing Office.

Walsh, W. F., & Vito, G. F. (2004). The meaning of CompStat: Analysis and response. *Journal of Contemporary Criminal Justice, 20*(1), 51–69.

Whisenand, P. M. (1981). *The effective police manager.* Englewood Cliffs, NJ: Prentice Hall.

Whisenand, P. M., & Ferguson, R. F. (1978). *The managing of police organizations* (2nd ed.). Englewood Cliffs, NJ: Prentice Hall.

Wilson, O. W., & McLaren, R. C. (1977). *Police administration* (4th ed.). New York: McGraw Hill.

2

Management Positions in Criminal Justice

Criminal justice includes the fields of police, prosecutorial court, and judicial administration; adult probation, parole, and custodial correctional administration; juvenile justice administration; and various public services to assist victims, witnesses, and criminal defendants (Quarles, Ethan, & Waldron, 2009; Schmalleger, 2009; Senna & Siegel, 2009; Travis, 2007; Wrobleski & Hess, 2005). Most agencies and organizations involved in American criminal justice are governmental, but private commercial and nonprofit, **nongovernmental organizations (NGOs)** also are involved in American criminal justice. The growth of nongovernmental justice-related services, agencies, and alternative programs to support the traditional government justice organizations has expanded the field considerably in recent years. These new agencies and services have introduced new administrative and managerial challenges within the field of justice administration. The traditional justice system also has undergone much internal change in the past two decades; it was spurred on by the now-defunct **Law Enforcement Assistance Administration (LEAA)** in the mid-1960s and the 1970s and has continued under its own momentum ever since.

In spite of great change in the justice system, classical managerial strategies and priorities continue to be followed within most of the subfields of justice administration and management, especially in law enforcement (Wilson & McLaren, 1977) and corrections (U.S. Bureau of Prisons, 1973). These general administrative and managerial principles were first set out in the 1930s (Gulick, 1937). They have persisted because they have served justice administrators well in the past, but these managerial principles have needed updating to match the times.

Since the early 1930s, our justice system has been subjected to much well-deserved criticism. The **Wickersham Commission** began the trend, identifying numerous problems in the administration of justice during the Prohibition Era (National Commission on Law Observance and Enforcement, 1931). Much was done in the following two decades to professionalize the administration of justice, applying managerial principles taken from the field of public administration. In the 1960s and 1970s the criticism began anew. The police encountered considerable negative attention from the communications media and the public for allegations of police brutality, mishandled riots, and civil disturbances; resisting the civil rights movement; tragic applications of deadly force; and corruption scandals. All tarnished the image of policing in the United States

What is the sequence of events in the criminal justice system?

FIGURE 2.1 A General View of the Criminal Justice System (LEAA). This chart gives a simplified view of caseflow through the criminal justice system. Procedures vary among jurisdictions. The weights of the lines are not intended to show actual size of caseloads.

and forced police departments all over the country to take action to correct their problems and improve their public images. In the same period, bloody prison riots and the attention paid to prison conditions put the correctional establishment in the spotlight, forcing much-needed reforms. The image of justice improved somewhat in the 1970s, as community relations efforts began to bear fruit (especially for police departments). In the 1980s, the judicial process came under much criticism and adverse attention as the insanity defense, seemingly incredible acquittals, and inappropriately light or heavy sentences were heavily publicized and criticized. Civil cases over rather inconsequential issues and the scandalous behavior of some personal injury lawyers brought discredit to the courts and the legal profession. The death penalty continues to be a sore spot in the relationship of the justice system with many community elements.

It is the duty of criminal justice managers to devise and recommend remedies to the problems of the criminal justice system. Indeed, criminal justice managers over the past four centuries have risen as leaders and reformers who have done exactly that. That promise and opportunity remains possible today, as new problems and issues arise for criminal justice agencies. So who are the managers of criminal justice agencies who need to deal with such matters?

The Police and Law Enforcement Management

The best-known and most visible officials of our justice system are the police. They serve the law enforcement function by aiding in crime prevention, traffic regulation, criminal investigation, criminal apprehension (arrest), and many additional public safety, service, and order-maintenance responsibilities. Managerial ranks in law enforcement often parallel the ranks and titles of the military, with such terms as *sergeant, lieutenant, captain,* and *commander.* The chief executive officer of many local police agencies is spoken of as "the **chief**," but in a sheriff's department, the managers are the sheriff and the chief deputy sheriff. In many state and federal investigative agencies, the senior manager is designated a **director.** The number of middle managers and the rank titles used will reflect the size of the agency. When in uniform, these managers often wear chevrons, metal bars, oak leaves, eagles, and stars generally copied from military ranks.

FIGURE 2.2 Military-style rank insignia often are used in American police and corrections organizations, including various styles of sergeants' chevrons ("stripes"). *Examples and photo by Richard R. E. Kania, from his collection.*

The police function in the United States is divided among many entities at five different jurisdictional levels. Police services are authorized under the jurisdiction and

FIGURE 2.3 Senior Rank Insignia: Samples of lieutenant, captain, major, colonel, and generals (chiefs) rank insignia. *Examples and photo by Richard R. E. Kania, from his collection.*

authority of: (1) private entities, (2) localities, (3) the state, (4) the federal government, and (5) international organizations. The police also are given power over law enforcement matters of special, limited jurisdiction. There are both general and specialized law enforcement agencies. The general law enforcement agencies are obliged to enforce a wide range of laws, while specialized agencies focus on one category of laws, such as wildlife and environmental protection laws, occupational safety laws, liquor and drug control laws, banking regulations, or postal laws.

Private Police and Law Enforcement

The **private investigator** (the PI), so well known from television and the movies, and the highly visible uniformed private security firms doing business in our communities are the most conspicuous representations of private law enforcement. In detective fiction, they are often loners like Sam Spade or Philip Marlowe, maybe having a partner or two and a secretary. Such small offices may have office managers, but managerial functions are often handled by the PIs themselves.

The lone-eagle private investigators are not alone in the private security industry, though. Private law enforcement includes the investigative offices of commercial utilities companies, the railroad police, a variety of corporate police, large security corporations, the security offices of private colleges and universities, as well as numerous other entities. These entities often work closely with the police and are an important element in public safety and security (Ortmeier, 2009, pp. 16–17).

The key feature of private law enforcement is that their policies and services are designed to fulfill the needs of the private persons or corporations employing them. This is the most rapidly growing sector of law enforcement employment. Because the laws of each state differ, some have powers equal to those of public law enforcement officers, while others have very limited law enforcement powers. Management of most of these private law enforcement organizations will follow business models because the organizations exist to achieve a profit as well as to provide public service. Even so, they also apply the same basic principles of management and organization theory followed by public police and security organizations (Ortmeier, 2009, pp. 199–214).

Most of the larger private security services are modeled on public police agencies. Many issue their officers uniforms and use the rank insignia and titles of public law enforcement. Their midlevel and top management positions typically are filled by merit hiring and promotion from within.

Local Police

The first echelon of publicly controlled police operate at the local level, in our towns, cities, and counties. These are the police we think of most often when the word *police* is spoken. Local law enforcement includes the **sheriffs** and their deputies who provide law enforcement services to our counties, the town and city police who serve our urban communities, and specialized local law enforcement officials who are not as often thought of as police, but perform local policing functions (e.g., building inspectors, dog catchers, health inspectors, and other local regulatory officers). In most American cities and towns, police chiefs usually are chosen by their city governments. The exact method of selection varies from location to location. A strong mayoral system allows the mayor of a city to appoint a police chief, thus making the office somewhat political. However, in municipal governments with a city manager, the chief is not appointed by a politician and therefore is more sheltered from politics (in theory, anyway). How a chief gets the job has an impact on the authority and control he or she has over the department. Midlevel police managers are chosen by some variety of civil service or merit selection process. Sheriffs, however, are elected within their counties, and their deputies often are personal, patronage appointees of those elected sheriffs.

State Law Enforcement

Many, but not all, of our state governments have general law enforcement police agencies. Others have state highway patrols that are specialized traffic law enforcement agencies, while still others have state investigative agencies modeled on the Federal Bureau of Investigation. There are many additional specialized law enforcement agencies at the state level of jurisdiction. Most states have some form of motor vehicle or drivers licensing law enforcement agencies, wildlife or game protection officers, tax investigation units, and liquor licensing agencies with law enforcement powers. Their top managers often are political appointees, but usually are chosen from a pool of experienced professionals. Midlevel managers are chosen, usually from within, by a civil service or merit selection process. Most use paramilitary ranks and titles. Some refer to managers using the title **inspector,** indicating one of the managerial functions of that office: the inspection of the subordinates they supervise.

Federal Law Enforcement

The U.S. Marshal's Service is the oldest federal law enforcement agency, formed in 1789. Other federal law enforcement agencies followed: the Internal Revenue Service (IRS) in 1862, the U.S. Secret Service (formed within the Treasury Department) in 1865, and the

Immigration and Naturalization Service (INS) in 1891. INS is now called Immigration and Customs Enforcement (ICE), and falls within the **Department of Homeland Security (DHS).** The most publicized federal law enforcement agency is probably the Federal Bureau of Investigation (FBI), founded in 1908 within the Department of Justice (Wrobleski & Hess, 1986, pp. 20, 23). Other specialized agencies involved in federal law enforcement include the Drug Enforcement Agency (DEA), the U.S. Postal Inspection Service, the Occupational Safety and Health Administration (OSHA), the Coast Guard (USCG), the Transportation Security Administration (TSA), and many more. The growth in federal regulations and legislation since the 1930s has produced the requirements for an ever-increasing number of specialized law enforcement officers and agencies within the federal government. The senior managers of these federal agencies are political appointees of the president, with senatorial advice and consent. Midlevel federal managers are promoted internally based on merit and civil service procedures. Several federal agencies use the term **special agent-in-charge** to identify managerial officers.

International Law Enforcement

U.S. representatives serving with **INTERPOL** and the CIA and officials of the U.S. State Department are involved in law enforcement and policing on an international basis. These international police are officers of our federal government or other national governments cooperating with ours who function extraterritorially, beyond our own national political borders, and typically are appointed within the executive ranks of their organizations. Some federal agencies have international jurisdiction, such as the Drug Enforcement Agency, which can operate both within and outside our national borders. The police units of our military services also operate both at home and internationally, but usually only in dealing with U.S. service people and in accordance with "status of forces" agreements with the host countries in which they are deployed.

Managing the Prosecution of Criminal Suspects

The **prosecution** function includes submission of criminal charges and supporting evidence to grand juries and preparation of cases for trial. Also known by such titles as district, state, or commonwealth "solicitor" or "attorney," in most states prosecutors are elected. In the federal system, they are political appointees of the Justice Department. Whether an appointee or an elected official, a prosecutor often is a highly visible public figure, especially when involved with a celebrated criminal case. The prosecutor manages the office of the district attorney and in larger offices will appoint managerial deputy DAs to help with supervision and case management.

The prosecutor has several functional roles to play in the American justice system, some reflecting the personalities of the office holders. Abraham S. Blumberg (1979) has identified five (pp. 133–139). The "collection agent" facilitates the payment of civil judgments, threatening to file criminal charges if the debts are not paid. For merchants holding bad checks or those entitled to child support, this help in recovering overdue payments is an important but nonglamorous aspect of the prosecutorial role. The "dispenser of justice" works closely with law enforcement agencies, bringing criminal cases to trial or disposition by plea bargaining. The "power-broker/fixer" enjoys the exercise of power in bringing highly visible cases, often involving prominent individuals or important social issues, to quick solutions. The "political enforcer" uses the office to attack political opponents, to "get" someone by public embarrassment and legal harassment, even if no criminal conviction will result. The mass media are much more important to these unethical prosecutors than juries. The "overseer of police" role involves monitoring police cases and activities closely. By screening police cases, these prosecutors are reviewing the quality of the police work, often requiring more investigation, dismissing weak cases, and bringing to trial only those that are well prepared.

The relationship of the prosecutor to the grand jury is one worthy of special attention. A grand jury is comprised of private citizens, who often have little or no experience or training in criminal procedures or law. The investigative grand jury operates in secret, and the actions of the prosecutor are not subject to the normal review. Prosecutors have been known to present hearsay, illegally acquired evidence, and other categories of evidence not admissible in a court case. Suspects may not be given the opportunity to hear the charges made against them. Witnesses who might be able to speak in the defense of suspects might be excluded. Testimony given before a grand jury is not subject to cross-examination. These factors give an unscrupulous prosecutor license to use the grand jury to damage the reputations of personal or political opponents by bringing charges and inspiring indictments against persons whose rights and protections in a courtroom would preclude conviction.

The high visibility of the prosecutor in a major criminal case, and occasionally in major government-initiated civil litigation, can make the incumbent of the office an instant celebrity. Highly successful prosecutors have used this fact to garner free publicity in their quest for higher political office. Among those who have used the prosecutor's office to seek still higher civic offices were Thomas E. Dewey, a DA who became governor of New York and was the Republican presidential candidate in 1948; Robert Kennedy, from the U.S. Attorney General to U.S. Senator and a leading candidate for the Democrat presidential nomination in 1968; and, more recently, former U.S. Attorney of New York Rudolph W. Giuliani as the Republican mayor of New York City and a candidate for the Republican presidential nomination in 2008.

Defense Attorneys: Public Defenders and Private Counsel

The right to legal counsel in a criminal case is guaranteed under the provisions of the Sixth Amendment to the U.S. Constitution. The *Gideon v. Wainwright* and *Miranda v. Arizona* rulings of the U.S. Supreme Court extended this right to persons charged under state laws and to those too poor to afford counsel. Previously, private lawyers hired by those accused provided this counsel. The expanded rights meant that the states and the federal government had to provide legal **defense counsel** to people who could not pay for these services (indigents). Some of this indigent defense is provided by appointed counsel, lawyers in private practice who are assigned criminal cases by the court and are paid by the state. In other jurisdictions, full-time defense attorneys are employed by public defender offices.

The defense attorney performs several roles before, during, and after trials. In addition, attorneys develop personal styles. Abraham Blumberg has observed and named several of these. The lawyer who undertakes "social causes" is the "pro bono ideologue." Usually financially independent and often personally quite colorful, this defender of causes rather than cases often achieves major reforms within the system (Blumberg, 1979, p. 237). Years ago, Clarence Darrow and William Jennings Bryan met in a small town in Tennessee to contest the legal aspects of the creationism-versus-evolutionism debate in the celebrated "monkey trial." This trial was given a fictional treatment in Stanley Kramer's 1960 film *Inherit the Wind.* In the 1960s, Abe Fortas achieved fame in his defense of Clarence Gideon in the *Gideon v. Wainwright* case, widely publicized by Anthony Lewis's book, *Gideon's Trumpet.* Another such figure was William Kunstler, who was involved in numerous important, high-visibility civil rights cases in the 1960s and 1970s.

A second type, the "star," is similar to the ideologue, being equally visible and colorful (Blumberg, 1979, p. 239). He or she too seeks out high-visibility cases, but not necessarily for the issues they represent. The star is often likely to be representing famous people or bringing suit against celebrities. Another of Blumberg's types is the "hired gun," the talented attorney without an ideology, prepared to argue whatever side of an issue in whatever case comes his or her way (1979, p. 239). The "patrician" or "courtly gentleman" lawyers are among the best and brightest in the legal profession (Blumberg, 1979, p. 239). Their stellar reputations often result in their being asked to head investigative commissions or serve as special prosecutors in highly sensitive cases. Although few attorneys in local practice will ever rise to the national recognition levels of Blumberg's characterizations, many attorneys pattern their careers and approaches on these styles. Every major city has its own stars, ideologues, hired guns, and patricians in daily practice.

Managing Bail, Bond, and Pretrial Detention Services

The U.S. Constitution provides the guarantee of reasonable bail for those held for trial. Bails and bonds are securities that are pledged or paid to ensure the appearance of a criminal suspect, and sometimes a civil litigant, at the trial. The security pledged against the promise of appearance is returned if the person appears as promised and is forfeited if the person does not appear. The amount is set by a judicial official, usually either a magistrate or a lower-court judge, but can be appealed in higher courts if the defendant feels the amount is excessive and unreasonable. Usually there is a chief magistrate for each district, but in some states this function is managed in the courts.

The **magistrate** or a judge is called upon to make decisions about the appropriate bail or conditions of bond. If the bail or bond cannot be met, the defendant must remain in pretrial detention until the trial date. In some busy court jurisdictions, this can mean serving many months of jail time without being convicted. If a conviction comes later, this pretrial jail time usually will be counted against the punishment, but there is no compensation if the defendant is later acquitted or the charges are dropped.

Managing Victim and Witness Services

Informative data on criminal justice victimizations became available after 1973, when the first of the LEAA-sponsored national surveys of victimization were released. From it and subsequent national victimization surveys, the *National Crime Victimization Surveys (NCVS)*, the scope of underreporting and a clearer image of criminal victimization arose, and the new subdiscipline within criminology, **victimology**, emerged (Lab & Doerner, 2008). In the 1980s, victims and witnesses in our system were given considerably more attention than in decades past (Viano, 1978, p. 438). Without the active support of these parties, the criminal justice system would be ineffective. Although the importance of witnesses and victims in the workings of the criminal justice system is significant, critics of the justice system have decried their apparent neglect and have identified many legitimate complaints and deal with various controversial aspects of providing services to crime victims (Moriarty, 2008). Agencies have therefore been established (both NGOs and governmental services) to provide services to victims and witnesses (Yeldell & Brown, 2002).

Community organizers and reform activists have taken up the causes of victims of rape, homicide, child and spouse abuse, and drunk driving, among others, to call attention to the patterns of neglect and abuse that they have encountered. The critics often charge that the civil rights of accused criminals have been assigned such high priority that their victims are all but forgotten. Two powerful films on rape, *A Case of Rape* in 1974 and *The Accused* in 1988, make this point very clearly. The rape victim in each story is victimized a second time by her treatment by justice officials, defense attorneys, and the media.

The families of homicide victims are also victims of those crimes. They have endured the losses of loved ones in murders and in fatal drunk-driving accidents. Their personal losses are too great for compensation, but they can expect some support and comfort from the justice system and the information media. Because so many homicides are committed by people who know their victims well, the survivors often are treated as the prime suspects. Bodies are held by police pathologists and coroners for what may seem like indeterminate or unreasonable lengths of time. Body parts and personal effects remain in police labs and evidence vaults for years as the case proceeds through investigation, trial, and appeals. Status reports on investigations often reach the press before they reach the survivors. Grisly photographs of their loved ones often appear on television and in newspapers and magazines, sometimes weeks, months, or years after the crime.

The witness in the justice system often has fared no better. Without receiving the sympathy that victims and victims' families often do, they too are victimized by the process of justice. Time is lost from work or other pursuits while witnesses wait for their time to testify. When a plea bargain terminates a case without a trial, occasionally witnesses are not notified and show up to testify unnecessarily, or are left sitting in witness chambers forgotten, as the other principals in the case go home or to their offices or to jail. They are rarely thanked and even less often compensated for their time and effort.

Some abuse of witnesses is deliberate. The common defense attorney strategy of recurring postponements is aimed specifically at witnesses. If a witness becomes discouraged, he or she may fail to appear, leading to a motion to dismiss the charges against the accused. If a witness endures the delays, the duration between the events they witnessed and the date of testimony will be cited as his or her ability to recall is questioned. Defense attorneys are not alone in abusing witnesses. The prosecutor often will use similar tactics against opposing witnesses. If witnesses are offered any financial compensation for their time and effort, the opposing attorney will attempt to make it appear that their testimony has been purchased and is tainted. If the opposing attorney is especially aggressive in cross-examination, he or she will attack the reputation, integrity, intelligence, motives, and character of the witnesses.

There have been some improvements. The appearance of witness assistance programs has been a major boon to helping overcome these problems. Changes in trial dates are announced, times for testimony are more carefully scheduled, and various services are provided to witnesses while they are waiting. Judges have also been helpful by discouraging postponements and in thwarting the efforts of opposing attorneys attempting to attack witnesses without just grounds.

Managing the Judicial System

The image of the black-robed judge presiding over a trial from his or her elevated bench in the courtroom is a powerful one. It is an impression that actually runs counter to many of our national democratic ideals. There is no question about the basic inequality of people in the courtroom. The **judge** is almost an imperial presence. Even more than the police officer, the judge personifies the power of the state over our lives. Judicial rulings are nonnegotiable orders backed by the power of government. They may be appealed, but they cannot be ignored. Only other judges have the power to correct fellow judges. Their formal role as interpreters, arbiters, and defenders of the law and the state and federal constitutions places them above all other civil servants and public service managers, legislators, mayors, governors, and even presidents on occasion.

A judge on the bench is not, however, a manager, but there are chief judges in judicial units and chief justices in the state and federal supreme courts whose off-bench duties are managerial. Many states and the federal courts provide assistance to these judges by operating offices for courts administration. Their directors are managers.

The selection of judges at the state level can be divided into five general methods, with minor variations from state to state even within these general descriptions (See Box 2.1). The variation reflects two goals, which are sometimes conflicting, that the states are

---

BOX 2.1 METHODS OF JUDICIAL SELECTION

---

1. Partisan election.
2. Nonpartisan election.
3. Merit commission selection, also known as a **Missouri Plan**.
4. Legislative appointment.
5. Gubernatorial appointment.

---

trying to balance. The first goal is the desire for an independent and unbiased judiciary. The second is to maintain among the members of the bench a sense of accountability to the public. The method of judicial selection that a state chooses reflects, to some degree, the importance that is placed on one goal or the other.

With a partisan election system, a judge seeking office first must seek the nomination of a political party and be selected as the candidate for that party before running for the office in the general election. A second method of elective selection is the nonpartisan election. This allows voters to hold judges accountable for the job that they do without having them become too tied up in party politics. Judges in these states appear on the ballot without any party affiliation listed. The idea is that the voting public can make a decision based on the issues or in many cases the perception of the job that an incumbent judge is doing. Elections are often a referendum on the incumbent regardless of whether the election is partisan or nonpartisan. However, the lack of a partisan label makes a candidate's "record" even more at issue because the factor of one's party affiliation is not involved.

Election of judges has always created concerns of a judiciary lacking in independence. Independence is indeed considered to be the most important function for the judicial branch. How can judges who accept campaign contributions from interest groups or who must stand for reelection after hearing high-profile cases maintain their independence from political pressures and do the right thing? The answer to this question, as with many others, depends on whom you ask (see Box 2.2: **Getting Reelected**).

The most common method of judicial selection is merit selection through a nominating commission, more commonly referred to as a **Missouri Plan**. Merit selection takes on various methods and does vary somewhat from state to state. A Missouri Plan implements a system that attempts to establish merit—that is, qualifications for the job—without taking all discretion from the selection. It is essentially an attempt to increase judicial independence while maintaining public accountability.

A nonpartisan commission is formed for the purpose of making recommendations for the appointment of members of the bench. The members of these commissions are appointed in a variety of ways but are usually a mixture of lawyers and nonlawyers. There are some states that combine merit selection with other methods of selection (including Missouri), depending on the level of court they are dealing with.

Even states that have implemented a merit system require judges to face the electorate periodically. Under the merit system, judges must periodically be subject to retention elections in which voters go to the polls to cast a vote either to retain or not retain a

---

BOX 2.2 GETTING REELECTED

There have always been self-imposed restrictions on what a judge can do or say in the course of a political campaign. Judicial ethics essentially only allow candidates to provide their personal and professional background and a promise to faithfully carry out the duties of the office. Judges are not allowed to adopt a platform of issues or promises to make policy, as are legislators. However, this code does not completely censor judicial candidates from making promises or criticizing opposing candidates. Campaign promises often center around issues such as cutting case backlogs or increasing the court's efficiency. Criticism of opponents is likely to include issues such as lack of experience or poor court management. Judicial candidates are expected to avoid inflammatory language and negative campaigning of any type.

---

judge. This provides an opportunity for interest groups to be very much involved in judicial politics even in merit-system states.

The least common method of judicial selection is legislative appointment to the bench. Currently, two states use this method—South Carolina and Virginia. Gubernatorial appointment is used in only three states: California, Maine, and New Jersey. However, several states authorize their governors to appoint judges to fill vacancies until such time as elections or commission actions can be completed.

Accountability to the public is quite important because some judges have been known to become overawed by their own power. Those who flaunt their powers are soon widely known within the court community and much disliked, but they are hard to deal with, discipline, or dispose of in a justice system that has sought to provide them with great protections from outside pressures. In states with elective judiciaries, the polling place provides one avenue of relief, but federal judges serve for life unless removed by impeachment by the U.S. Congress, a rare event even when obviously warranted.

Even judges who do not become despots often acquire other unappealing personal traits—or bring these traits with them—to the displeasure of attorneys, victims, witnesses, media representatives, and/or defendants who must deal with them. Abraham S. Blumberg (1979, pp. 264–266) identified six role patterns in the judges he observed. The roles of "intellectual" and "hack" carry the burdens of court work with little attention or public visibility. "Political adventurers" use their current judicial post to rise higher in public life; this type of judge will cultivate good media and public relations. The "bench-warmer" has been given a judgeship as the final step in a political career, becoming a "judicial pensioner," as if the post were a retirement reward. The "hatchet man" is a close ally of the prosecutor's office who functions to expedite high-visibility cases. The final role described by Blumberg has three aspects: "tyrant-showboat-benevolent despot." This type of judge is egocentric and uses the judicial bench as a stage for his or her personal advantage, especially enjoying media attention.

The judge is only one of a collection of key personalities in the judiciary. In each courtroom are other justice officials who are also important functionaries. The court reporters, bailiffs, clerks of court, and magistrates all play important roles in the operation of the court and in the shaping of the image of the judicial system in the eyes of the public.

The **clerks of court** are among the most influential of these other officials. They schedule the trials, manage the paper flow, keep the records, and have the most frequent dealings with persons outside the judiciary. Clerk's offices are managed by a chief clerk, often an elected official. When efficient, helpful, and courteous, clerks are effective entities, but unfortunately this is not always the case. Because most clerks work for judges, or perceive themselves as doing so, some are uninterested in serving their other clients. It is common for a visitor to the clerk's office to find stuffy formality, indifference, and a lack of cooperation among the clerical staff.

Also serving in the courts are **bailiffs** and **court reporters,** not the journalists who cover trials, but the officials of the court who transcribe testimony. These professionals were formerly called **court stenographers,** but this term is going out of use gradually as the practice of **stenography** has become obsolete. In some states they are called **court recorders.** Often the bailiffs are employees or deputies of the sheriff. In other states, they are civil service employees of the court itself, as are most court reporters/recorders/stenographers. **Magistrates,** also known as **justices of the peace** in many states, are lower-ranking judicial officials. Some are elected; others are appointed by the courts or by other public officials.

The courts have not escaped criticism for their faults. Judges, clerks, and other judiciary officials have been called to task for their more serious shortcomings. The awe and esteem given the courts and judges require them to pay great attention to their responsibilities to the public they are there to serve. Maintaining public accountability of the judicial system is indeed an important task for the criminal justice system and for us all.

Managing Adult Corrections

Adult offenders convicted of crimes can experience a wide range of punishments, ranging from simple admonishments not to violate the law again to the death penalty. The potential penalty usually is set in law, but the penalty is the product of judicial decision-making. The severity of the offense, circumstances associated with the offense, the victim's role in the crime and relationship to the offender, prior criminal record, degree of cooperation with the authorities leading up to trial, efforts taken to make restitution, prospects for rehabilitation, and numerous other factors are taken into consideration in rendering sentences, often under legal guidelines. Other, extralegal factors also come into play in sentencing: sex; race; ethnicity; unorthodox political, sexual, religious, or ideological views; social standing of the victims; and economic status of the offenders and victims among them.

A wide range of formal correctional options and penalties may be used by a judge. The laws set limits, but judges are given varying degrees of autonomy in selecting sentences within these limits. Some of these are explained in Figure 2.1, but the list is neither exhaustive nor in absolute rank order of severity. Other punishments exist. Some corrections options can be combined and often are. Furthermore, once a person is under sentence to prison, there are additional correctional options available.

Custodial Corrections—The Jails

Jails are used for pretrial detention and for short terms of punishment under the supervision of the county. The sheriff is the manager of the county jail, but many sheriffs will appoint a jail manager to run day-to-day operations.

Custodial Corrections—The Prisons

Prison often is the first option that most people outside the justice system think of when they consider possible criminal penalties. However, it is not the most common penalty assessed. Fines, probations, and short jail terms are used more frequently, if only because most criminal offenses are relatively minor and do not justify prison terms. Most states use their limited prison resources to house only the most serious and dangerous criminals, using other correctional alternatives for less risky offenders. Prisons are managed by **wardens**, usually merit-selected from the civil service, and larger prisons have large numbers of middle-level managers, usually using officer ranks borrowed from the military. Because prisons operate 24/7, shift managers represent the managerial team on duty, whatever the hour.

Discharge from Prison

Once offenders are in prison, they can exit legally via several means. One is discharge of sentence. They serve their full time or are granted clemencies or pardons and are discharged, with no more time left to serve. There are few prisoners who exit under these terms. Most are released conditionally. The institution of parole is the means most commonly used to discharge prisoners before the end of their full sentence terms. Various other programs, such as furloughs, also readmit sentenced criminals into the general population.

Correctional theorists argue that as prisoners near the end of their active prison sentences (even before parole in many cases), they need an opportunity to be reintegrated into the society that has excluded them by exiling them to prisons. This can be achieved by a number of means. Three of the most popularly used are furloughs, work release, and halfway-house placements.

FURLOUGHS

A furlough is a temporary release from custody, a brief vacation from confinement. It may be either supervised or unsupervised, according to the rules of each state. When supervision is provided, a correctional officer can be assigned to be the constant companion of the convict, but this is rare. More often, there is little actual supervision, and the offender merely has to check in at preappointed times to meet the conditions of the furlough.

WORK RELEASE AND STUDY RELEASE

Related to the furlough programs are work release and study release programs that allow recurring furloughs to allow inmates to attend schools or engage in regular jobs outside prison walls. These programs have been especially attractive because the work or classroom environment provides some supervision for the convicts while they are outside the walls and because they are either acquiring work skills or an education that can serve in their rehabilitation.

HALFWAY-HOUSE PLACEMENT

A halfway house is a facility in a community in which prisoners must stay overnight but can go out to workplaces or educational institutions during the normal hours for these activities. The residence is supervised by a special group of correctional officers who function much like probation officers, ensuring that the stipulations of conditional release from prison are met. Violations can result in immediate return to secure custodial institutions and even lengthening of sentences (Hartman, Friday, & Minor, 1994; Walsh & Beck, 1990).

Community Corrections, Probation, and Parole Officers

Furloughs, work release, and halfway houses use the resources of the community to prepare an offender to readapt to the world outside prison. They are typically managed by prison officials. **Probation** is used for a similar purpose, but prior to an active term of incarceration, and typically is administered by the courts or a local probation office headed by a senior **probation officer. Parole** is used after a term in custody, and it is usually administered by the state correctional system, with a civil service staff of **parole officers** and appointed managers (Abadinsky, 2000). Collectively these are classified as "**community corrections**."

Parole

Parole is conditional release from prison. As long as the conditions are met, the former prisoner can remain in society without having to return to prison. Those conditions and their supervision operate much like probation. Parole supervision is managed from community offices. Violations are a matter for parole or correctional authorities to deal with administratively. A parole revocation hearing does not involve the sentencing judge. The parole officials can order the reincarceration of a parole violator if the hearing concludes that the conditions were violated (Leary & Chiles, 1965).

Community Organizations

The role of private citizens in the justice system has grown in recent years. Far more community organizations have taken over functions that were once exclusively reserved for the government. This has been most obvious in juvenile and adult corrections, victim assistance, and judicial oversight activities.

Most correctional activities are under the control of either states or localities. However, in recent years a number of private institutions have become active in rehabilitation efforts and have offered some communities sentencing options not previously available. Most of these private efforts have been in the area of counseling and therapy, but some are even semicustodial, providing housing for clients directed to them as conditions of probations or paroles.

Among the more successful and well known of these private semicustodial efforts is the Delancey Street Foundation, a program that began in California, and has branched out to other parts of the country. A typical Delancey Street Foundation program will provide a group residence, like a halfway house, under strict discipline of the staff, many of whom are reformed offenders themselves. The client population will be employed in industries and enterprises run by the Delancey Street Foundation. Profits from these enterprises are used to sustain the houses. The clients are given wages for their work, from which they are expected to contribute to the operating expenses of the residence. Like every correctional effort, these programs have their failures, but they have had a good success rate with referral clients and have cost the public far less than either prisons or close supervision parole.

Victim assistance programs were not given much attention within criminal justice studies until the feminist movement selected rape victimization as one of its causes (Kania & Mackey, 1983; Resick, 1987, p. 468). Women often experienced secondary victimization by the system and the investigative process (Campbell & Raja, 1999). The attention given to women as victims helped direct public attention to victims more generally, and new programs to assist crime victims were developed across the United States (Viano, 1987, p. 441). From these rape victim assistance programs have come many similar services designed to help all types of victims. In addition to counseling victims and helping them cope with the psychological, financial, and physical consequences of their victimization, these programs have been quite successful in mounting lobbying efforts in state legislatures on behalf of victim compensation legislation and improved standards for the treatment of victims by the police, prosecutors, and the courts.

Other private community groups are attempting to bring about additional improvements in the judiciary. Several groups have targeted the courts for special attention. Because judges are relatively immune from public criticism and critique from within the legal profession, these groups have undertaken to provide this service. Court accountability projects, such as Court Watch of North Carolina, have undertaken the evaluation of judges of the civil family courts, using trained volunteer observers in the courtrooms. The judges are critiqued with regard to their demeanor on the bench, their treatment of litigants, and their efforts to facilitate justice and help litigants (usually women seeking help in collecting court-ordered child-support payments). Several state and local chapters of Mothers Against Drunk Driving (MADD), a nonprofit organization opposed to the criminal act of drunk driving, have undertaken the evaluation of criminal court judges and their handling of drunk-driving cases. The records of judges in bringing convictions are contrasted, and the imposed sentences are compared. Judges who are characteristically prone to acquit or to render light sentences are publicly identified. This attention to their activities has put judges on notice that they are not a privileged elite immune from critical evaluation. It also has helped them reform their profession and correct their mistakes without resorting to more radical remedies.

Juvenile Justice

The place of juveniles in our justice system differs somewhat from that of adults. Beginning late in the 19th century, the courts began to treat younger offenders differently, establishing the notion of *parens patriae,* the idea that the state stands in place of the parents when a juvenile comes into conflict with the law. Under this doctrine, in theory, the courts act in the best interest of the juvenile, not to punish but to guide and reform the youthful offender. As a result, separate reform and training schools replaced jails and prisons as the places where juveniles were held in custody.

The courts set up a separate **juvenile justice system** of intake officers to review cases involving juveniles and probation officers and counselors to work with those found in violation of the laws. These officials are responsible for determining what is in the best interests of the child. Punishment of the guilty is not the objective of the court's judgment. Instead the objective is the correction, rehabilitation, and reintegration of the juvenile offender into society. Although penalties are assessed in some juvenile court cases, the findings and judgments are not usually severe. Court findings of what is best for the juvenile offender can include loss of freedom by assignment to training schools and reformatories, which can be viewed very much like being sentenced to prison (Lab & Whitehead, 2008).

After the U.S. Supreme Court ruling in the case ***In re Gault***, the courts were obliged to provide juvenile defendants with the same legal rights that adults possess: the right to counsel, the right to confront their accusers, the right to trial, and so forth. The federal courts had come to view some state juvenile courts as predominantly punitive entities that did not afford juveniles "due process of law" and occasionally denied juveniles the full opportunity to defend themselves against complaints. The Supreme Court has taken the position that juvenile suspects have all the same rights as adults, plus some additional protections because of their status as minors. For example, a juvenile cannot be called upon to waive his or her legal rights to legal representation or the protection against self-incrimination without parental consultation; juveniles in police custody or in correctional institutions must be kept separate from adult offenders; and educational opportunities for juveniles cannot be denied as a consequence of correctional custody.

There exists a shadow system of juvenile justice that parallels the adult criminal justice system. In police departments, there are juvenile officers specializing in juvenile law enforcement. Intake officers serve a role similar to that of magistrates in reviewing charges against juveniles and deciding whether to release them or hold them in custody while pending trial on the charges. If held, offenders are placed in juvenile detention centers, rather than local jails, to await trial. Cases are heard by juvenile courts and judges specializing in juvenile law. Juvenile probation officers and counselors work with those found in violation of the laws but not ordered into state custody. Some offenders are assigned to foster care for intensive probation within a family environment. Those ordered to be held in secure custody go to reform or training schools to serve their time. Halfway houses are used to reintegrate them into society, and aftercare programs function like supervised parole.

Summary

Some years ago there was a running debate about whether the American approach to criminal justice constituted a system. In the final analysis of that debate, everything depended on how an author defined or meant to use the concept of a "system." The debate served us well, though, because it allowed scholars to make the point that the American approach to justice is very disjointed and decentralized. It is not an efficient system by any measure of efficiency. Its actors are in conflict or in competition as often as they work in cooperation.

The criminal justice system in the United States is uniquely American. Although many of its institutions are derived from English models, the American criminal justice system ceased being like the English long ago. The **decentralization**—that is, the lack of formal integration of agencies into cooperating entities—that characterizes the American criminal justice system is unparalleled in the rest of the world. The division of responsibilities defies logic or easy explanation. It is organizationally "ugly." Nevertheless, it seems to work—although not always well—in achieving its competing objectives of protecting society and protecting the civil rights of our citizens, even the criminally inclined of them; identifying and punishing the guilty; and preventing crime and reintegrating criminal offenders into the general population. The American justice system exists to respond to the demands of a diverse nation. Because Americans are not of one mind about what the justice system should be doing for whom, the laws and the parties who are called upon to enforce (or not enforce) them are given conflicting requirements to fulfill.

These conflicting requirements introduce upsetting contradictions and give rise to much of the criticism that is attached to American justice. The system hires the lawyers who try to exonerate the offenders whom we hire police and prosecutors to put away. The legal system employs lawyers for the convicts who are suing our correctional officials. When public officials crack down on crime, their critics decry the encroachments on the civil liberties of us all. When they faithfully protect the rights of criminal suspects, they are criticized for being soft on crime. One segment of America objects to the inhumane conditions produced by prison overcrowding, while another segment (including some of those in the first segment) resists the construction of prisons. Moreover, a third segment (including some of those in the second segment) demands that we keep our criminals locked up. All of these contradictions are part of the price of representative democracy. In a totalitarian state, we would be free of these conflicts. Only one role would be assigned to our justice system, and it would respond to that singular obligation. Only where there is very broad consensus is the system relatively immune from criticism.

While the American justice system may not always function smoothly and efficiently, it is a system that has at least the potential to function as it should. A criminal case can come to the attention of the system, be solved, arrests made, and a trial set. Suspects are defended, tried fairly, given the opportunity to confront their accusers as well as the evidence against them, and acquitted if found not guilty. If found guilty, they will be sentenced, given ample opportunity to appeal, and will serve sentences that are at least humanely executed in relatively good conditions by world standards. Not all cases follow this ideal sequence, but enough do in a timely enough fashion to give some critics at least hope that the whole system can be made to work better.

Similarly, the civil justice system appears to have the potential to function well. Justice too often is slow and costly, but important personal and social issues do get resolved in the civil courts. Both rich and poor are heard. Influential and invisible people alike have their days in court. Both socially significant and inconsequential cases eventually are resolved. Like the American criminal justice system, civil justice has the potential to be improved.

Knowing how the justice system should work is a first step toward making it work. Whether the interested person reading this book is a justice administration student, a justice system volunteer, a professional practitioner, a journalist, or a private citizen simply interested in the connection between the American justice administration and information media relations, a basic understanding of the fundamental organization and functions of the major justice system components is essential. This chapter leaves far too much unsaid and should be seen only as an introduction to the subject matter. In the bibliography that follows are numerous titles that can be consulted for further information. Especially useful as reference materials are the reports of the two national commissions studying American criminal justice institutions in the 1960s and 1970s: the **President's Commission on Law Enforcement and Administration of Justice** and the **National Advisory Commission on Criminal Justice Standards and Goals.** Knowing the system well is a duty for those whose careers include serving in it, managing it, and reporting on it, and is prudent for those whose lives will be touched by it.

LEARNING OBJECTIVES

Upon finishing this chapter, you should be able to do the following:

1. Name and identify the primary functions of each major component of the American criminal justice system.
2. Identify the most commonly used titles of rank in American law enforcement and corrections.
3. Identify the activities of nongovernmental agencies and individuals in providing criminal justice services.
4. Name and identify the investigative responsibilities of several major federal law enforcement agencies within the Departments of Justice and Homeland Security.

IMPORTANT TERMS AND NAMES

- *bailiff*
- *chief*
- *clerks of court*
- *community corrections*
- *court recorder*
- *court reporter*
- *court stenographer*
- *decentralization*
- *defense counsel*
- *Department of Homeland Security (DHS)*
- *director*
- *In re Gault*
- *Gideon v. Wainwright*
- *inspector*
- *INTERPOL (International Police Organization)*
- *jails*
- *judge*
- *justice of the peace*
- *juvenile justice system*
- *Law Enforcement Assistance Administration (LEAA)*
- *magistrate*
- *Missouri Plan*
- *Mothers Against Drunk Driving (MADD)*
- *National Advisory Commission on Criminal Justice Standards and Goals*
- *National Crime Victimization Surveys (NCVS)*
- *nongovernmental organizations (NGOs)*
- *parole*
- *President's Commission on Law Enforcement and Administration of Justice*
- *prison*
- *private investigator*
- *probation*
- *prosecution*
- *sheriffs*
- *special agent-in-charge*
- *stenography*
- *victimology*
- *warden*
- *Wickersham Commission (National Commission on Law Observance and Enforcement)*

References and Supplemental Sources

Abadinsky, H. (2000). *Probation and parole* (7th ed.). Upper Saddle River, NJ: Prentice Hall.

Blumberg, A. (1979). *Criminal justice: Issues and ironies* (2nd ed.). New York: New Viewpoints, Franklin Watts.

Campbell, R., & Raja, S. (1999). Secondary victimization of rape victims: Insights from mental health professionals who treat survivors of violence. *Violence and Victims, 14*(3), 261–275.

Champion, D. J. (2003). *Administration of criminal justice.* Upper Saddle River, NJ: Prentice Hall.

Feldman, M. S., & Khademian, A. M. (2001). Principles for public management practice: From dichotomies to interdependence. *Governance, 14*(3), 339–361.

In re Gault, 387 U.S. 1 (1967).

Gideon v. Wainwright, 372 U.S. 335 (1963).

Gulick, L. H. (1937). Notes on the theory of organization. In Gulick, L., & Urwich, L. (Eds.), *Papers on the science of administration.* New York: Institute of Public Administration.

Hartman, D. J., Friday, P. C., & Minor, K. I. (1994). Residential probation: A Seven-year follow-up study of halfway house discharges. *Journal of Criminal Justice, 22*(6), 503–515.

Kania, R. R. E., & Mackey, W. C. (1983). A preliminary analysis of feminist views on the crime of rape. *Southern Journal of Criminal Justice, 8*(1), 88–104.

Lab, S. P., & Doerner, W. G. (2008). *Victimology* (5th ed.). Burlington, MA: Anderson.

Lab, S. P., & Whitehead, J. T. (2008). *Juvenile justice: An introduction* (6th ed.). Cincinnati: Anderson Publishing Company.

Leary, J., & Chiles, C. L. (1965). Parole administration in the United States. *Crime and Delinquency, 11*(3), 265–271.

Lewis, A. (1964). *Gideon's trumpet.* New York: Random House.

Miranda v. Arizona, 384 U.S. 436 (1966).

Moriarty, L. J. (2008). *Controversies in victimology* (2nd ed.). Burlington, MA: Anderson.

National Advisory Commission on Criminal Justice Standards and Goals, *Corrections.* Washington, DC: Government Printing Office.

National Advisory Commission on Criminal Justice Standards and Goals, *The courts.* Washington, DC: Government Printing Office.

National Advisory Commission on Criminal Justice Standards and Goals, *The criminal justice system.* Washington, DC: Government Printing Office.

National Advisory Commission on Criminal Justice Standards and Goals, *The police.* Washington, DC: Government Printing Office.

National Advisory Commission on Criminal Justice Standards and Goals, *Juvenile justice and delinquency prevention.* Washington, DC: Government Printing Office.

National Advisory Commission on Criminal Justice Standards and Goals, *Private security.* Washington, DC: Government Printing Office.

National Commission on Law Observance and Enforcement (Wickersham Commission), *Wickersham commission reports.* Washington, DC: Government Printing Office.

Ortmeier, P. J. (2009). *Introduction to security: Operations and management.* Upper Saddle River, NJ: Pearson Education/Prentice Hall.

Peak, K. J. (2008). *Justice administration: Police, courts, and corrections management* (6th ed.). Upper Saddle River, NJ: Pearson/Prentice Hall. (Chapter 1)

President's Commission on Law Enforcement and Administration of Justice, *Task force report: Juvenile delinquency and youth crime.* Washington, DC: Government Printing Office.

President's Commission on Law Enforcement and Administration of Justice, *Task force report: The courts.* Washington, DC: Government Printing Office.

President's Commission on Law Enforcement and Administration of Justice, *Task force report: The police.* Washington, DC: Government Printing Office.

Quarles, C. L., Ethan, D., & Waldron, R. J. (2009). *The criminal justice system: An introduction* (5th ed.). CRC Press.

Radelet, L. A. (1980). *The Police and the community* (3rd ed.). New York: Macmillan.

Resick, P. A. (1987). Psychological effects of victimization: Implications for the criminal justice system. *Crime and Delinquency, 33*(4), 468–478.

Senna, J. J., & Siegel, L. J. (2009). *Introduction to criminal justice* (12th ed.). Belmont, CA: Wadsworth.

Schmalleger, F. (2009). *Criminal justice: A brief introduction.* Engelwood Cliffs, NJ: Prentice Hall.

Travis, L. F., III (2008). *Introduction to criminal justice* (6th ed.). Newark, NJ: LexisNexis Matthew Bender.

U.S. Bureau of Prisons, *Jail management: Administration of jail operations.* Washington, DC: Government Printing Office.

Viano, E. (1987). Victim's rights and the constitution: Reflections on a bicentennial. *Crime and Delinquency, 33–34,* 438–451.

Walsh, C. L., & Beck, S. H. (1990). Predictors of recidivism among halfway house residents. *American Journal of Criminal Justice, 15*(1), 137–156.

Wilson, O. W., & McLaren, R. C. (1977). *Police administration* (4th ed.). New York: McGraw-Hill.

Wrobleski, H., & Hess, K. M. (2005). *Introduction to law enforcement and criminal justice* (8th ed.). Belmont, CA: Wadsworth.

Yeldell, S., & Brown, M. (2002). *Victim assistance handbook.* Dubuque, IA: Kendall Hunt.

3 ∷

Historical Antecedents

From the earliest times, people have been seeking better ways to manage large-scale human activities and provide good governance. In ancient Greece, both Socrates and Plato considered questions anticipating the development of the managerial sciences some 2,400 years ago. **Socrates** noted that the basic concepts of organizing an army and staging a chorus for a play required similar managerial talents. **Plato** asked rhetorical questions about the training and selection of the ideal "guardians" for society, and offered answers he attributed to Socrates. About 2,000 years ago Romans created a standing army and established outposts across Europe where the soldiers were based and imperial governors managed the Roman colonies for another 400 years. The Byzantines carried on their practices for another thousand years. Concurrently, the Roman Catholic Church established a system of church self-governance parallel to the Roman and Byzantine civil authorities. A thousand years ago the Chinese were developing a professional civil service and the institution we now call a **bureaucracy**. Yet these developments also faced setbacks as these empires fell and the church underwent a schism. As a result, both governance and criminal justice suffered in Europe until the Enlightenment.

A new form of the state was emerging in Europe in the 17th century. In France, **Cardinal Richelieu** (1585–1642), prime minister to King Louis XIII, was calculating ways to reduce the feudal privileges of the hereditary nobles and begin the modern political state with early notions of bureaucracy and merit selection of **civil servants** (i.e., career civilian public-sector employees working for a government department or agency). **Merit selection** is a way of choosing employees that uses objective selection criteria and a nonpartisan commission or neutral staff to locate, recruit, investigate, and evaluate applicants. What Richelieu created developed into Europe's most advanced public bureaucracy. Under his leadership, new judicial institutions were created in France that employed an educated, merit-selected judiciary under the authority of the King to supplement and replace older, more corrupt, and less effective practices of inherited office holding and patronage appointments (Carey, 1981, pp. 14–21; Richelieu, 1688/1947, pp. 230–249; 1688/1961, pp. 75–89).

At about the same time, the English were undergoing the final stage of their "Great Rebellion" (1648–1649), which established the practice of holding even the King accountable to the law, at the expense of the head of King Charles I (Durant & Durant, 1961, pp. 219–221). Thereafter, the British monarchy learned the necessity of sharing power with its legislature, the Parliament. Although they seemed to have forgotten it by 1776, it was a lesson that the colonial Americans heeded in creating a three-branch government in 1789.

BOX 3.1 CARDINAL RICHELIEU, ORIGINATOR OF EUROPEAN MERIT-BASED BUREAUCRACY

Armand-Jean du Plessis, the Cardinal de Richelieu, from the painting by Phillippe de Champaigne of the Cardinal, now displayed in the Louvre, Paris. Cardinal Richelieu introduced a merit-based criminal justice bureaucracy to Europe while reforming the French judiciary in the service of King Louis XIII. Although a cardinal of the Roman Catholic Church, he served the king of France as the prime minister of the French government from 1624 until his death in 1642.

FIGURE 3.1 Triple Portrait of Cardinal Richelieu. *en.wikipedia.org*

In Chapter 1, you were introduced to eight principles of public management: leading, organizing, deciding, evaluating, staffing, training, allocating, and reporting. These were relatively recent creations among the ideas of humankind. Three intellectual threads involving them have been crossing since 1776 to bring us to where American criminal justice stands today. They are ideas taken from political philosophy, merged with ideas from managerial science and reform ideals within criminal justice.

Pioneers and Predecessors of Modern Public Service Management Theory

In the 17th and 18th centuries, several important pioneers in the social, managerial, and organizational sciences developed concepts applicable to criminal justice. Cesare Beccaria and Jeremy Bentham offered rational, utilitarian ideas on justice and crime control, and Bentham also contributed novel ideas in sentencing and penology. In the new American republic, new ideas about a democratic civil service were proposed and implemented by Thomas Jefferson. In the 19th century, the United States was an established entity. Prominent American figures such as Andrew Jackson, Dorothea Dix, Zebulon

Brockway, and Woodrow Wilson made significant contributions to public service and criminal justice.

Europeans continued to make contributions, especially in the areas of management science. Robert Owen, Charles Babbage, Augusta Ada Byron, Henri Fayol, and Max Weber all contributed. John Stuart Mill expanded on the libertarian concepts found in the public philosophy of Thomas Jefferson, while conservative Tory political leader Sir Robert Peel created an original synthesis of organizational and managerial concepts to give Britain and then the United States a new model for municipal policing. At the same time, Alexander Maconochie pursued reforms in corrections.

The pioneers of the early 20th century—including Frederick W. Taylor, Luther Gulick, August Vollmer, O. W. Wilson, Bruce Smith, Raymond Fosdick, and Roscoe Pound—built upon these ideas to expand social, managerial, and classical organizational theory and added ideas that were applicable to criminal justice.

As mentioned before, interest in management and organizational principles dates back many centuries to the earliest large-scale human enterprises. Indeed, most of the basic principles of organization and management arose from military applications, and as such, they were heavily influenced by the coercive, order-giving style of militaristic leadership. However, in the 18th and 19th centuries, new factors came into play that created the noncoercive approach to management and organization that is now more in favor. It is in this new, more democratic, performance-based model on which American public service management concepts are founded. As we will learn, though, not everyone was of one mind on how to manage public service, and the roots of current disagreements rest deep in our history.

The American public service ideal was forged from three elements: managerial concepts borrowed from commercial enterprise; political concepts about representative, democratic institutions; and scholastic social science theories about what does and does not work. Thus, we must be prepared to study management, political science, and the social sciences to grasp fully what is expected of a person entering a career in the public service.

Cesare Beccaria

Cesare Bonesano Marquis of Beccaria (1738–1794) was an Italian political philosopher and social reformer who was deeply troubled by the practices in the administration of justice in the 18th century. He wrote *On Crimes and Punishments* in 1764 [in the original Italian, *Dei Delitti e Delle Pene*]. French (1766) and English (1767) translations soon followed. In this book, Beccaria clearly established his view that crime was a rational choice, influenced by three deterrent factors: the swiftness, surety, and sufficient severity of punishment. He felt that it was important to forgo torture to extract confessions, and generally believed that the death penalty was an excessive punishment. He also felt that the laws needed to be publicized, the public needed to be educated on the law, and the laws needed to be consistently enforced.

BOX 3.2 *OF CRIMES AND PUNISHMENTS,* BY CESARE BECCARIA

Cesare Beccaria wrote his booklet, **Dei Delitti Delle Pene,** in Italian in 1764 as a critique of the administration of justice in Europe in the middle of the 18th century. Soon translated into French and English, it became a major influence on legal reforms in Europe and America, read by the likes of Thomas Jefferson and John Adams (Yar, 2010: 4).

FIGURE 3.2 **Title Page of** *Dei Delitti e Delle Pene* (en.wikipedia.org) **by Cesare Beccaria, and his statue in Italy** (free-photos.biz).

His small book was highly influential in his lifetime, and among its many readers were Voltaire, Thomas Jefferson, and John Adams. Beccaria became a prominent criminal justice reformer in Europe. He was selected to serve on a board revising the judicial code for the region around Milan in 1791. His reforms applied important 18th-century philosophical ideas, natural law, the social contract, and utilitarianism (Yar, 2010, p. 5). He was an early advocate of what we refer to today as deterrence theory, but was strongly opposed to torture, cruelty, and punitive excess. He thought that the death penalty, in most cases, was just such an excess, and that better deterrents to crime could be found (Internet Encyclopedia of Philosophy, 2001). His ideas were greatly appreciated in the emerging United States and still underlie our system of jurisprudence.

Adam Smith

Adam Smith (1723–1790) is best known for his book, *The Wealth of Nations* (1776/1937). In Chapter 1 of that work, titled "Of the Division of Labor," he illustrated how an industrious individual pin-maker, a master craftsman, could make fewer than 20 pins a day, but 10 men dividing the tasks into 18 distinct operations could make 48,000—240 times as many per worker as could be made by one highly skilled craftsman. Three basic principles were involved in the **division of labor:** increased dexterity in doing a few simple

BOX 3.3 ADAM SMITH AND "OF THE DIVISION OF LABOR"

Adam Smith was both a civil servant and a moral philosopher who, in 1776, introduced Europeans and Americans to the productive and economic virtues of the division of labor, a key element in organizational theory to this day. Smith's work influenced Benjamin Franklin, Alexander Hamilton, Thomas Jefferson, James Madison, and John Adams among our "founding fathers" (Moriarty, 1986).

FIGURE 3.3 **Adam Smith.** *Portrait by Jauneth Skinner ©2011. All rights reserved to the artist.*

operations per worker, time savings by not shifting from one task to another, and the application of labor-saving machines. This reduced costs, while improving the quality of life for everyone. Common people could afford inexpensive pins, hence demand rose to create even more work and higher incomes for the pin-makers. This economic advantage is now known as supply-side economics. Criminal justice officials do not make pins, but the abstract concepts of the division of labor behind pin-making do apply to criminal justice occupations: task specialization, work coordination and integration, and the application of labor-saving technologies. All modern criminal justice agencies now use the concept of the division of labor first described and advocated by Adam Smith.

Smith also explained how social and economic trends occurred as if brought about by some "invisible hand." These "caused" events were brought about not by deterministic forces but by the cumulative effect of many thousands of individual decisions, each reflecting individual reasoning and free will. This point of view on trends is particularly valid for the analysis of change. Instead of seeking some single causal force to explain what we now speak of as a "megatrend," the researcher should examine the event as each individual does, looking for the common elements that all the decision-makers consider. Hence, by this view, the abstraction of "poverty" does not cause the behaviors known collectively as "crime." Certain particular conditions, which taken collectively are known as "poverty," are critical factors in the individual decision-making of all rational individuals, some of whom will decide to act criminally.

Smith himself was a bureaucrat, a customs inspector for Scotland. He wrote one other influential book, *The Theory of Moral Sentiments* (1759/2007), reflecting his interest in moral philosophy. As an economist, he made major contributions to the promotion of free markets and capitalism. In management theory, his major contribution is his explanation and defense of the concept of the division of labor.

Thomas Jefferson

Thomas Jefferson (1743–1826) was the principle author of the Declaration of Independence in 1776; third president of the United States, from 1801 to 1809; founder of the University of Virginia; and a life-long champion of the ideal of a limited government

---

BOX 3.4 THOMAS JEFFERSON, AUTHOR OF THE DECLARATION OF INDEPENDENCE

The Jefferson Memorial in Washington, DC, has a statue of Thomas Jefferson set in front of the inscribed Preamble of the Declaration of Independence. Thomas Jefferson was the principle author of the Declaration of Independence and third president of the United States. As a political philosopher he called for limited government and wanted public officials to function as servants of the people, rather than overseers of them.

FIGURE 3.4 Statue of Thomas Jefferson at the Jefferson Memorial. *en.wikipedia.org*

designed to serve the people rather than rule them. He felt that there were social elites who were responsible for serving the public—an undemocratic *noblesse oblige* concept—but he also believed in the native dignity of all men (other than Indians, African Americans, and those "men" who were born female), which allowed for the rise of those not hereditarily ennobled based on their individual merits and accomplishments.

Jefferson and those who followed his vision for more than a century saw the role of government enterprise as very limited, and the role of the public service manager as that of noble servant, not overseer. His ideas on public service are seminal in the development of the ethical principles of governance in the United States.

Similar views were held by later philosophers, most notably John Stuart Mill, who believed that governments were obliged to act in some situations and ought be constrained in others. The art of political science was distinguishing one from the other.

BOX 3.5 SOME KEY IDEAS OF THOMAS JEFFERSON IN HIS OWN WORDS

"Free government is founded in jealousy, and not in confidence; it is jealousy, and not confidence, which prescribes limited constitutions, to bind down those whom we are obliged to trust with power" (Jefferson, 1798/1904, p. 474).

"Still one more thing, fellow citizens—a wise and frugal government, which shall restrain men from injuring one another, which shall leave them otherwise free to regulate their own pursuits of industry and improvement, and shall not take from the mouth of labor the bread it has earned. This is the sum of good government, and this is necessary to close the circle of our felicities" (Jefferson, 1801).

FIGURE 3.5 Thomas Jefferson. *Portrait by Rembrandt Peale, 1800. en.wikipedia.org*

John Howard

John Howard (1726–1790) became involved in correctional reforms when he became a sheriff in Britain. In the 18th century, the British experimented with more humane

---

BOX 3.6 JOHN HOWARD, PENAL REFORMER AND HUMANITARIAN

John Howard was a sheriff in Britain who was touched by the appalling conditions of the jails [gaols] of his time. He committed his life to the improvement of the condition of prisoners. To this day the John Howard Society continues his efforts around the world.

FIGURE 3.6 John Howard Halfpenny. This special English halfpenny is inscribed on the reverse, "Remember the Debtors in Gaol" and "Go Forth." Such halfpennies were given to the poor in Howard's name to help spread the message of his penal reforms. *Coin from the collection of Richard R. E. Kania.*

FIGURE 3.7 John Howard. *Portrait by Jauneth Skinner ©2011. All rights reserved to the artist.*

---

approaches to law enforcement: the hulks (old warships used as floating prisons), work houses, and jails for short-term offenders. These were not humane places in practice, however. The government did not care for its prisoners properly, and the prisoners or their families had to provide food and other necessities. So awful were the conditions that John Howard wrote *The State of the Prisons* in 1777 as an exposé of the terrible conditions he found in British prisons, hulks, and jails. This embarrassed the British government into making minimal improvements. Originally used as a more humane device for controlling lesser offenders, the hulks sank occasionally, taking all their inmates with them (Campbell, 1993). Even so, they were in use into the 1850s.

Howard is remembered to this day because of the existence of John Howard societies and associations in several English-speaking countries, including Great Britain, Canada, New Zealand, and the United States.

Jeremy Bentham

As a leader in the cause of **utilitarianism** (i.e., the balance of pain and pleasure in making rational decisions), Jeremy Bentham (1748–1832) also was a pioneer in social, judicial, and penal reform. He saw humankind as potentially rational, and thus subject

---

BOX 3.7 JEREMY BENTHAM, A PIONEER IN SOCIAL, JUDICIAL, AND PENAL REFORM

Jeremy Bentham was a penal reformer and quite an eccentric figure. In his will, he gave his fortune and his mummified body (called an "auto-icon") to University College of London, where it remains on display (O'Malley, 2010, p. 12). The head today is a wax replica. Among his many reforms was the "panopticon" prison. His penal reforms applied the philosophy of rational choice and utilitarianism to sentencing.

FIGURE 3.8 Jeremy Bentham. *Portrait by Jauneth Skinner ©2011. All rights reserved to the artist.*

to influence by rational policies. For him and his followers, utility and efficiency were higher-order values. Trained in the practice of law, and influenced by Cesare Beccaria, he in turn influenced both British and American social policy on many matters, including penology. Jeremy Bentham was a wellspring of utilitarian ideas. From the influence of Bentham, the British built the "panopticon" prison, in which a central guard station and cells in tiers around this central "hub" allowed the guards to look into all the cells, and thus fewer guards could monitor the behavior of the prisoners.

Bentham also recommended sentences calculated to fit the crime, and established six rules for punishment:

1. Punishment should be designed to outweigh the advantages of crime.
2. The more severe the offense, the more a scaled, increasingly severe punishment is justified.
3. Punishment should move people to choose lesser criminal options, if it cannot discourage them from crime altogether (to steal to meet one's needs rather than to murder or rob).
4. Each offense should have its own, unique punishment, appropriate to the character and the gain of the offense (a punishment to fit the crime).
5. Punishment should be no more than that minimally necessary to achieve deterrence; excessive punishment is needless cruelty.
6. The usual penalty designed with general deterrence in mind, but sentences calculated with circumstances added in (O'Malley, 2010: 10–11).

Wealthy and politically influential, Bentham was successful in influencing both law and public opinion. In his last book, *Constitutional Code* (1830), he expressed his views that government officials should be selected by competitive examination and that the work of politicians and government officials should be subject to continuous public inspection. Like Jefferson before him, Bentham felt that public officials needed to be reminded continually that they are the "servants, not the masters, of the public" (Simkin, 2003).

Andrew Jackson

Andrew Jackson (1767–1845) was the seventh president of the United States (serving from 1829 to 1837) and the first modern "democrat," and a true "populist," speaking and acting on behalf of the common man. He was a backwoods man, Indian fighter, war hero, and rabble-rouser of a politician. He won the popular vote but not the majority of the electoral college, losing the presidency in 1824. He won it in 1828 and again in 1832.

Jackson's greatest contribution to public affairs was the institutionalization of the spoils system (a practice in which the incoming political party gives government jobs to its party loyalists) in American government. The patronage appointment was not just the norm for this age, it was viewed as the expression of a political ideal. At the national level,

BOX 3.8 ANDREW JACKSON, AN ADVOCATE OF EGALITARIANISM AND OF THE "COMMON MAN"

Andrew Jackson was the seventh president of the United States and an advocate of the common man. He brought ordinary citizens into public service, expanding participation in government, but he also advocated partisan selection of political loyalists as a key criterion for public service appointment.

FIGURE 3.9 Andrew Jackson. *en.wikipedia.org*

Andrew Jackson had announced that the spoils system was to be official government policy when he came to office in 1829, but he certainly was not the first politician to see it this way. In New York City in 1816, the city watchmen who preceded the police force were political appointees of the prior Federalist administration and went out with the party that named them (Richardson, 1970, p. 21).

With his announcements on the spoils system Jackson provided it with an ideological rationalization. As an advocate of **egalitarianism,** Jackson operated from the assumption that a common man of normal intellect could perform a government job as well as any aristocratic Federalist holdover. If the new, politically loyal appointee could perform as well as the outgoing incumbent, then no harm could come to government by the exchange. In this period, which Frederick C. Mosher (1968, pp. 61–63) has described as "government by the common man," the spoils system was viewed as an integral part of the democratic process. President Jackson was careful to select educated and capable men for his appointments, aware in practice that not just anyone could do the work of government. However, not all those who followed his words also followed his example:

> *Jackson's view of public office as a central tenet of an egalitarian philosophy nevertheless became a symbol and guide for his colleagues and successors, not only at the national level of government but in the states and local units as well. Among the consequences of the spoils system, run rampant, were: the periodic chaos which attended changes in administration during most of the nineteenth century; the popular association of public administration with politics and incompetence; the growing conflicts between executive and legislature over appointments . . .; the development of political machines in states, counties, and cities (where most government actually was); and the rise to pre-eminence of lawyer-politicians in every branch of government and at every level. (Mosher, 1968, pp. 62–63)*

The patronage system of appointments introduced dramatic personnel changes to the civil service. Experienced appointees of one administration were discharged en masse to make room for the untrained followers of the new administration (Richardson, 1974, pp. 35–41). An extreme example of this flux was the Cincinnati Police Department, which saw 239 of its 295 officers depart in 1880 and 246 of its 305 police discharged in 1886 as the political fortunes rotated the parties in and out of power (Walker, 1977, p. 9).

Some of the patronage-induced changes were not as negative. Ethnic and racial minorities secured some government positions through political alliances, making those government administrations more representative of the communities they served (Walker, 1980, p. 61). The numerous advantages prolonged the patronage system well into the 20th century, but its problems already were well known and led to numerous calls for its reform. Among those seeing both the pluses and minuses of patronage appointments was Woodrow Wilson (1887), who, long before he was elected president, had advocated a blended system of patronage appointments for decision-makers and merit-based civil service appointments for midlevel and lower-level public servants. To this day we retain some patronage appointments in government, although usually only at the upper-managerial levels.

Robert Owen

Robert Owen (1771–1858) was a Welsh industrialist who sought to create a utopian workers' community around his textile mills. A social reformer, he hoped to create an ideal employment climate. Thus, he previewed what was to become, a century later, the Human Relations School of industrial relations. He saw his workers as **"vital machines"** who had to be cared for with the same attention given to other machines (Ott, 1989, p. 11). The mill town of New Lanark, Scotland, was his experimental utopian town. In cooperation with fellow investors, Quaker William Allen and social theorist Jeremy

BOX 3.9 ROBERT OWEN, IMPROVING PRODUCTIVITY BY TREATING WORKERS AS "VITAL MACHINES"

Robert Owen was a 19th-century British industrialist and advocate for the "vital machines" of commerce, his workforce. By the criteria of the times, he paid well and provided many benefits to workers and their families.

FIGURE 3.10 Robert Owen. *Portrait by Jauneth Skinner ©2011. All rights reserved to the artist.*

Bentham, he provided his workers with a wide range of employment benefits and services and a fair wage. He used productivity data to show that these extra expenses paid dividends in employee stability and high productivity.

Owen's book, *A New View of Society* (1813) was published in the United States in 1825, and its concepts were employed in the building of many American mill towns, such as New Harmony, Indiana, which were America's first "planned communities."

Alexander Maconochie

Alexander Maconochie (1787–1860), a naval officer and well-respected geographer, became a penal reformer later in his life. In 1840, he was named to be the superintendent of the penal colony on Norfolk Island, Australia. Conditions there were brutal, and he initiated many humane reforms. Maconochie established a system of sentence reduction earned by good behavior. He was replaced in 1844, and many of his reforms were ended (*Gazetteer for Scotland*, 2005). However temporary his reforms were at Norfolk Island, he publicized his ideas widely, influencing later reformers who used his penal policy innovations worldwide.

BOX 3.10 ALEXANDER MACONOCHIE, A PENAL REFORMER AND HUMANITARIAN

Alexander Maconochie began his career of public service as an officer in the British navy, attaining the rank of captain. In 1833, he was named the Professor of Geography at the University of London. His interest and knowledge of the Pacific took him to Australia in 1836. He was named governor of the British penal colony of Norfolk Island between 1840 and 1844 and there instituted numerous humane reforms.

FIGURE 3.11 **Alexander Maconochie.** *Portrait by Jauneth Skinner ©2011. All rights reserved to the artist.*

Sir Robert Peel

Sir Robert Peel (1788–1859) was a British politician who put together the political compromise that became the model for modern policing: the London Metropolitan Police of 1829. Municipal policing is a relatively new concept when viewed against the expanse of human history. It was a social reform as much as it was a practical response to the serious crime problems of that city. It offered all of the advantages of the traditional decentralized English social control system, while matching the efficiency of the military-model state police forces of the continent in combating crime and disorder. Peel was the Tory Home Secretary who implemented this social innovation. The Tories, the English conservatives, felt threatened by political unrest and the maneuvering of their political opponents, but they also had to deal with the suspicion of government

BOX 3.11 SIR ROBERT PEEL, INNOVATOR OF THE MODERN MODEL FOR URBAN POLICING

Sir Robert Peel was Home Secretary and later Prime Minister of Great Britain. He led the reform of law enforcement in 1829 that resulted in the "new model" London Metropolitan Police.

FIGURE 3.12 Sir Robert Peel. *Portrait by Jauneth Skinner ©2011. All rights reserved to the artist.*

BOX 3.12 SIR ROBERT PEEL'S INSTRUCTIONS TO THE LONDON METROPOLITAN POLICE

"It should be understood at the onset, that the object to be attained is the prevention of crime.

To this great end every effort of the police is to be directed. The security of person and property and the preservation of a police establishment will thus be better effected than the detection and punishment of the offender after he has succeeded in committing crime. …

He [the constable] will be civil and obliging to all people of every rank and class.

He must be particularly cautious not to interfere idly or unnecessarily in order to make a display of his authority; when required to act, he will do so with decision and boldness;

He must remember that there is no qualification so indispensable to a police-officer as a perfect command of temper, never suffering himself to be moved in the slightest degree by any language or threats that may be used; …

In the novelty of the present establishment, particular care is to be taken that the constables of the police do not form false notions of their duties and powers force." (Peel, 1829, quoted in Critchley, 1972, p. 52)

inherent in the Utilitarian doctrines of the rising English middle class. The leading Utilitarians, Jeremy Bentham, Edwin Chadwick, and Patrick Colquhoun, provided the compromise solution that a Tory government could accept: a degree of local control over law enforcement was maintained, under Home Office regulation, and a strong military-style law enforcement organization was formed. The English ideals of liberty were unthreatened, while the Tories acquired a police force strong enough to bring order back to London (Critchley, 1972, pp. 49–50). It was a political compromise in the best English political tradition.

Like any new idea, the police force experienced problems from its inception, some of which continue to this day. The first police constables were recruited from the ranks of the existing parish night watches and various foot and horse patrols. Although considerable effort was directed toward the selection of suitable men, many of the first recruits were not fit to be police. In the early years, there were charges of drunkenness, brutality, spying, and other forms of political tyranny (Critchley, 1972, pp. 52–55). The British Home Secretary anticipated many of the problems and drafted instructions and regulations for his new police.

Thus, the new model police had features that, when brought together in one agency at the same time, were novel law enforcement arrangements. These police:

1. Were selected for merit, for being moral, and for being able to read and write.
2. Were paid fixed salaries in a time when most still earned fees.
3. Were tax-supported, with both municipal and national funds.
4. Were municipal in orientation and obligations; but quasi-municipal in their control, with the Home Office having a regulatory role.
5. Patrolled in geographic beats, out among the citizens.
6. Were uniformed, but not in the Army style.
7. Carried no firearms, only wooden batons.
8. Were responsible to every citizen equally.
9. Were recruited from working classes, rather than elites.
10. Were apolitical, unable even to vote initially.

Charles Babbage

Charles Babbage (1792–1871) was an advocate of technological innovation and the inventor of a precursor of the computer. He called it his "difference engine," but never completed a successful prototype. He attempted to apply new technologies to reduce the labor intensity of early industrial work. He argued that industrialists should evaluate the utility of machines and the division of labor, using criteria of the quality of output and the costs of production (Swade, 2001). He demonstrated how using labor-saving technologies produced greater efficiencies and increased productivity, giving us the concept of **applied technology.** He published his views in his book, *On the Economy of Machinery and Manufactures* (1835, original published 1832), which previewed most of the ideas now associated with "scientific management."

BOX 3.13 CHARLES BABBAGE, EARLY ADVOCATE OF APPLIED TECHNOLOGY FOR EFFICIENCY

Charles Babbage was a 19th-century British industrialist and inventor who advocated using labor-saving machines to improve both the efficiency of organizations and to reduce the physical demands on his laborers. He also designed a precursor to the computer, which he called the "difference engine." Babbage's computer design was built in 1991 and worked just as Babbage supposed it would (Swade, 1993).

FIGURE 3.13 Charles Babbage. *en.wikipedia.org.*

Augusta Ada Byron King

Widely known in modern times as Ada Lovelace, Augusta King (1815–1852), the Countess of Lovelace, and daughter of the famous poet, Lord Byron, is recognized as one of the earliest computer programmers. Lovelace applied her wealth and influence to support early work into calculating machines. Her sponsorship of the work of Charles Babbage's difference engines went far beyond financial investment, for she was well known for her mathematical skills and mastery of symbolic logic, which she directed to computer applications, translating and annotating works on the subject (Crawford, 1983, pp. 241–242). She acquired her interest in mathematics from her mother, Anne Isabella Milbanke, Baroness Wentworth (1792–1860), who was a recognized mathematician in her own right. The computer language "Ada," formerly used by the U.S. Department of Defense, was named in her honor (Uglow, 1982).

Augusta Ada Byron King, the Countess of Lovelace, daughter of the famous poet, Lord Byron, was a 19th-century British associate of Charles Babbage, who helped him develop the algorithms for his difference engine—in essence, the first person to develop computer software. Independently wealthy, she also helped finance his research.

FIGURE 3.14 Augusta Ada Byron King. *Portrait by Jauneth Skinner ©2011. All rights reserved to the artist.*

John Augustus

John Augustus (1785–1859) is credited with introducing probation to American courts. In 1841, he posted a bail bond for a criminal suspect and took responsibility for that person. Before he did so, he undertook an investigation into the background and circumstances of the man—what some now credit as start of presentencing investigations—and was selective in bonding offenders (Jones, 2005, p. 178). He used his legal control over that man to guide him toward reform and keep him out of prison. In the next two decades, he similarly bailed out and tried to reform about 2,000 people. Prior to John Augustus it was common for sheriffs to discharge offenders into the custody of citizens for involuntary servitude, selling convict labor. In the South, it was a discredited way of reconstituting slavery. In 1878, the Commonwealth of Massachusetts passed a probation statute making official what Augustus and his successor, Rufus Cook, had been doing for decades. By 1920, every state had a similar system.

BOX 3.15 JOHN AUGUSTUS, THE ORIGINATOR OF PRESENTENCING INVESTIGATIONS AND PROBATION

John Augustus was a Boston entrepreneur who has been called the "Father of Probation" in the United States. He advocated for lenient treatment for some convicted criminals, based on an in-depth investigation into their background and circumstances, what was the start of presentencing investigation.

FIGURE 3.15 **John Augustus.** *Portrait by Jauneth Skinner ©2011. All rights reserved to the artist.*

Elam Lynds

Elam Lynds (1784–1855) was the first warden of the Auburn, New York, prison and creator of the "Auburn system" of correctional practice, named after the 1816 Auburn Prison, (Pettigrove, 1910, pp. 31–34). The Auburn system was characterized by the "tier" or "congregate" arrangement. Its rows and tiers of cells were used for solitary and silent confinement, mixed with periods of closely supervised labor and supervised interaction among inmates (congregation). From Auburn Prison, Lynds moved to Ossining, New York, where he used convict labor to build a new prison, Sing Sing, which opened in 1826. So important and profitable was this inmate labor that Lynds contracted with private entrepreneurs to use this convict slave labor to make many useful consumer goods (Gado, 2003). These were sold to the public for the profit of the prison and the entrepreneurs. As exploitive as this was, the work also helped inmates learn useful skills that they could use profitably after release.

Today Lynds is criticized as a harsh warden, but in his era he was a progressive reformer. Only troublesome inmates were kept in total silence and isolation all day. Hard work, controlled interaction, and silence were the key features of this system, and as a result it is often referred to as the **"silent system"** (Reid, 1999, p. 243). Violations were met with severe physical punishment, usually whippings. Prisoners were chained together in the infamous chain gangs, and taught how to march in lockstep when chained so as not to tangle their chains under the feet of other inmates. At Auburn, beginning in 1821, prisoners were classified by the character of their crimes and segregated within the penal institution. Dangerous offenders were in perpetual isolation, while less dangerous offenders were given some limited social time and were allowed to attend workshops, at which they labored in total silence (Reid, 1999, p. 244).

BOX 3.16 ELAM LYNDS, PRISON ADMINISTRATOR AND INNOVATOR OF PRISON INMATE PROGRAMS

As warden of Auburn Prison and later Sing-Sing Penitentiary, Elam Lynds innovated a penal method for controlling and employing inmates, which allowed them to work together during the day (congregation) and kept them in solitary confinement at night, with enforced silence. The inmates were moved in chains in "lockstep," a 19th-century innovation developed under Elam's direction at Auburn Prison.

FIGURE 3.16 Elam Lynds. *Portrait by Jauneth Skinner ©2011. All rights reserved to the artist.*

Dorothea Lynde Dix

Dorothea Dix (1802–1887) was an American social reformer who was deeply concerned with the welfare of the insane (Tiffany, 1890). She toured the country and lobbied for the establishment of humane mental institutions. As a result, a number of states opened such institutions, and existing institutions improved the treatment of their inmates. During the American Civil War, Dix was the Superintendent of Army Nurses. She used that post to extend care to Confederate prisoners in Union prison camps. She directed some of her efforts to improving prison conditions for conventional offenders, and she also worked to improve the treatment of people with various handicaps, such as the blind, the deaf, and the mute. Dix's efforts at prison reform were in part inspired by Elizabeth Gurney Fry (1780–1845), a noted prison reformer of the early 19th century and a Quaker, a member of the Religious Society of Friends.

BOX 3.17 DOROTHEA DIX, 19TH-CENTURY AMERICAN SOCIAL REFORMER

As a reformer, Dorothea Dix was an advocate for the mentally ill and the imprisoned. She used her social standing and position to bring about major reforms in the way inmates were treated and cared for in American prisons.

FIGURE 3.17 **Dorothea Dix.** *Portrait by Jauneth Skinner ©2011. All rights reserved to the artist.*

Because of the connections between insanity and criminality, many of the people Fry and Dix helped were identified as criminally insane. On a visit to a local jail in Boston in 1841, Dix was teaching a Bible class for a group of incarcerated women. She then visited other parts of the jail, including the areas where insane inmates were chained to the walls. What she saw there led her to begin her reform campaigns on behalf of inmates and the mentally ill (Jones, 2005, p. 182).

Zebulon Reed Brockway

Zebulon Reed Brockway (1827–1920) was another reform-oriented warden. At the prison in Elmira, New York, he instituted the Elmira model, which offered inmates the hope of parole for good behavior and cooperation and provided training and educational opportunities to inmates (Jones, 2005, pp. 195–196). He advocated novel correctional concepts such as indeterminate sentences and improved on the system of inmate classification. The Elmira

---

BOX 3.18 ZEBULON REED BROCKWAY, INNOVATIVE PRISON MANAGER AND REFORMER

Under Warden Zebulon Reed Brockway, Elmira Prison in Elmira, New York, became a model for innovative programs for inmates, which included education, the acquisition of useful work skills, and parole for good behavior. Brockway introduced an improved system of prisoner classification and other managerial reforms to create a more efficient and humane institution.

FIGURE 3.18 Zebulon Reed Brockway. *Portrait by Jauneth Skinner ©2011. All rights reserved to the artist.*

institution was an industrial facility that used the inmates for uncompensated slave labor, but it did provide job skills and minimal education to its inmates. As such, it was a major reform in its time (the 1870s through the 1920s). It may be that Reed borrowed these ideas from Maconochie and his publicist and supporter, Sir Walter Crofton (Reid, 1999, pp. 245–246), for they also had recommended rewards, population size control, progressive restriction reduction, and parole eligibility for well-behaving inmates long before Brockway had. But it was Brockway who implemented such ideas at Elmira, both to control the inmate population and to achieve the moral rehabilitation of inmates. He publicized his success, and progressive correctional managers across the United States followed his example.

John Stuart Mill

As Jacksonian democracy began to supplant Jeffersonian idealism, the government was playing an ever-larger role in people's lives. In Britain, as in the United States, there were individuals who found this objectionable and called for the restoration of the earlier values. As the author of the essay "On Liberty" (1859/1956), John Stuart Mill (1806–1873) expressed many of the views of the Benthamites (Utilitarians) and the 19th-century liberals and radicals of Great Britain. His advocacy of limited government was not unlike that

---

BOX 3.19 JOHN STUART MILL, MORAL PHILOSOPHER AND ADVOCATE FOR HUMAN LIBERTY

John Stuart Mill was a 19th-century British political philosopher who, like Thomas Jefferson, believed in limited government and minimal governmental regulation of human activity, except when that activity was harmful to others.

FIGURE 3.19 John Stuart Mill. *Portrait by Jauneth Skinner ©2011. All rights reserved to the artist.*

favored by Jefferson. He was not an anarchist, as some imply, but believed that governments were obliged to act in some situations and ought be constrained in others. The art of political science was sorting one from the other:

> *The object of this essay is to assert one very simple principle, as entitled to govern absolutely the dealings of society with the individual in the way of compulsion and control. . . That principle is that the sole end for which mankind are warranted, individually or collectively, in interfering with the liberty of action of any of their number is self-protection. That the only purpose for which power can be rightfully exercised over any member of a civilized community, against his will, is to prevent harm to others. His own good, either physical or moral, is not a sufficient warrant (Mill, 1859/1956, p. 13).*

Human liberty was not without some reasonable restriction. There was justification for requiring people to act in the best interests of others when such actions were not to their own disinterest.

> *A person may cause evil to others not only by his actions but by his inaction, and in either case he is justly accountable to them for the injury. . . .*
>
> *The only freedom which deserves the name is that of pursuing our own good in our own way, so long as we do not attempt to deprive others of theirs or impede their efforts to obtain it. Each is the proper guardian of his own health, whether bodily or mental and spiritual. Mankind are greater gainers by suffering each other to live as seems good to themselves than by compelling each to live as seems good to the rest. (Mill, 1859/1956, pp. 15, 17)*

Mill was a true 19th-century liberal and a Jeffersonian idealist. As Mill aged, he became more socialistic in his viewpoints. He did not quite abandon his earlier advocacy of classical liberalism, but became more interested in helping the disadvantaged, especially women, and began to argue in favor of governmental interventions to reverse discriminatory patterns in law and custom.

Woodrow Wilson

Best known as the president of the United States from 1913 through 1921, Woodrow Wilson (1856–1924) also was governor of New Jersey, and before that, a college professor at Princeton. As a professor of government, he helped create the field of public administration within political science and political philosophy.

His major scholarly work was an article, "The Study of Administration," printed in 1887 in *Political Science Quarterly*. In it, he wrote: "It is the object of administrative study to discover, first, what government can properly and successfully do, and, secondly, how it can do these proper things with the utmost efficiency. . . ." He argued for the separation of routine administrative functions of government, which he felt should be assigned to career, merit-selected, civil service employees, from the political and policy-making positions of elective and appointed government officials (the politically loyal leadership). His bifurcated model is widely followed today in criminal justice and the public service generally.

BOX 3.20 WOODROW WILSON, COLLEGE PROFESSOR, GOVERNOR, AND PRESIDENT

Woodrow Wilson was the 28th president of the United States and an advocate of civil service reform. He was the United States' only Ph.D. president (other than presidents who were given honorary doctorates). He believed that patronage appointments should be limited to policy-making positions only, with all other public servants selected primarily for merit.

FIGURE 3.20 **Woodrow Wilson.** *Library of Congress, Prints & Photographs Division, photograph by Harris & Ewing, LC-USZ62-123456.*

Roscoe Pound

Educated at Harvard Law School, Nathan Roscoe Pound (1870–1964) practiced law in Nebraska, then returned to Harvard Law to teach from 1910 to 1916 and then serve as its dean from 1916 to 1936. Pound was a prolific author with at least 15 published books, among them including *Introduction to the Philosophy of Law* (1922), *Criminal Justice in America* (1930), *Social Control through Law* (1942), and *The Lawyer from Antiquity to Modern Times* (1953), and many articles (Setaro, 1942; Online Library of Liberty, 2011). His pioneering use of sociological concepts and studies in these works set the model for most modern criminal justice research. He and future Supreme Court Justice Felix Frankfurter applied content analysis to measure newspaper coverage of crime, and discovered that crime waves were more hype than substance (Pound & Frankfurter, 1922). He is credited with bringing social sciences and law together as "**sociological jurisprudence.**" His application of social science research to the study and analysis of criminal justice issues has been a common feature of late 20th- and 21st-century criminal justice studies.

BOX 3.21 ROSCOE POUND, JUDGE, LEGAL AND JUDICIARY REFORMER

Roscoe Pound was a legal reformer who influenced the manner in which the American judiciary looked at the law itself. He used empirical scientific methods to study crime problems, and he wrote a history of the legal profession in 1953.

FIGURE 3.21 Roscoe Pound. *en.wikipedia.org*

Summary

The brilliant minds and carefully considered ideas of a great many men and women have been applied to the question of how best to manage a public service or criminal justice organization or how best to provide criminal justice services to the public. Our modern approaches to these issues are rooted in the contributions of these men and women; merit selection of public servants; the notion of government officials as public servants and not rulers; the humane treatment of both workers and the people in custody; the intelligent application of labor-saving technologies and principles, such as the division of labor; new and better ways of providing public services, such as the London police model or the panopticon prison; and the application of social science research to criminal justice police and practices are all early innovations that are still with us today. Contemporary criminal justice managers have the capacity and the duty to propose new approaches and bring innovations into the modern criminal justice workplace, just as these reformers and leaders did in the past.

The study of historical developments in criminal justice can be of great value to a future criminal justice manager. Knowing how we got to where we are now can offer insights to the problems our predecessors had to face and the solutions they were able to utilize. Excellent studies of major pioneers in criminal justice and important past studies can be found in several valuable collections (Hayward, Maruna & Mooney, 2010; Jones, 2005, Thistlethwaite & Wooldredge, 2010).

LEARNING OBJECTIVES

Upon finishing this chapter, you should be able to do the following:

1. Identify the three intellectual sources of the ideas on which American public service stands.
2. Identify three American presidents whose ideas contributed significantly to the development of the American civil service.
3. Identify leading reformers in policing, corrections, and jurisprudence in Europe and the United States and know their specific contributions.
4. Identify leading managerial theorists whose ideas have been incorporated into the American criminal justice system.

IMPORTANT TERMS AND NAMES

- *John Augustus*
- *Charles Babbage*
- *Cesare Beccaria*
- *Jeremy Bentham*
- *bureaucracy*
- *civil servants*
- *division of labor*
- *Dorothea Dix*
- *egalitarianism*
- *John Howard*
- *Andrew Jackson*
- *Thomas Jefferson*
- *Augusta Ada Byron King*
- *Elam Lynds*
- *Alexander Maconochie*
- *merit selection*
- *John Stuart Mill*
- *Robert Owen*
- *patronage system*
- *Sir Robert Peel*
- *Plato*
- *Roscoe Pound*
- *Zebulon Reed Brockway*
- *Cardinal Richelieu*
- *silent system*
- *Adam Smith*
- *sociological jurisprudence*
- *Socrates*
- *utilitarianism*
- *Woodrow Wilson*

References and Supplemental Sources

Babbage, C. (1835). *On the economy of machinery and manufactures* (4th ed.). London: C. Knight.

Beccaria, C. (1764/2004). *On crimes and punishments* (original title in Italian, *Dei delitti e delle pene*). Reprint of English edition: Whitefish, MT: Kessinger Publishing Co.

Bentham, J. (1830). *Constitutional code.*

Campbell (1993). *The intolerable hulks: british shipboard confinement, 1776-1857.* Bowie, MD: Heritage Books.

Carey, J. A. (1981). *Judicial reform in France before the Revolution of 1789.* Boston: Harvard University Press.

Crawford, A. (Ed.). (1983). *The Europa biographical dictionary of British women.* London: Europa.

Critchley, T. A. (1972). *A history of police in England and Wales.* Montclair, NJ: Patterson Smith.

Durant, W., & Durant, A. (1961). *The story of civilization, Part VII: The Age of Reason begins.* New York: Simon & Schuster.

Gado, M. (2003). The profit of slave labor. In: Stone upon stone: Sing Sing Prison. New York: New York Correction History Society. Retrieved from <http://www.correctionhistory.org/auburn&osborne/bighouse1.htm/>; and TruTV Crime Library © 2010 Turner Broadcasting System, Inc. A Time Warner Company. Retrieved from <http://www.trutv.com/library/crime/notorious_murders/famous/sing_sing/2.html/>.

Gazetteer for Scotland (2005). The Gazetteer for Scotland ©1995–2005, the Robertson Trust, Royal Scottish Geographical Society, Institute of Geography, University of Edinburgh. Retrieved from <http://www.geo.ed.ac.uk/scotgaz/people/famousfirst733.html/>

Hayward, K., Maruna, S., & Mooney, J. (Eds.), (2010). *Fifty key thinkers in criminology.* New York: Routledge.

Howard, J. (1777). *The state of the prisons.*

Internet Encyclopedia of Philosophy (2001). Cesare Beccaria (1738–1794). Retrieved from <http://www.iep.utm.edu/beccaria/>

Jefferson, T. (1798/1904). The Kentucky Resolutions of 1798. In: Ford, P. L. (Ed.), (1798/1904). *The works of Thomas Jefferson* (vol. 8 of 12). New York: Putnam, Knickerbocker Press.

Jefferson, T. (1801). First Inaugural Address, March 4, 1801. The Avalon Project at Yale Law School. Retrieved from <http://avalon.law.yale.edu/19th_century/jefinau1.asp/>

Jones, M. (2005). *Criminal justice pioneers in U.S. history.* Upper Saddle River, NJ: Prentice Hall.

Kim, E. E., & Toole, B. A. (1999). Ada and the first computer. *Scientific American, 280*(5), 76–81.

Mill, J. S. (1859/1956). *On liberty.* Indianapolis: Bobbs-Merrill.

Moriarty, D. (1986, November). Adam Smith: America's "adopted" founding father. *The Constitution.*

Mosher, F. C. (1968). *Democracy and the public service.* New York: Oxford University Press.

Nelson, M. (1982). A short, ironic history of American national bureaucracy. *The Journal of Politics, 44*(3), 747–778.

Online Library of Liberty (2011). "Law and liberty by Roscoe Pound," Online Library of Liberty. Retrieved on 14 August 2011 from < http://oll.libertyfund.org/option=com_content&task=view&id=337&Itemid=284 > .

O'Malley, P. (2010). Jeremy Bentham. In: Hayward, K., Maruna, S., & Mooney, J. (Eds.), *Fifty key thinkers in criminology* (pp. 7–12). New York: Routledge.

Ott, J. S. (1989). *Classic readings in organizational behavior* (1st ed.). Pacific Grove, CA: Brooks/Cole.

Owen, R. (1813). *A new view of society.*

Owen, R. (1825). *A new view of society* [first American edition].

Pettigrove, F. G. (1910). State prisons of the United States under separate and congregate systems. In: Henderson, C. R. (Ed.), *Penal and reformatory institutions, Vol. 2: Corrections and prevention* (pp. 27–67). Philadelphia: Press of William F. Fell.

Plato. (1961). *The republic* (P. Shorey, trans.). In: Hamilton, E., & Cairns, H. (Eds.), *The collected dialogues of Plato.* Princeton, NJ: Princeton University Press.

Pound, R. (1922). *Introduction to the philosophy of law.* New Haven, CT: Yale University Press.

Pound, R. (1930). *Criminal justice in america.* New York: Henry Holt.

Pound, R. (1942). *Social control through law.* New Haven, CT: Yale University Press.

Pound, R. (1953). *The lawyer from antiquity to modern times.* St. Paul, MN: West.

Pound, R., & Frankfurter, F. (1922). *Criminal justice in Cleveland.* Cleveland: Cleveland Foundation.

Reed, Z. (1912). *Fifty years of prison service.* New York: Charities Publications Committee.

Reid, S. T. (1999). *Crime and criminology* (9th ed.). Boston: McGraw-Hill.

Richardson, J. F. (1970). *The New York police.* New York: Oxford University Press.

Richardson, J. F. (1974). *Urban police in the United States.* Port Washington, NY: Kennikat Press, National University Publications.

Richelieu, A. J. P., Duke and Cardinal (1688/1947). *Testament politique, edition critique* (L. Andre, ed. and annotater). Paris: Robert Laffont.

Richelieu, A. J. P., Duke and Cardinal (1688/1961). *The political testament of Cardinal Richelieu* (H. B. Hill, trans.) Madison, WI: University of Wisconsin Press.

Setaro, F. C. (1942). *Bibliography of the writings of Roscoe Pound.* Cambridge, MA: Harvard University Press.

Simkin, J. (2003) Bentham. *Spartacus Educational.* Retrieved from <http://www.spartacus.schoolnet.co.uk/PRbentham.htm/>

Smith, A. (1776/1937). *The wealth of nations.* New York: Random House.

Smith, A. (1759/2007). *The theory of moral sentiments.* Champaign, IL: Standard Publications, Inc.

Socrates discovers generic management [an extract from Xenophon] (1992). Article 1 in Shafritz, J. M., & Ott, J. S., *Classics of organization theory,* 3rd ed. Pacific Grove, CA: Brooks/Cole.

Swade, D. D. (1993). Redeeming Charles Babbage's mechanical computer. *Scientific American, 268*(2), 86–91.

Swade, D. D. (2001). *The difference engine: Charles Babbage and the quest to build the first computer.* New York: Viking.

Tiffany, F. (1890). *The life of Dorothea Lynde Dix.* Boston: Riverside Press.

Uglow, J. S. (Ed.). (1982). *International dictionary of women's biography.* New York: Continuum.

Walker, S. (1977). *A critical history of police reform.* Lexington, MA: Lexington Books.

Walker, S. (1980). *Popular justice: A history of American criminal justice.* New York: Oxford University Press.

Weber, M. (1922). In: Roth, G., & Wittich, C. (Eds.), *Economy and society* (2 volumes). Berkeley, CA: University of California Press.

Wilson, W. (1887). The study of administration. *Political Science Quarterly, 2*(2), 197–222.

Yar, M. (2010). Cesare Beccaria. In: Hayward, K., Maruna, K., & Mooney, J. (Eds.), *Fifty key thinkers in criminology* (pp. 3–7). New York: Routledge.

4

Leading in Criminal Justice

"Leading" is the first of the "LODESTAR" functions of every public service manager. Leadership is a fine art, not a science. It has been a frequent topic of books in management science (Burns, 1978; Drucker, 1967). Peter Northouse (2009) sees it as consisting of traits, abilities, skills, behaviors, and relationships. Eric Beebe's (2010) examination of the leadership literature finds six paradigms of leadership: the great man, trait, behaviorist, situational, role-based, and relational (pp. 1–2). His analysis draws heavily on the work of Bernard Bass and Ralph Melvin Stogdill (Bass, 1990; Stogdill, 1974). Others have added a seventh paradigm (King, 2008; Price, 2003; Rippy, 1990), focusing on the "transformational leader," a change agent, a concept introduced by James MacGregor Burns (1978). In criminal justice, many men and women have brought about significant improvements in the way criminal justice services are delivered and criminal justice organizations are run.

Everyone who studies leadership can ascertain its key ingredients and components, but knowing the right mix of these ingredients is an art. Just as knowing the materials and techniques of painting does not ensure the production of great art, knowing the methods and techniques of leadership does not guarantee you will be a great leader, or even a good one. Leading involves giving direction and supervision. It requires authority and, in criminal justice organizations, an office from which to exercise it.

Leadership Selection

Selecting a criminal justice manager in our democratic system of public service can be done in several ways. Each has its appropriate place, sometimes selected by custom and sometimes by sophisticated thought and reasoning. However derived, the decision to appoint a criminal justice manager to lead a criminal justice organization will occur via one of two basic approaches: (1) direct election, or (2) appointment.

Elections are conducted in accordance with the laws of the political entity or the bylaws of the public service agency using elective selection. Decision by election can require:

- unanimity—total agreement of all entitled to vote;
- a weighted majority—some percentage greater than half;
- a simple majority—any number more than half of the total; or
- a plurality—the greatest number of votes, but not necessarily the majority of those cast.

Popular election, usually by plurality or simple majority, is used to select some of the key managers in the criminal justice system: sheriffs, many clerks of court, some judges,

71

district attorneys, police commissioners, and directors of public safety. In most cases, these are the chief executive positions within the organization.

Most managers in public service are not elected, however. They are appointed. **Appointments** can occur according to several criteria:

- **Performance-based merit selection**—selecting the best qualified candidate, or one fully qualified, using rational, performance-based criteria.
- **Nonmerit selection**—using noncompetitive criteria that are not directly performance-based, such as political affiliation, kinship, friendship, contributions and donations (and even bribes), settlement of debts and outstanding obligations, racial or sexual preference, etc.
- **Combined merit/nonmerit criteria**—selection of one of those fully qualified by additional nonmerit criteria (the ideal of affirmative action programs).

Managers in criminal justice are expected to be both leaders and policy-makers. Those who are elected to office or serve as political appointees can expect to stay in or lose their positions as a direct consequence of the quality and effectiveness of their policy-making abilities.

This was one of the key points made by Woodrow Wilson (1887) in his advocacy of the division between politics and administration: the people who work in politics (elected officials and their personal appointees) are subject to the approval or disapproval of the people by means of the ballot box. However, in Woodrow Wilson's bifurcated model, administrators would in general be immune from the harsh realities of elective politics, safe within the civil service system.

Yet these civil servants often also make policy. Ought they not also to be held accountable to the public through the elective political processes? The answer he gave is "no," and his reason was that these civil service administrators are making "second-order policy," designed only to carry out the "first-order policy" of those elected and the patronage officials who are subject to the ballot.

Chester Barnard discussed the concept of "executive work" (1938/1989): those tasks the leader performs that are not the functional work of the organization. In criminal justice contexts, a police chief does not usually investigate crimes, direct traffic, or write motor vehicle violation tickets. He or she has duties that are quite different from the rank and file of the organization, Barnard's "organization work." Barnard observes that executives do a fair measure of nonexecutive work, but it is not the justification for their employment. In his essay, he offers yet another answer to Luther Gulick's question, slightly modified to "What is the work of the executive?" His answer: maintaining a system of cooperative effort (coordinating), organizational communication (reporting), defining the scheme of organization (organizing), recruiting and dealing with personnel matters (staffing), including acquiring their loyalty and influencing them (leading), and formulating purposes and objectives for the organization (deciding, including planning).

First-order policy-making, also called **primary policy-making**, includes the policies that set the major goals and objectives of the organization. **Second-order policy-making**, also called **secondary policy-making**, includes the policies that are made to implement the major goals and objectives of the organization. For example, the Congress or the state legislature will pass legislation that creates a new program and outlines in general terms what the goals and objectives of that program are. The president or governor and the top cabinet officials then task and organize their agencies to create implementation mechanisms to carry out these mandates, clarifying these goals and objectives. Setting and refining these goals and objectives are political first-order policy matters.

The manager of the federal or state agency assigned to carry out the program mandated by the Congress or state legislature will establish specific policies and procedures to implement the program. These will be in compliance with the legislated goals and objectives; hence, this is second-order policy-making.

Attributes of Successful Leaders

The Traits of a Leader

Numerous authorities have developed lists of attributes that they feel are needed to be an effective leader. This is the *laundry-list approach;* it offers a compilation of worthwhile traits. Many such lists have been proposed, including those of Joseph Massie (1987) and General Mark Clark and Rensis Likert (Souryal, 1995). Massie takes the viewpoint of academic expertise in criminal justice management (1987, p. 102). General Mark Clark was a distinguished army commander in World War II, with a long record of public service after the war, and offers the perspective of a military mind. Rensis Likert is a social psychologist, researcher, and management theorist who has given leadership serious study and consideration. Likert's list takes the approach of a social psychologist with a strong interest in management research. A quick examination of Box 4.1, with comparisons of leadership trait lists, shows that the three perspectives agree on very little. Yet it would be hard to argue against the inclusion of any of the traits each lists.

The **Leader Behavior Descriptive Questionnaire (LBDQ)** was developed at Ohio State University as a project undertaken by the Ohio State Leadership Studies Office, at the time directed by Carroll L. Shartle. The LBDQ provides a work group the opportunity

---

BOX 4.1 COMPARISONS OF LEADERSHIP TRAIT LISTS

Joseph Massie (1987, p. 102): age, maturity, extroversion, intelligence, verbal skills, physical bearing, attractiveness, height, charisma, education, popularity, decisiveness, aggressiveness

   General Mark Clark (Souryal, 1995, pp. 106–107): confidence, energy, timing, clarity, tenacity, boldness, concern, morality, faith

   Rensis Likert (Souryal, 1995, p. 107): unselfishness, sympathy, cooperation, enthusiasm, intellect, interest in workers, friendliness, morality, planning ability to describe the behavior of their leader in any kind of organization. The primary condition is that the subordinates must routinely have observed their leader in action (Fisher College of Business, 2008). The LBDQ allows a researcher to examine the leadership traits workers use to evaluate their leaders. The questionnaire is available for nonprofit use by any organization that can make use of such information. Two dimensions emerge:

Considerations: These include such traits as trust, respect, support, rapport, and communication.

Initiating Structures: The factors defining and structuring the leadership role, including active or passive approaches to planning, directing, and scheduling work activities.

When employees are asked what they like, admire, or appreciate in their managers, they cite certain important qualities:

- patience
- kindness
- wisdom
- trust
- virtue
- knowledge
- empathy
- self-control

Task Analysis

Another approach to determining what makes a good leader involves task analysis. What skills must the leader master to be effective? Robert Katz (1974) places emphasis on three areas of the **skills of a leader:**

- technical skills
- human relations skills, including empathy, tolerance of ambiguity, and the ability to work within a team
- conceptual skills

Four ideas about leadership in public service organizations have emerged from this skill-focused approach to leadership (Klofas, Stojkovic, & Kalinich, 1990, pp. 124–125):

- It is a process for accomplishing organizational goals;
- It can be learned;
- It is a group process, to include:
  1. legitimate request,
  2. instrumental compliance,
  3. coercion,
  4. rational persuasion,

   5. rational faith,
   6. inspirational appeal,
   7. indoctrination,
   8. information distortion,
   9. situational engineering,
   10. personal identification,
   11. decision identification.
- Within the criminal justice system, it is inherently political.

As discussed in Chapter 1, Luther Gulick was an American authority on public admin-istration. His approach to the study of leadership also focused on the tasks of the public service executive. He sought to define and explain the role of the senior public service manager by asking and then answering the question, "What is the work of a chief exec-utive? What does he do?" The answer he gave to his own question was the acronym POSDCORB—planning, organizing, staffing, directing, coordinating, reporting, and bud-geting. These were the essential functions of the chief executive of any public agency. This mnemonic device was to become the accepted definition of the functions of public service executives for the next three-quarters of a century.

Leadership and Managerial Styles

A third approach deals with **managerial style,** the manner in which a manager operates. Much of the literature on managerial styles recognizes three major variants (Souryal, 1985, p. 71; 1995, pp. 104–106), **authoritarian, democratic,** and **laissez-faire**. These are defined or explained first in terms of the level of control the manager seeks to impose over his or her subordinates, and the degree of concern for those subordinates; two major variables are *involvement* and *control*. In this discussion, we will introduce a fourth type to supersede the inappropriate "authoritarian" classification.

   Authoritarian leadership reduces discretion and reduces the input of the workers, thus maximizing control. Some authors refer to this style as *autocratic,* and some do not view it as negatively as do some others. Indeed, it is best to divide the original authoritar-ian style into two variants, *autocratic* and *despotic,* so that the negative aspects of the style can be distinguished from the positives.

   Democratic leadership gives up some control by giving the workers significant say in the decision-making of the agency. Input is welcome, and subordinates are encouraged to contribute ideas. This democratic approach seeks to build a team and provide for the collective interests of the members of the work team by giving them genuine input into agency policies and practices. To acquire input, this type of manager is skilled at measuring consensus and valuing the inputs of others. Being both involved in and concerned with the lives of others, the democratic manager can become a busybody with a kindly disposition.

   The *laissez-faire* manager also relinquishes much control over his or her subor-dinates, but differs in subtle ways from the democratic manager. The laissez-faire model allows the workers much autonomy, but without team-building. In this style of management, concern for the needs and welfare of the workers is not an important issue for the manager, as each worker is expected to attend to his or her individual needs. Either the laissez-faire manager has no concern for these group interests or feels he or she simply has no business becoming involved in them. This style of manager will provide guidance by passive example, the manager being neither directly involved in nor showing concern with the lives of others. This manager will stress autonomy, liberty, and freedom of action.

Autocratic managers will maintain firm control and be comfortable with the exercise of their authority and powers, but they also reveal a genuine concern for the well-being of those they supervise. An excellent example of the autocratic manager is the traditional drill sergeant at a police academy. An order-giving, controlling leader, he or she is very much interested in the welfare and the progress of the trainees under his or her control. The autocratic manager is a bossy busybody. Frequently—and often erroneously—associated with the Army and Marines, this order-giving, demanding, close-supervision style requires a great deal of commitment and involvement in the work output of others, thus showing concern for the lives and needs of those workers, though less than for the mission or outcome.

The *despotic* manager is a self-serving, controlling leader who shows no interest or concern in the well-being of the workers and rejects any input from them. This manager is quite different from the autocratic manager, who does demonstrate concern for the needs of his or her subordinates (Carey, 2004). The stereotype of the cruel and corrupt prison warden so often seen in prison films is a version of the despotic manager. Control takes precedence over the interests of both prisoners and the prison staff in this stereotype. Ruling by decrees, and never showing an interest in the personal consequences of those decrees, the despotic tyrant seeks total compliance with his or her directions, but has little concern with the workers or their problems in complying.

Authority versus Power versus Influence

Around the time Luther Gulick introduced us to POSDCORB (1937), *leadership* in public service in general and criminal justice in particular was one and the same with *command,* simply the exercise of power. For this reason the "D" in POSDCORB is *directing*. Telling people what to do and expecting them to obey is out of place in most public service work settings. Instead, the leader is expected to motivate the workers to achieve common aims. Thus, the modern leader selects among leadership styles based on factors such as subordinate characteristics, preferences for or distaste for authoritarianism, locus of control, abilities of the leader and the workers, the formal authority and disciplinary system, and work-group dynamics.

In reality, there is a ***continuum of leadership behaviors,*** ranging from boss-centered to subordinate-centered leadership. General George S. Patton once said, "Never tell people how to do things. Tell them what to do and they will surprise you with their ingenuity" (2008). Robert Tannenbaum and Warren Schmidt, in a frequently cited and reprinted *Harvard Business Review* article (1958, 1973), described this continuum as follows:

- Manager makes decisions and announces them.
- Manager "sells" decisions to subordinates.
- Manager presents ideas and invites questions.
- Manager presents tentative decisions and accepts ideas from subordinates.
- Manager presents problems, seeks suggestions, and makes decisions based on all input.
- Manager defines limits, supplies key data, and asks subordinates to make the decision.
- Manager permits subordinates to operate on their own, within broad, general limits defined by the manager or their position descriptions.

Which Represents What Style?

Tannenbaum and Schmidt conducted interviews with a group of highly effective and successful managers working in closely related fields. Each was asked about his or her managerial and decision-making styles. These are some of the statements they collected (1958, 1973):

> "I put most problems into my group's hands and leave it to them to carry the ball from there. I serve merely as a catalyst, mirroring back people's thoughts and feelings so that they can better understand them."

> "It's foolish to make decisions oneself on matters that affect people. I always talk things over with my subordinates, but make it clear to them that I'm the one who has to have the final say."

> "Once I have decided on a course of action, I do my best to sell my ideas to my employees."

> "I'm being paid to lead. If I let a lot of other people make the decisions I should be making, then I'm not worth my salt."

> "I can't waste time calling meetings. Someone has to call the shots around here, and I think it should be me."

True leadership requires the willingness of subordinates to accept authority and to follow the example of or decisions of the nominal leader. So why do people obey a leader? Max Weber undertook to answer that question, as discussed next.

Authority or Coercion?

All people will obey if sufficiently coerced. This is one expression of power. In some cases, that must suffice as a basis for compliance, but it is not cooperation. People will follow willingly and rationally under some circumstances, especially when they accept the authority and legitimacy of the leader. According to Max Weber, authority has three ideal types:

> *Charismatic:* The "natural leader," emotion- and confidence-inspiring. People are attracted to such a leader and follow willingly.

Traditional: By custom, a king because he is a king's son, the occupant of a status because that status is a leadership status regardless of the incumbent. Ascription! *Rational-Legal:* A person selected because of his or her technical competence, or other merit principles—as enforced by "legal" procedural selection, relying on credentials.

In actuality every leader shows aspects of all these types of authority. A police chief, warden, or parks director is chosen by rational-legal civil service or merit selection criteria. The job title of "police chief," "warden," or "director" is a traditional office of leadership, but the person ideally selected has "something extra," a charismatic appeal that makes him or her stand out from other qualified applicants.

In his classic work on the power of the American presidency, Richard Neustadt (1960) discusses the importance of the "power to persuade." Strong leadership, whether in the White House or in a criminal justice agency, involves much more than authority. It is about building relationships and convincing others to follow. Neustadt remarks on how employees can be persuaded to follow in more than one way and managers can be effective and still be themselves. Many great leaders are inspirational or charismatic, but many others can simply convey a sense of competence and foster trust. Whatever the approach, a leader must convince followers of his or her vision of success for the organization.

In *A Comparative Analysis of Complex Organizations* (1961), Amitai Etzioni offered another approach to understanding power in organizations:

1. coercion: the threatening aspect of leadership
2. remuneration: the rewards that the leader can bestow
3. normative: the commitment that both the leader and the subordinate have toward complying with the rules of organization, society, or the law

Applying Managerial Styles

Early in the 20th century, leaders were expected to be controlling, autocratic managers, giving orders, supervising closely, and using coercive measures to ensure discipline. By the latter part of the century, other approaches were in favor. Among the leading voices in the first approach were Henri Fayol, Frederick Taylor, Luther Gulick, and Max Weber.

Henri Fayol (1841–1925) was a French engineer and industrialist who was the leading proponent in Europe of the ideas now known as "principles of scientific management" (Fayol,

FIGURE 4.1 **Henri Fayol** Fayol was a French engineer and advocate of "scientific management" in the workplace. His ideas were widely applied in Europe at the end of the 19th century, and later were carried to the United States.

1916/1949). His ideas arrived late to the United States. The English translation of his major work, *General and Industrial Management,* was released in the United States in 1949 (translation by Constance Storrs). Fayol's ideas preceded the translation, though, and he was an influence—even if only indirectly—on the rise of American scientific management concepts at the start of the 20th century.

Fayol's principles included the division of work, authority, discipline, unity of command, unity of direction, subordination of interests to the general interest, remuneration, centralization, "scalar chain" (established lines of authority), order, equity, personnel stability, initiative, and esprit de corps (morale). All were to reappear in the works of American advocates of scientific management, including both Frederick W. Taylor (1911/1967) and Luther Gulick (1937), who cites Fayol directly.

Frederick W. Taylor (1856–1915), renowned in the United States as the founder of "scientific management," is best known for *The Principles of Scientific Management* (1911/1967). He was emphatic about the use of the scientific method to observe, categorize, and quantify work as a preliminary step to better job design. His ideas led to time and motion studies, better workplace layouts, and even some engineering improvements to tools and machines.

Taylor offered four principles about matching workers to the workplace:

1. Use empirical observations to reduce each job to its component parts, formulating discrete rules for the most efficient performance of each;
2. Scientifically select workers who are capable of doing the work for which they were hired, giving them additional training on the specifics of their employment once hired;
3. Bring the employee, the technology, and the manager into cooperative harmony; but
4. Divide the responsibilities of management from labor.

Taylor observed how the workplace had become too complex for the average novice worker to know his or her job. Therefore, training was necessary. He also was aware that being a good laborer did not make one suited to being a good manager or foreman. He felt that managerial skills had to be present in prospective managers, just as mechanical skills had to be possessed by prospective mechanics. His approach became quite popular, and

FIGURE 4.2 Frederick W. Taylor Taylor was an American advocate of "scientific management" and efficiency studies applied in the industrial workplace, and later in government. His ideas influenced public service management decisively for the first half of the 20th century. *en.wikipedia.org*

his adherents called the approach "Taylorism." Essentially, Taylor was treating workers as if they were interchangeable replacement parts in the machinery of commerce, industry, and government. The scientific management leader establishes and enforces performance criteria and is goal-oriented.

Luther Gulick (1937)was influenced by Taylorism and approached public service leadership in much the same way. August Vollmer and Orlando W. Wilson were influenced by both Taylor and Gulick as they brought scientific management ideas into policing.

Human Relations School Theorists and the Hawthorne Studies

At about the same time that Gulick was penning his mnemonic POSDCORB and Orlando Wilson was applying the ideas of scientific management to American police management, a new approach was being developed in American workplaces. Led by several professors of management at the Harvard Business School (among them Elton Mayo, Frederick Roethlisberger, and William J. Dixon), the "human relations school" emerged. In this approach, a leader seeks to fulfill needs of employees in order to make the work satisfactory. Workers and managers were expected to communicate with one another. Order-giving was not considered good practice. As Mary Parker Follett (1868–1933) advocated, "not the face-to-face suggestion ... so much as the joint study of the problem." Follett (1926), an intellectual predecessor to the human relations school, also favored circular or reciprocal communications and advised against order-giving. (See Chapter 11.) The school took shape in the 1930s in the lessons learned in what have become known as the Hawthorne Studies.

The **Hawthorne Studies** were a series of management experiments done for the Western Electric corporation. They began in the structure of the "scientific management school," but their unexpected findings gave rise to a new way of approaching management theory: the "human relations school." The key figures in this transition were Elton Mayo and Frederick J. Roethlisberger.

Elton Mayo (1880–1949) was an Australian-born Harvard professor, often credited with bringing about the shift from scientific management to human relations. He helped organize the **Hawthorne Studies**. His major works are *The Human Problems of an Industrial Civilization* (1933) and *The Social Problems of an Industrial Civilization* (1945). In earlier research, he was able to demonstrate with scientific precision that requiring less in terms of actual time worked would result in more productivity. Workers were protected from exhaustion and thus could complete their work day as productively as they had begun it. He and Roethlisberger and Dixon, his Harvard associates in the Hawthorne Studies, later discovered the role of the workplace social environment in productivity.

F. J. Roethlisberger (1898–1974) provided the research details of the Hawthorne Studies in his 1941 book *Management and Morale* and in a book written with William Dickson, *Management and the Worker* (1939). The studies were done in the 1930s, during the Depression. Workforce reductions were in progress. Other cost-cutting schemes were being considered. Western Electric commissioned a study of the impact of illumination on productivity. It was a controlled experiment. A test group whose lighting was varied upward in intensity was compared with a control group whose lighting was kept at a constant level. Productivity records were compared for the two groups and contrasted with prior production records for the plant. Then lighting was reduced in the test group. In both sets of experiments, production improved for both groups. Further experiments were designed. Teams were organized, and tests were made with variations in several factors, including temperature, illumination, humidity, the physical condition of workers, and workers' eating, sleeping, and rest periods. When "better" working conditions were introduced, productivity went above the old base levels. When the experiments ended after a year and a half, and the old "bad" conditions were restored, productivity remained at the new level rather than returning to the pre-experiment level.

What Was Going On? The Four Sentiments

Social—not mechanical—engineering was the key to what was discovered in the Hawthorne Studies. Four basic "sentiments" were identified from the study findings (Roethlisburger & Dickson, 1939, p. 522):

1. Don't bust rate
2. Don't chisel
3. Don't squeal
4. Don't be officious

The first pair set the "normative" work pace for each work group. The next two defined relationships among workers and between workers and management. If these sentiments are satisfied, a worker becomes a part of the social group of the workplace, and this keeps up morale in the workplace. "Workers are not isolated, unrelated individuals; they are social animals and should be treated as such. ...A human problem to be brought to a human solution requires human data and human tools" (Roethlisburger, 1941).

Abraham Maslow: Hierarchy of Human Needs

Abraham Maslow (1908–1970) was the next major contributor to the human relations school. He wrote "A Theory of Human Motivation" (1943) in *Psychological Review*, and expanded upon it in a subsequent book, *Motivation and Personality* (1954; 1970). He introduced a *hierarchy of human needs (basic goals)* that can be satisfied by work:

- physiological (homeostasis and appetites; food and shelter)
- safety (obsessive–compulsive neurotics lock in here)
- affiliation (close social relationships); "love"
- achievement and esteem (self-respect)
- self-actualization (need to develop one's skills and responsibilities to the maximum)

To motivate an individual, the manager must find the means to associate the organizational goals with the laborers' level of needs. In the nature of human needs, we are often unaware of our own requirements and only vaguely sense that something is bothering us. The manager has to be quite perceptive to discover what it is that the worker is lacking in order to find a way to bring the worker fulfillment.

Frederick Herzberg: Motivation and Hygiene

Frederick Herzberg (1923–2000) was very much influenced by Maslow and the Hawthorne Studies. He wrote *The Motivation to Work* with Mausner and Snyderman (1959) and expanded upon "Motivation-Hygiene Theory" in *Work and the Nature of Man* (1966), wherein he discussed motivational and hygienic factors in work. He followed up on this with an often-cited article, "One More Time: How Do You Motivate Employees?" in the *Harvard Business Review* (1968/1987).

Hygiene versus Motivators

Herzberg's explanation of the differences between true motivation and more subtle forms of coercion focused on what he called the **hygiene factors** involved in the latter. These are the factors that generate potential dissatisfaction. People are unhappy if hygiene factors are insufficient. However, people are not automatically happy if those hygiene factors are satisfied. In contrast, **motivational factors** are the factors that generate potential satisfaction.

Hygiene (cited as sources of workplace problems):

- Company policy
- Supervisor/supervisor relations
- Working conditions
- Salary
- Peer relations

Motivation (cited as bringing workplace satisfaction):

- Achievement
- Recognition/rewards
- Work content/challenges
- Responsibility
- Advancement/growth

Douglas McGregor and Theory X versus Theory Y

Douglas McGregor (1906–1964) wrote *The Human Side of Enterprise* (1960), in which he struck a contrast between what he described as *Theory X*, associated with scientific management and what he called the **Type A manager**, and *Theory Y*, associated with human relations and what he called the **Type B manager**. McGregor clearly was advocating Theory Y.

Theory X Assumptions (1960, pp. 33–44):

1. Management is responsible for the key productive elements (Taylor, separate the functions of labor and management).

2. Workers are there to be directed, motivated, controlled.

3. Workers are passive or resistant to organizational needs.

4. The average worker does as little as possible.

5. The average worker lacks ambition.

6. The average worker is self-centered and indifferent.

7. The average worker will resist change.

8. The average worker is easily duped by charlatans.

Theory X is associated with the military model (structured, hierarchical, and command control–oriented). It relies on coercive practices, negative reinforcement, and punishment. It is preferred by both autocratic and despotic managers. It is useful among novices, the unskilled, and those clearly not motivated.

Theory Y Assumptions (1960, pp. 45–57):

1. Management retains responsibility for the key productive elements, but can count on support from the work force.

2. People are not passive or resistant to organizational needs.

3. Self-motivation, potential, capacity for responsibility, and the ability to be a team player are in all workers.

4. The essential role of the manager is to arrange working conditions and resources so that the work force can best achieve their personal goals while serving the organizational goals.

Theory Y is associated with the cooperative work model and teamwork. It relies on true motivation via self-actualization. It is used by both democratic and laissez-faire managers. It relies on positive reinforcement and offers workers positive feedback and rewards. It is most useful among the talented, competent, and motivated.

Not everyone agrees with McGregor that Theory Y is preferable. Indeed, several studies, including that noted in the Tannenbaum and Schmidt article, demonstrated that there are highly successful managers who use Theory X approaches. As a result, several subsequent authors have argued that the style used should vary to match the leadership situation. Ideas like *contingency management, reality leadership,* and *situational leadership* are the result. Deciding which factors should determine which style to use is a leadership decision.

Fiedler, Luthans, and Contingency Management

Fred Fiedler

Fred Fiedler (1922–) wrote *A Theory of Leadership Effectiveness* (1967), in which he advocated "The Contingency Model: A Theory of Leadership Effectiveness." He saw leadership constrained by three situational dimensions:

1. leader–member relationships (trust, affection, respect, fear)
2. task structure within the organization (organizational mission and objectives)
3. leader's ability to exercise genuine power (e.g., the power to hire and fire)

Fiedler held that once these are determined, a management style could be selected that best fit these contingencies.

Fred Luthans

Fred Luthans (born in 1939) expanded these ideas in *Introduction to Management: A Contingency Approach* (1976), which was essentially a textbook. In it, he identified problems with both Theory X (scientific management) and Theory Y (human relations) approaches. Solutions to these problems gave rise to alternatives, including what some call a "systems approach," others call **situational management**," and Luthans called a "contingency approach." All three concepts pointed out the flaws in trying to apply rigid principles to the workplace and that excessive interest in human relations concepts put the workplace employee at the center at the expense of productivity. Moreover, Mary Parker Follett's idea of "taking orders from the situation" was rediscovered, most conspicuously in the contingency approach of Fred Luthans. He advocated that the contingency leader should project likely situations and use if–then plans for each, rather than follow rigid principles to govern management decisions. Such a leader considers "environmental" factors, "resource variables," and "management variables" in making decisions.

Environmental factors, resource variables, and management variables include:

- organization size
- interaction possibilities
- personalities of workers
- goal congruence
- decision-making echelons
- technology
- organizational performance record

Proper management requires determination of the impact of such variables on each organization and fitting a managerial strategy to the situation and circumstances of a particular workplace. **"Contingency Theory"** often is used in modern police organizations (Zhao, Ren, & Lovrich, 2010, pp. 212–213), which cannot deal successfully with ever-changing circumstances with rigid policies, some of which, like 9-11, simply cannot be anticipated, but do require immediate decisions.

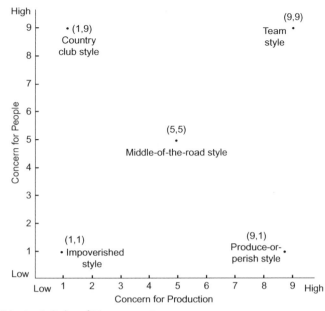

FIGURE 4.3 Blake and Mouton's Styles of Management.

Paul Hersey and Kenneth H. Blanchard's "**Situational Leadership Theory**" (1977) is important in its description of the leader–follower relationship. Observing that because different employees are at different maturity levels, leader behavior must be determined by those different job maturity levels. They describe leader behaviors that range from high interaction with less mature employees to simply delegating responsibility to more mature employees. Leadership, therefore, is "situational" because employees have these differences in maturity, abilities, and needs. There also are maturity factors inherent in the leader-manager. Schubert (1988) found that the relative age of the manager was a significant factor in leadership style, but only because older managers consulted more and invited more participation in decision-making than did younger managers.

The *management leadership grid* is an illustrative model developed by R. R. Blake and J. S. Mouton in *The Managerial Grid* (1964) to identify and measure managerial styles (see Figure 4.3). A psychological questionnaire was administered to score each manager on two scales:

1. Vertical scale for concern for people (rated from 1 to 9).
2. Horizontal scale for concern for production (also rated from 1 to 9).

Five styles of management emerged:

1. **The Country Club Style** (1,9): This style has a high concern for people and a low concern for production. Managers using this style will pay a great deal of attention to the needs, security, and comfort of their subordinates in the hope that this will increase their performance. The resulting atmosphere is usually cohesive and friendly but not necessarily highly productive.

2. **The Produce-or-Perish Style** (9,1): With a high concern for production, and a low concern for people, managers using this style will provide their subordinates with adequate wages and benefits and expect high levels of performance in exchange. Managers using this style also pressure their employees by using rules and punishments to achieve the organizational goals. This style is associated with McGregor's Type A manager of Theory X, and these will merge in crisis situations.

3. **The Middle-of-the-Road Style** (5,5): Managers using this style try to strike a balance between organizational goals and the needs of their subordinates. By showing concern for both people and production, managers who use this style hope to maintain a balance to achieve acceptable performance.

4. **The Team Style** (9,9): In this style, high levels of concern are given to both people and production. Managers choosing to use this style encourage teamwork and commitment among their subordinates. This method seeks to help them feel themselves to be integral, contributing parts of the organization. The Team Style closely approximates McGregor's Theory Y.

5. **The Impoverished Style** (1,1): This style reflects the absence of leadership. The manager ranks low on both concerns. Such a manager is a "seat holder," one who occupies the position and collects the salary, but does little to justify having either.

Leading by Negotiation

Modern leaders have learned to motivate people by applying incentives. Implicit in Maslow's hierarchy and Herzberg's motivators is the idea that the manager will manipulate inducements to encourage and reward desirable behavior among subordinates. Clearly, the modern manager cannot hope to succeed by raw intimidation and coercion, at least not for long. As Mary Parker Follett's discussion about taking orders from the situation and joint study of the problem pointed out, a leader does better to negotiate solutions than to demand them. The old order-giving directional style is not viable in most cases. Give-and-take strategies will work better.

The 1938 essay by Chester Barnard, "Economy of Incentives," was an early statement of this awareness. He observed that incentives could be specific or general, the former suited to working with an individual to meet his or her needs and the latter open to all to meet commonly shared needs. Barnard identified several classes of such inducements:

1. material inducements (not just money, not even "perks" alone)
2. personal nonmaterial opportunities (prestige, power, titles)
3. desirable physical conditions (the perks of the job)
4. ideal benefactions, the opportunities to achieve personal objectives or fulfill personal values via the job, including satisfying feelings of loyalty, aesthetic, or spiritual feelings; pride in performance or workmanship; etc.

5. associational attractiveness
6. adaptive strategies, recognizing the weight of customary practices and shared attitudes and values, implicitly avoiding too much or radical change
7. expanded participation
8. "condition of communion," those highly "intangible and subtle" incentives, involving social relationships that are comfortable and rewarding (very close to the aspects of "associational attractiveness," but for Barnard, importantly different)

In an important 1959 article, "A Behavioral Theory of Organizational Objectives," Richard Cyert and James March view the organization as a coalition. They acknowledge that there are individual differences in what participants want from a decision, and that bringing people on board requires some side-bargaining to meet those wants and needs, but once these negotiations have been successfully concluded, the coalition can be considered a unit with a common purpose organizationally (implement Policy X) and many personal aims will be fulfilled at the same time. These side bargains could include money, personal treatment, and policy advantages.

Cyert and March conclude that five basic mechanisms are needed:

1. "a mechanism that changes the quantitative value of demands over time"; this has an ability to evolve situationally
2. an attention-focusing mechanism that can move among the three states (active-set, inactive-set, and non-considered-set), implicitly promising that everyone's needs will be met at some point, although not all right now
3. a mechanism to direct attention to problems and demands that are, or should be, organizational priorities
4. a mechanism that recognizes the potential weaknesses of participants and ensures performance consistency in spite of them—knowing how to use a weakness to an advantage
5. a mechanism for choosing which competing coalitions will serve best—applying "game theory" to group decision-making

March, in collaboration with Michael Cohen (1974/1992, pp. 195–229), went further in expressing this image of the organization as a coalition, suggesting several rules to help the manager make order out of organizational anarchy:

1. spend time
2. persist
3. exchange status for substance
4. facilitate opposition participation
5. overload the system
6. "provide garbage cans" (raise diversions)
7. manage unobtrusively
8. interpret history

Some of Cohen and March's ideas may seem subversive, but they are rules that keep most of the players in the game and keep the game being played while the leader guides the game toward his or her objectives. A manager must be prepared to manage his or her own schedule as well as the schedules of others. A manager needs to be satisfied with abstract (indirect) job satisfaction—being satisfied with the achievements of his or her subordinates rather than his or her own successes (like parental pride). A manager must be comfortable being an evaluator, judging others, and listening to the judgments of others. A manager must have the capacity to deal with long-term and unusual problems and must be able to leave routines to subordinates. A good manager is always aware that an agency's key resources are its people.

Direct Supervision

A leader is expected to be a supervisor over subordinates. In the days of the authoritarian scientific manager, this meant directing, as in the "D" in Luther Gulick's POSDCORB. With the focus shifted to less authoritarian styles, leadership is now expected to be less directional and more cooperative and consultative, but what does that do to the issue of supervision? The manager still has supervisory responsibilities that must be fulfilled. Theodore Caplow (1983) has suggested a list of 12 supervision principles for the modern workplace that fit the criteria, and also identifies major managerial mistakes.

Supervision Principles:

1. Set unmistakable goals (objectives).
2. Supervise the work, not the worker.
3. Distinguish essential or nonessential rules.
4. Reward sparingly; punish more sparingly.
5. Give credit where credit is due.
6. Listen to complaints; don't bitch back.
7. Defend the faith.
8. Form an inner circle.
9. Protect status of subordinates.
10. Retain final control.
11. Innovate democratically.
12. Take infinite pains to see things go right. (pp. 81–88)

Major Managerial Errors:

1. overcontrolling (authoritarian managers' problem)
2. undercontrolling (laissez-faire and democratic)
3. one-way communicators:

   - order givers
   - silent listeners (giving no guidance)
   - appeasers (yielding to subordinates too often)

- non-delegators (never giving subordinates independence)
- halfway delegators (assigning responsibilities but not sharing authority).

Summary

The art of leadership is vital to the criminal justice manager. Scholars continue to study what styles and approaches work for the successful leader (Shafritz & Ott, 1992), but the shift from scientific management to a human relations approach has had a considerable impact on the practice of management in the 20th century and beyond. Perhaps there is no one best way to lead. Situational and contingency management theories call for flexibility. The transformational leader, seeking to create purposeful change in an organization, can use a variety of approaches and will rely on a wide range of personal talents and traits. A wise and resourceful criminal justice leader today often will assume a role within the organization that will build positive social relationships with the subordinate workforce without losing sight of the organizational mission and objectives.

LEARNING OBJECTIVES

Upon finishing this chapter, you should be able to do the following:

1. Identify which criminal justices in your locality and state are elected.
2. Distinguish between first-order and second-order policy-making.
3. Discuss some of the traits that you consider to be very important in a criminal justice leader.
4. Discuss the skills you feel that a criminal justice leader should possess.
5. Identify four distinct managerial styles and compare them in terms of concern for subordinates and concern for maintaining control.
6. Compare and contrast scientific management and human relations approaches to leadership and management.
7. Discuss various models of contingency or situational management and leadership.
8. Identify incentives that can be used in criminal justice management.

IMPORTANT TERMS AND NAMES

- *appointment*
- *autocratic leader*
- *authoritarian leader*
- *considerations*
- *contingency theory*
- *continuum of leadership behaviors*
- *democratic leader*
- *elections*

- *Henri Fayol*
- *Fred Fiedler*
- *the Four Sentiments*
- *Hawthorne Studies*
- *Fred Herzberg*
- *hygiene factors*
- *influence*
- *initiating structures*
- *Leader Behavior Descriptive Questionnaire (LBDQ)*
- *laissez-faire leader*
- *Fred Luthans*
- *managerial style*
- *Abraham Maslow*
- *Elton Mayo*
- *merit selection*
- *Douglas McGregor*
- *motivational factors*
- *nonmerit selection*
- *performance-based merit selection*
- *primary/first-order policy-making*
- *F. J. Roethlisberger*
- *secondary/second-order policy-making*
- *situational management*
- *supervision principles*
- *task analysis*
- *traits of a leader*
- *transformational leadership*
- *skills of a leader*
- *Frederick Taylor*
- *Theory X assumptions*
- *Theory Y assumptions*
- *Type A manager*
- *Type B manager*

References and Supplemental Sources

Barnard, C. (1938/1989). Economy of incentives. In J. S. Ott (Ed.), *Classic readings in organizational behavior*. Pacific Grove, CA: Brooks/Cole.

Bass, B. (1990). *Bass & Stogdill's handbook of leadership*. New York: Simon & Schuster, The Free Press.

Beebe, E. S. (2010). *Paradigms of contemporary leadership theory*. Cincinnati: Bee Squared.

Blake, R. R., & Mouton, J. S. (1964). *The managerial grid: The key to leadership excellence*. Houston: Gulf.

Burns, J. M. (1978). *Leadership*. New York: Harper Torchbooks.

Caplow, T. (1983). *Managing an organization* (2nd ed.). New York: Holt, Rinehart and Winston.

Carey, B. (2004, June 22). Fear in the workplace: The bullying boss. *New York Times.* Retrieved from < http://www.nytimes.com/2004/06/22/health/fear-in-the-workplace-the-bullying-boss.html/>.

Cohen, M. D., & March, J. G. (1974/1992). *Leadership and Ambiguity.* Stanford, CA: Carnegie Foundation for the Advancement of Teaching. (Extract reprinted as Leadership in an organized anarchy. In: Shafritz, J. M., & Ott, J. S. (Eds.), *Classics of organizational theory,* 3rd ed. (pp. 432–448). Pacific Grove, CA: Brooks/Cole.)

Cyert, R. M., & March, J. G. (1959/1992). A behavioral theory of organizational objectives. In: Shafritz, J. M., & Ott, J. S. (Eds.), *Classics of organizational theory* (pp. 133–142) (3rd ed.). Pacific Grove, CA: Brooks/Cole.

Drucker, P. F. (1967). *The effective executive.* New York: Harper & Row.

Etzioni, A. (1961). *A comparative analysis of complex organizations.* New York: The Free Press, Macmillan.

Fayol, H. (1916/1949). *General and industrial management.* English translation by C. Storrs. London: Pittman.

Fiedler, F. E. (1967). *A theory of leadership effectiveness.* New York: McGraw-Hill.

Fisher College of Business, Ohio State University (2008). *Leader Behavior Description Questionnaire (LBDQ).* Retrieved from <https://fisher.osu.edu/offices/fiscal/lbdq/>.

Follett, M. P. (1926). The giving of orders. In: Metcalf, H. C. (Ed.), *Scientific foundations of business administration.* Baltimore: Williams & Wilkins.

Gulick, L. (1937). Notes on the theory of organization. In: Gulick, L., & Urwick, L. (Eds.), *Papers on the science of administration.* New York: Institute of Public Administration.

Hersey, P., & Blanchard, K. H. (1977). *Management of organizational behavior: Utilizing human resources* (3rd ed.). Englewood Cliffs, NJ: Prentice Hall.

Herzberg, F. (1966). *Work and the nature of man.* New York: Ty Crowell.

Herzberg, F. (1968/1987). One more time: How do you motivate employees? *Harvard Business Review, 46*(1), 53–62. (reprinted in the *Harvard Business Review, 65*(5), 109–120.)

Herzberg, F., Mausner, B., & Snyderman, B. B. (1959). *The motivation to work.* New York: Wiley.

Katz, R. (1974). Skills of an effective administrator. *Harvard Business Review, 52*(5), 90–101.

King, M. S. (2008). Problem-solving court judging, therapeutic jurisprudence and transformational leadership. *Journal of Judicial Administration, 17,* 155–177.

Klofas, J., Stojkovic, S., & Kalinich, D. (1990). *Criminal justice organizations: Administration and management.* Pacific Grove, CA: Brooks/Cole.

Luthans, F. (1976). *Introduction to management: A contingency approach.* New York: McGraw-Hill.

Maslow, A. H. (1943). A theory of human motivation. *Psychological Review, 50,* 370–396.

Maslow, A. H. (1954). *Motivation and personality.* New York: Harper & Row.

Maslow, A. H. (1970). *Motivation and personality* (2nd ed.). New York: Harper & Row.

Massie, J. L. (1987). *Essentials of management* (4th ed.). Englewood Cliffs, NJ: Prentice Hall.

Mayo, E. (1933). *The human problems of an industrial civilization.* Cambridge, MA: Harvard University Press.

Mayo, E. (1945). *The social problems of an industrial civilization.* Cambridge, MA: Harvard University Press.

McGregor, D. (1960). *The human side of enterprise.* New York: McGraw-Hill.

Neustadt, R. E. (1960). *Presidential power: The politics of leadership.* New York: Wiley.

Northouse, P. G. (2009). *Introduction to leadership: Concepts and practice.* Thousand Oaks, CA: Sage.

Patton, G. S. (2008). General George S. Patton, Jr. CMG Worldwide, Estate of George S. Patton, Jr. Retrieved from <http://www.generalpatton.com/quotes.html/>.

Price, T. L. (2003). The ethics of authentic transformational leadership. *The Leadership Quarterly, 14*(1), 67–81.

Rippy, K. M. (1990). Effective followership. *The Police Chief, 57*(9), 22–24.

Roethlisberger, F. J. (1941). *Management and morale.* Cambridge, MA: Harvard University Press.

Roethlisberger, F. J., & Dixon, W. J. (1939). *Management and the worker.* Cambridge, MA: Harvard University Press.

Schubert, J. N. (1988). Age and active-passive leadership style. *American Political Science Review, 82*(3), 763–772.

Shafritz, J. M., & Ott, J. S. (Eds.). (1992). *Classics of organizational theory* (3rd ed.). Pacific Grove, CA: Brooks/Cole.

Souryal, S. S. (1985). *Police organization and administration.* Cincinnati: Pilgrimage/Anderson.

Souryal, S. S. (1995). *Police organization and administration* (2nd ed.). Cincinnati: Anderson.

Stogdill, R. M. (1974). *Handbook of leadership: A survey of theory and research.* Urbana: University of Illinois at Urbana-Champaign.

Tannenbaum, R., & Schmidt, W. H. (1958). How to choose a leadership pattern. *Harvard Business Review, 36*(2), 95–101.

Tannenbaum, R., & Schmidt, W. H. (1973). How to choose a leadership pattern. *Harvard Business Review, 51*(3), 162–180. (reprinting the original article as a *Harvard Business Review* classic.)

Taylor, F. W. (1911/1967). *The principles of scientific management.* New York: Norton Library, Harper & Row.

Wilson, W. (1887). The study of administration. *Political Science Quarterly, 2*(2), 197–222.

Zhao, J., Ren, L., & Lovrich, N. (2010). Police organizational structures during the 1990s: An application of contingency theory. *Police Quarterly, 13*(2), 209–232.

5

Organizing Criminal Justice

The "O" in LODESTAR and the first "O" in POSDCORB both stand for "organizing." Organizing the workforce is one of the essential responsibilities of a criminal justice manager. In Chapter 1 we considered how the study of organization and management has been complicated by popular misunderstandings of the key terms. It is easy to limit the conceptualization of "organization" to only its corporate-entity meaning as a synonym for "agency" (e.g., the organization, as in the FBI), thereby ignoring its process meaning (e.g., organization is the process of arranging and structuring cooperative human effort). The study of organization is not the study of *an* organization but rather the science of how organizations are best organized, structured, and arranged (March and Simon, 1958; McGregor, 1960).

Often people join organizations and function within them with the assumption that they always have been as they are—that their structure is "set in stone" and immutable. This is absolutely false. Agency managers have both the authority (subject to laws) and the responsibility to alter and modify organizational arrangements to respond to new demands and changes in the work environment.

Bureaucracies

Most modern criminal justice agencies are bureaucracies. In the course of human history a criminal justice bureaucracy is a relatively new concept, not yet 400 years old. Until the time of Cardinal Richelieu (1585–1642) in France, there were no governmental or criminal justice bureaucracies in Europe. The Roman Catholic Church, a large and widely dispersed organization, did have a system of self-governance that approximated a bureaucracy, and Richelieu applied many of those concepts to French government. He selected government officials on the basis of objective merit, naming judges who were formally trained in law to replace some of the feudal nobles who had been judges by birthright. By the time of Emperor Napoleon Bonaparte (1769–1821), France possessed an advanced governmental bureaucracy that included the management of the courts, the police, and the prisons by trained, merit-selected officials. The occupying French forces replaced the governing institutions of conquered nations with bureaucrats trained by the French. The consequence was the rapid spread of bureaucracy across Europe in the first years of the 19th century. Even the final, total defeat of the French in 1815 did not set back the progress of bureaucracy as an institution of governance in Europe. It was especially successful in taking hold in the German states.

Bureaucracy, therefore, is an essential element to consider as we study organization in contemporary criminal justice organizations. German scholar Max Weber was the first to recognize and examine the key features of a modern bureaucracy. Nicely summarized by Sam Souryal (1995, pp. 10–11), its features include:

- a system of fixed jurisdictions
- enumerated tasks and duties
- predetermined goals and objectives
- explicit rules and procedures
- integration of the labors of large numbers of people
- hierarchical system of authority (chain of command)
- delegation of authority with supervised span of control
- career officials (bureaucrats)
- probationary appointments
- fixed salaries and benefits
- in-service training
- code of discipline
- information systems of internal communication, written records, and files

Maximilian Carl Emil Weber

Max Weber (1864–1920) was a German social scientist credited with being one of the founders of both sociology and public administration. Although best known today as a scholar and professor, he was active in German politics after World War I and served on the commission that drafted the Weimar Constitution.

Weber was a prolific writer on a wide range of subjects. His last work was *Economy and Society* (1922), published posthumously. Among his most important theoretical contributions were his analysis of power and authority and his detailed explanation of bureaucracy. He used the concept of the ideal type as an explanatory device, and his description of bureaucracy was an example of an ideal type. In his day, the concept of bureaucracy was seen as a positive development, as a superior way of managing and conducting public affairs. Its dependence on merit selection of public officials was a major improvement on earlier ways of appointing government officials from the petty nobility.

When Weber wrote about "bureaucracy," he introduced us to some of the key organizational principles of modern bureaucratic organizations:

1. fixed jurisdictional areas
2. hierarchal principle
3. documentation (the files)
4. trained office management
5. career commitment (official duties, a "vocation")
6. official, stable learnable rules.

Some of the elements of bureaucracy had their conceptual origins in earlier ideas. A system of fixed jurisdictions, enumerated tasks and duties, and predetermined goals and objectives are aspects of "the division of labor," attributed first to Adam Smith (1776) and a key feature of the scientific managerial principles of Henri Fayol.

Hierarchical arrangements have been part of human social structure since ancient times. The delegation of authority with supervised span of control also is quite ancient, being a feature of armies in the earliest historical records. But there were new features to be found in bureaucracy. The merit selection of career officials, chosen objectively for their educational preparations, talents, and skills; initially giving probationary appointments; and entitling these officials to fixed salaries and benefits all were original ideas. Keeping comprehensive files and establishing rules and procedures for the conduct of the work and the system of internal discipline required to follow them all were new as well. Bureaucratic work ceased to be the responsibility of an individual practitioner and became

FIGURE 5.1 Max Weber. Weber was a German social philosopher who approached the study of bureaucracy both historically and analytically, identifying within it the features that have given it its great strength in public service. He also studied the origins and exercise of noncoercive power as an aspect of leadership. *en.wikipedia.org*

instead the responsibility of the office he or she occupied. In this way, an incumbent in the office could share the duties, responsibilities, and records of the office with associates and subordinates, and pass them on to his or her successor.

In Weber's mind, bureaucracy was the solution to many problems of governance and human organization. Today, however, bureaucracy is seen by many as a problem. Bureaucracy has developed a reputation for being cumbersome, slow, inefficient, and officious.

BOX 5.1 ASTERIX THE GAUL VERSUS BUREAUCRACY

The French, who did so much to spread bureaucracy across Europe, often ridicule their own bureaucrats. The popular French-Belgian cartoon character Asterix must deal with the entrenched and unresponsive bureaucracy as one of the most difficult of *Les Douze Travaux d'Asterix [The Twelve Labors of Asterix]*, a parody of the "Twelve Labors of Hercules." In his eighth labor Asterix must secure "Permit A-38," contending with a multitude of bureaucrats and offices in an almost hopeless effort to secure this document. He does so only by playing the bureaucratic game against the bureaucrats themselves, demanding from them an imaginary permit to which he claims an entitlement.

While bureaucracy has become tainted by its abuses, done right, it still works better than most means for managing a large organization. Elliott Jaques (1990) wrote "In Praise of Hierarchy" as a defense of this essential aspect of bureaucracy, yet Jaques too identifies real problems in hierarchal arrangements:

1. There are too many layers and too much distance between managers and labor, poor communication, deflection of responsibility, stress and conflict.
2. Midlevel managers rarely add to the productivity of their line subordinates; and even can reduce its value.
3. Bureaucracies often play into the nasty aspects of human behavior, greed, insensitivity, selfish careerism, and unhealthy competition.

Jaques finds that hierarchy, like bureaucracy, when done right, works well. Both responsibility and accountability must be defined unambiguously. Someone must be held accountable for each of the tasks assigned to the organization—both for doing them and for seeing that they are being done. The focus must be on getting the job done; exercising authority is a very distant second. If getting the job done can be made easier by distributing authority, then that is the way to go; if centralization gets more done, then centralize. However, "group decisions" must still ultimately be the manager's decision. The manager is responsible for buying into the decision or into the decision-making process. To make **hierarchy** (which arranges the performers of tasks in a ranked or graduated series) actually work, several powers must be vested in the leadership:

1. The manager needs to retain the right to veto the employment or placement of any person not up to the standards of the organization or of the tasks to be performed.
2. The manager needs to have the right to make work assignments.
3. The manager needs the power to conduct performance appraisals and to allocate or withhold rewards based on them; not just to make inconsequential recommendations.
4. The manager needs the authority to initiate removal procedures for nonfunctional or low-productivity staff.

James Q. Wilson

James Q. Wilson (1931–) became a well-regarded expert on policing styles with the publication of his book, *Varieties of Police Behavior* (1968). He subsequently undertook a comprehensive examination of modern American public service bureaucracies in the 1980s (1989). He has identified two problem areas confronting modern bureaucracies: inefficiency and arbitrariness in decision-making. Wilson proposes that bureaucracies can be much more efficient if their **rank and file**—the individuals who actually do the work of the organization—are given more incentives, greater flexibility, and independence of action. They are not automatically prone to **red tape,** as the mass of paperwork often associated with bureaucracies is called, or to self-serving expansionism. They often develop a strong **sense of mission,** which keeps them focused on the tasks they were hired to perform. They are, however, responsive to political pressures.

BOX 5.2 JAMES Q. WILSON

James Q. Wilson has made considerable contributions to the study of police behavior, and to American crime policy, authoring the book, *Thinking About Crime* (1975). He served as a presidential advisor to Ronald Reagan on crime policy. He was awarded the Presidential Medal of Freedom in 2003.

Organizational Principles and the Courts

Some organizations do not fit the bureaucratic pattern well (e.g., the courts). Court officials, both judges and clerks of court, are elected in many states. The courts are a meeting place for multiple bureaucracies with competing goals and objectives. Here the court staff, the police, the prosecutor, the public defender, and representatives of the probation office meet to determine complex questions of law, innocence or guilt, and consequences of convictions. Each of these represented bureaucracies has a different interest in the case before the court. Nevertheless, leaders in the judiciary have made significant organizational improvements in the courts. Among the most noteworthy of these court reformers was Arthur Vanderbilt.

Arthur T. Vanderbilt

In the area of the courts, major organizational innovations were introduced by Arthur Vanderbilt (1888–1957). A New Jersey native and politically active community leader, Vanderbilt helped bring about major constitutional changes in the organization of the New Jersey court system, and thereafter became its Chief Justice (1948–1957). In that capacity, he also served as the director of the newly created Administrative Office of the Courts, the first such entity in the United States. Previously, Vanderbilt had been the president of the American Bar Association (1937–1938). He had served as Dean of New York University Law School and founded the Institute of Judicial Administration at New York University in 1950. He was a strong advocate of states establishing court administration agencies in a period when judges expected virtual autonomy in running their courts (Vanderbilt, 1976). He edited *Minimum Standards of Judicial Administration* (1949) (standardizing court practices) and wrote *The Challenge of Legal Reform* (1955). Today, his ideas form the basis of modern court administration. State agencies ensure that their courts are consistent and uniform in their documentation, record-keeping, and routine procedural matters. Judges get training on routine judicial administration upon entering office.

Organizational Principles and Law Enforcement

Introducing the concepts of organizational theory to law enforcement were Leonhard F. Fuld, August Vollmer, and Orlando W. Wilson. Fuld penned the first American book on police administration (1910), intended primarily for police executives. Vollmer and Wilson were mentor and protégé. Together, these two men substantially altered the path of law enforcement in the United States in the first half of the 20th century. Both were prolific writers on police organization and administration (Vollmer, 1936; Wilson, 1950). Raymond Fosdick (1920), Elmer Graper (1921), and Bruce P. Smith (1940) were other pioneers in the application of scientific management principles to law enforcement.

August Vollmer

The first law enforcement position held by August Vollmer (1876–1955) was as an elected town marshal in 1907. Vollmer had earned a national reputation as an innovator and publicist of new ideas while serving as police chief in Berkeley, California. He was an advocate of the selection of college-educated men for police work. In an age when many police departments still did not even require a high school diploma, the need for college-educated police was not immediately appreciated.

Often called the "father of modern law enforcement," Vollmer reorganized the Berkeley Police Department, created new units within it, and increased its capacities with motor vehicles outfitted with one-way radios that could monitor the police dispatchers (but could not, at that time, reply to them). Never feeling bound by the old ways of doing things, he was willing to experiment with organizational experiments. He wrote many articles about his innovations, and in 1936 published a compilation of his progressive ideas in *The Police and Modern Society* (1936).

FIGURE 5.2 August Vollmer. Vollmer was a leading American law enforcement innovator and reformer. He introduced many ideas into policing that we now take for granted: patrol cars, radio dispatch, MO files, and criminal profiling among them. He also recruited and hired the first college-educated police officers, and helped create criminal justice education in the United States. *en.wikipedia.org*

Orlando W. Wilson

Orlando W. Wilson (1900–1972) was a police chief and educator who was instrumental in applying managerial concepts to police agencies. His book, *Police Administration* (1950), is a classic in the application of scientific management concepts to police practices. Wilson was one of the first college-educated police officers (a street cop, not a college-educated police executive).

Wilson created the School of Criminology at UC–Berkeley in 1950 and served as its first dean. As a police manager and as an academic, he sought to apply the basic principles of good management to law enforcement and did much to create the emphasis on "professionalism" in policing that has characterized its development in the past half century (Wilson & McLaren, 1977).

FIGURE 5.3 Orlando W. Wilson. Wilson was an expert on police administration and management, who applied the principles of scientific management to policing. Wilson was hired by another great leader in law enforcement, August Vollmer, to be an officer in the Berkeley Police Department in 1921. He earned his bachelor's degree while a police officer and then took his first chief of police post in Fullerton, California, in 1925. In later years he directed police departments in Wichita, Kansas, and Chicago, Illinois, and was involved in public safety in Italy and Germany in the war-time occupations of those nations. *SoxPhotos.*

Bruce P. Smith

Bruce Smith (1892–1955) was a leading advocate of **economies of scale,** arguing that the consolidation of smaller police forces into larger ones, replacing sheriffs with state police, and other centralizing efforts would provide for greater efficiency in law enforcement. He helped develop the Uniform Crime Reports (UCR) for the International Association of Chiefs of Police (IACP) and the FBI (Wilson, 1956, p. 235). His book, *Police Systems in the United States* (1940), was the peak expression of the reform ideal merging with the rising focus on better managerial practices.

Organizational Principles and Corrections

Leaders in correctional management began making contributions to the better organization of prisons and jails in the 19th century. Such early leaders as John Howard, Jeremy Bentham, Alexander Maconochie, Dorothea Lynde Dix, Elam Lynds, and Zebulon Reed Brockway already were mentioned in Chapter 3 in the discussion of the historical antecedents to criminal justice management. In the 20th century, new ideas were offered by reform-minded leaders seeking to further improve on prison and jail organization. Three

FIGURE 5.4 Katharine Bement Davis. Davis was a reformer and pioneer in corrections, as the first woman to be appointed New York City Correction Commissioner, in 1914. Having earned a Ph.D. at the University of Chicago in 1900, she was a social reformer and activist for much of her life. She undertook a highly controversial sex study of 2,200 women, which began in 1920. *en.wikipedia.org*

famous 20th-century correctional reformers were Katharine Bement Davis, Mary Belle Harris, and George Beto.

Katharine Bement Davis

Katharine Bement Davis (1860–1935) was the first woman to run a major municipal agency in New York, and her selection made news around the world. She managed an agency with 650 uniformed and civilian employees; 5,500 inmates in nine city prisons and jails; and a $2 million annual budget. Between 1918 and 1928 she served as the head of the Bureau of Social Hygiene, funded by the Rockefeller Foundation. With her sponsorship, the Bureau published *Women Police* and Edith Spaulding's "Experimental Study of Psychopathic Delinquent Women" (Spaulding, 1924). Among her achievements was the recruiting of Mary Belle Harris, another prison reformer (McCarthy, 1997).

Mary Belle Harris

Mary Belle Harris (1874–1957) was appointed superintendent of the women's workhouse on Blackwell's Island, New York, by Katharine Davis. She revised institutional rules to transform the workhouse, which was badly overcrowded and one of the worst on Blackwell's Island, into a model institution, with a library, an exercise yard, and an inmate classification system. Harris later moved to New Jersey to head the State Reformatory for Women at Clinton. Harris later served in corrections posts in Pennsylvania and the U.S. Bureau of Prisons women's prison in Alderson, West Virginia, where she was the first woman to be a warden in the federal system. In a 1936 book about her career in penology, *I Knew Them in Prison,* Harris recounted her life, accomplishments, and penal reforms, and credited Davis with having a major influence on her correctional career (McCarthy, 1997; Rogers, 2000).

George John Beto

George Beto (1916–1991) was appointed to the Texas Prison Board in 1953 (later renamed the Texas Board of Corrections), serving until 1959. Soon after that he served on the Illinois Parole and Pardon Board. In 1962, he returned to the Texas Department of Corrections. The prisoners called him "Walking George" because he unexpectedly visited the prisons to observe them. He helped secure legislative approval and funds for prison system reforms. Among the reforms he helped bring about were an 8-week prerelease program, giving prisoners counseling and education. In 1969, he helped institute a special work-release program and also expanded college-education programs at prisons in cooperation with Sam Houston State University. He helped the university develop its criminology program, and the American Correctional Association elected him its president for 1969–1970. Though a reformer, Beto favored authoritarian disciplinary practices.

Each of these leaders and reformers— and many others—have found creative ways to reorganize and revitalize criminal

FIGURE 5.5 Mary Belle Harris. Harris was a correctional innovator as the superintendent of the women's workhouse on Blackwell's Island, New York, and later headed the State Reformatory for Women at Clinton, New Jersey. She joined the U.S. Bureau of Prisons to become the first female warden in the federal prison system. She also earned a Ph.D. at the University of Chicago. *Bucknell College Yearbook.*

FIGURE 5.6 George Beto. Beto was an expert on correctional administration and management who applied the principles of both the scientific management and human relations schools to prison management and reform. After he retired as director of the Texas Department of Corrections, Beto was a professor of criminology and corrections at Sam Houston State University from 1972 to 1991. He is described as being "one of the visionaries who brought about the building of the Criminal Justice Center" at Sam Houston State University (Roth, 1997, p. 46). He was member of the National Advisory Commission on Criminal Justice Standard and Goals from 1972 to 1973 (Horton & Nielsen, 2005; Lucko, 2007).

justice agencies to better provide the services they were created to deliver. In various ways, they each applied the principles of organization to achieve these innovations and improvements.

Principles of Organization

In the fourth edition of *Police Administration*, by O. W. Wilson and Roy C. McLaren (1977), the following principles were set down, with application to police work first in Wilson's mind. However, the principles have much more general application in all public service organizational contexts:

1. Tasks should be grouped together in one or more units under the control of one person. In order to facilitate their assignment, these tasks may be divided according to:
   a. similarity in purpose, process, method, or clientele (functional),
   b. the time (temporal),
   c. the place of their performance (spatial), and
   d. the level of authority needed in their accomplishment.
2. Specialized units should be created only when overall departmental capability is thus significantly increased; they should not be created at the expense of reduced control and decreased general interest.
3. Lines of demarcation between the responsibilities of units should be clearly drawn by a precise definition of the duties of each,
   a. duties of a unit should be made known to all members of the unit.
   b. responsibility within the unit and between units should be placed exactly.
   c. such definition should avoid duplication in execution and neglect resulting from the non-assignment of a duty.
4. Channels should be established through which information flows up and down and through which authority is delegated.
   a. These lines of control should correspond to the delegation of authority, the placement of responsibility, the supervision of work, and the coordination of effort.
   b. Lines of control should be clearly defined and well understood by all members so that all may know to whom they are responsible and who, in turn, is responsible to them.
   c. Exceptions to routine communication of information through channels should be provided for emergency and unusual situations.
5. Structure and terminology should facilitate the understanding of the purposes and responsibilities of the organization by all its members. Avoid exotic arrangements and obscure jargon.
6. Each individual, unit, and situation should be under the immediate control of one, and only one, person, thus achieving the principle of unity of command and avoiding the friction that results from duplication of direction and supervision.

7. The span of control of a supervisor should be large enough to provide economical supervision, but no more units or persons should be placed under the direct control of one person than he or she is able to manage.

8. Each task should be made the unmistakable duty of someone; responsibility for planning, execution, and control should be definitely placed on designated persons.

9. Supervision should be provided for every member of the organization and for every function or activity. (If the supervision is not immediately available at the actual level of execution, it should be obtainable through referral to a predesignated authority.)

10. Each assignment or duty should carry with it commensurate authority to fulfill the responsibility.

11. Persons to whom authority is delegated should be held accountable for the use made of it and for the failure to use it. (pp. 73–74)

These principles of organization often are depicted in the form of an organizational chart (see Figure 5.7). Known by such terms as a "block chart," "plumbing chart," or a "wiring diagram," the organizational chart is the embodiment of the ancient adage that a picture is worth 1,000 words. These box charts use rectangular boxes to represent offices, units, or important individual officers in an agency. One of the learning objectives of this unit is teaching each student how to read, use, and later how to draw a correct organization chart.

Police patrol units take messages from the 911-dispatch center and respond to them as if they were taking orders (e.g., "Unit B-57, respond to a disorder at 123 4th Avenue"). Such a communication sounds like an order being given by a dispatcher to a uniformed

---

BOX 5.3 READING AN ORGANIZATION CHART

Solid lines represent command and supervisory relationships.

Dashed or dotted lines represent communications and coordination channels and interrelationships such as attachment, operational control (Op Con), liaison, and detail.

Boxes represent an "office," "department," or some other unit with a functional, temporal, or spatial division of labor.

Very similar units are often merged, by overlapping (stack) or **"comb" arrangements,** meaning that all such units are very similar in their organization/function.

The chart should show all elements supervised by a superior element/person with a single clear path from top to bottom.

A chart ought not create fictional relationships (yet some do, leading to people saying "I don't report to him!").

No box should be unconnected, but some will be in reality because of managerial or political compromises; for example, the "independent" agency such as the office of the ombudsman, the "special prosecutor," or the "independent counsel."

No box should be connected to two or more supervisory boxes with a solid line, yet some can linked by a dotted or dashed line, reflecting such relationships as attachment, operational control (Op Con), liaison, detail, or preauthorized direct communication channels.

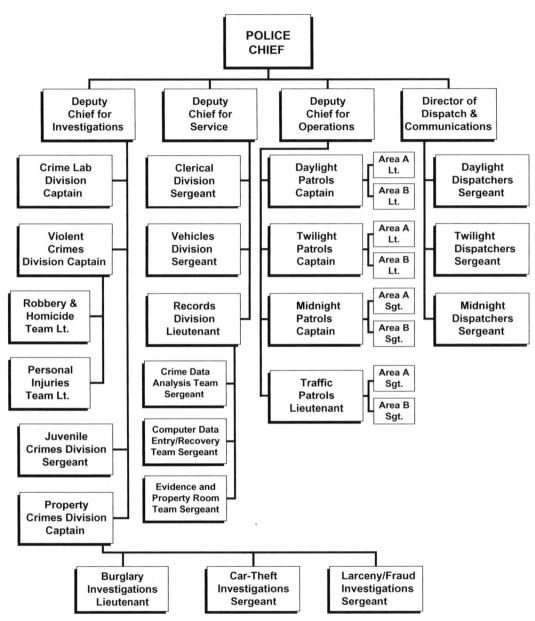

FIGURE 5.7 Sample Organization Chart.

officer. In organizational practice, it is not. The dispatcher is "sharing information" with the officer. If the officer feels he or she should not respond to the call, the officer can decline it or request direction from his or her direct supervisor (e.g., "Unit B-03, this is B-57. I am monitoring suspicious activity at 8th and Market Street. Request that another unit respond to the disorder on 4th Avenue"). The field supervisor, shown as the solid line on the organization chart, has the authority to reassign the officer to take the call or assign another patrol unit to respond to it.

The way dotted-line, dual relationships can be handled includes concepts of *attached, operational control* (OPCON), *liaison,* and *detailed.*

Attached: When a unit (or an individual) is detached from its own agency and attached to a different organization, the receiving organization becomes responsible for that unit, providing its logistics, supervision, and duty assignments. A criminal justice example would be a judge, temporarily transferred from his or her home district to a different district to help reduce case backlogs in the receiving court district. For most purposes, that judge functions as if he or she had been transferred to the new district. Logistics support, such as office space, a courtroom, clerical support, and a wide range of other support activities, is provided by the receiving district. Eventually the attachment will end and the judge will return to his or her home district.

Operational Control (OPCON): When an entire unit from one organization takes its direction from another organization that is not normally part of its chain of command, it can be considered to be under operational control. Common examples in law enforcement are combined task forces of federal, state, and local law enforcement agencies that agree to protocols that place one of them in charge of the activities of the others. The Drug Enforcement Agency (DEA) often has operational control of drug investigations that have the full participation of state and local antidrug agencies. The state and local units remain the "property" of their larger organizations, which provide most of their support and logistics, but their actual task assignments, direction, and supervision are transferred to the DEA agent in charge.

Liaison A liaison officer is an official of one agency who is assigned to work with a different agency as a means of facilitating coordination and communication between or among agencies. A common criminal justice example would be police, fire, rescue, and public health officials assigned to an emergency operations center established to respond to a major community crisis. They interact with each other and inform each other of what their home agency can contribute to the joint operation. Some liaison relationships are long-lasting; others are temporary. The long-lasting relationships take on the features of a detail.

Detailed When a unit or an individual is detailed, that person or unit works for one department or agency but is "detailed" to support a different department for a specific function or a limited time. A common criminal justice example is an experienced police investigator being detailed to the prosecutor's office to conduct further investigation into a case being prepared for trial. Such an investigator remains an employee of the police department and will eventually return to the police department, but for the duration of the detail will work under the direct supervision of the prosecutor's office.

It might be worthwhile to clarify some of the terminology in common use in criminal justice agencies. An **officer** is an employee empowered to act on behalf of the agency or organization, and can be a part of the management team, having some supervisory duties. Formally speaking, a "police officer" would not be an "officer" within the police department in this sense, but a police sergeant or lieutenant with managerial duties would be. On the street, though, a police officer is authorized to act independently and takes on duties in his or her relationship to the public that imply being an "officer" of the police department. An "employee" need not be an officer. A clerk has a task to do but no supervisory or managerial powers to exercise on behalf of the agency. An agent will include a nonemployee engaged for specific acts (e.g., a lawyer hired to represent the agency or organization on a limited question or case). Agents who are not employees often do not appear on the organizational charts. (See Figure 5.8.)

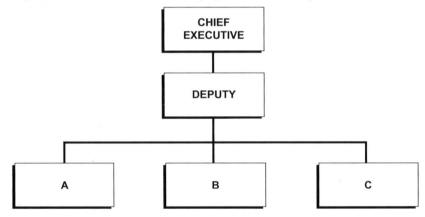

A common error in organization chart drawing implies that people who are in Departments A, B, or C must see the deputy boss before seeing the boss.

Unless this is so, that is, if deputy is traffic controller like president's secretary or chief of staff, the deputy should be drawn off to the side of the manager.

FIGURE 5.8 Common Organization Chart Error.

Organizational Structure and Function

Weber and Wilson both approached organization as a rational exercise, with an underlying assumption that workers are analogous to identical replacement parts in a working machine. This was also evident in Frederick Taylor's writings. However, the Hawthorne Studies invited questions about this assumption. Workers were "vital engines" even more than Robert Owen might have assumed. This gave rise to the human relations school and its model of human organizational behavior. In time, other models have been proposed, so that now we can consider three major options that a leader may use in organizing his or her agency: the bureaucratic–scientific management model, the human relations model, and the situational and contingency models.

Bureaucratic–Scientific Management Model

In the bureaucratic–scientific management model (Gulick, 1937; Taylor, 1911/1967; Weber, 1922; Wilson, 1950): Organizational principles are applied somewhat rigidly, with the hierarchy principle given very high priority. Authority is very precisely allocated, with those higher up in the hierarchy having more power. Rules are explicit, and organizational discipline is enforced. The agency's organizational chart clearly defines areas of jurisdiction and command–control relationships. Organizational communications, command, and control are expected to follow the chain of command. This approach dominated organization in criminal justice well into the middle of the 20th century.

Human Relations Model

The human relations model (Herzberg, 1968/1987; Maslow, 1970; Mayo, 1933; Roethlisberger 1941) was preceded by the ideas of Mary Parker Follett, and arising with the discoveries of the Hawthorne group (Mayo and Roethlisberger), older scientific management organizational principles were called into question. Hierarchy and command aspects were not abandoned, but their importance declined. Lines of command, control, and communication were often ignored in favor of work groups, operating as equals, even when they were comprised of different ranks. Rules were replaced by flexible guidelines. Rising in popularity in the 1960s, these ideas never fully replaced scientific management organization in criminal justice. They found expression in the 1970s as team policing, community policing, and empowerment of client populations in criminal justice priority-setting became popular.

Situational and Contingency Models

Situational and contingency models (Fiedler, 1967; Luthans, 1976) promoted flexibility and situational management, and revived Mary Parker Follett's 1926 recommendation that leaders should take their orders from the situation. The application of CompStat in law enforcement and problem-oriented policing are both expressions of this approach. Criminal justice work teams are created, reorganized, and disbanded as needed. There is more use of delegation and operational control practices than in scientific management, but less workplace democracy than was the case in human relations applications. The older scientific management–based principles reemerged as good practices, but not rigid formulas, for organizing criminal justice agencies.

Applying Organizational Principles

The **division of labor** in a criminal justice organization must reflect functional, temporal, and spatial demands placed on it by its mission.

Functional Divisions of Labor

The tasks or functions of a criminal justice agency will be reflected by the internal divisions it adapts. Souryal (1995, pp. 12–13) identified several factors to be considered, among them major purposes (missions), processes used, subjects (specific services to be provided), and clientele.

A municipal police department needs to provide crime prevention, public safety, order maintenance, public service, and crime investigation services to the public. If the workload justifies it, there can be functional divisions to reflect each of these. Even a smaller police department will have patrol, services, and investigative units. The courts are called upon to hold bail and bond hearings, conduct civil and criminal trials, sentence people, collect fines, supervise probation conditions, hear appeals, and perform many other judicial functions. Court managers create units within the court system to provide these services. Corrections managers must classify, house, educate, medicate, treat, and release inmates. They will pay attention to classifications of inmates based on their danger to correctional staff and society at large, and thus correctional units will be developed that are maximum security, medium security, and minimum security. There will be classification units. There will be medical, counseling, education and vocational training, parole-hearing, and other correctional units.

Clientele will include the aforementioned security grades in a prison population, youth offenders, victims, witnesses, the public at large, the staffs of the agencies, and many others. Specific units can be established to deal with the special requirements of various client groups. Police, court, and corrections units exist to meet the needs of juveniles. Prosecutors need to handle offenders, witnesses, and victims in different ways, and may choose to create divisions within their offices to provide those services.

The processes used by modern criminal justice agencies often rely on complex technologies the average agency employee simply will not possess. Police will rely on crime scene investigation (CSI) experts and other advanced scientific elements to provide such technical support. Computers are very important in all the components of the criminal justice system, and having support staff who can manipulate data efficiently on computer platforms is critical to all criminal justice agencies. Highly sophisticated communications equipment can be entrusted to centralized 911 dispatch and communications centers.

Henry Mintzberg (1979) identified five basic parts of an organization, and these are a modern reflection of the functional divisions of labor:

1. **apex**—the top leadership and management team
2. **middle line**—midlevel managers and supervisors
3. **techno-structure**—specialists in the applications of complex technologies
4. **support staff**—clerical-administrative personnel who deal with internal matters
5. **operating core**—the actual workforce to do the labor of the organization

Temporal Divisions of Labor

Municipal police agencies, 911 centers, and correctional units operate 24 hours a day, 7 days a week. In some larger cities magistrates also are available 24/7, and lower courts hold night sessions. Juvenile justice units have to respond to cases whenever they arise, not just between 9 A.M. and 5 P.M., Monday through Friday. On the other hand, state and federal investigative agencies and higher courts often can maintain "banker's hours" with 40-hour-a-week work schedules, so the organization of the criminal justice agency must reflect accurately the times when their services are needed.

Spatial Divisions of Labor

Many criminal justice agencies serve large geographical areas. Federal agencies need field offices across the entire nation. State agencies must be present statewide. Police in large cities need to operate divisions or precincts to provide police services citywide. Patrol operations must be provided over the entire jurisdiction being served. The courts have established districts so that every community has local or regional access to judicial services.

The **span of control** refers to the number of individuals routinely supervised by an officer of the agency. Tight control exists when a supervisor oversees only two or three subordinates. Loose control exists when a supervisor oversees a large number of subordinates. Therefore, span of control exists in inverse relation to the intensity of supervision. When supervision does not need to be intense, the span may be increased without loss of manageability and productivity. This is often the ideal case in Theory Y scenarios. When supervision must be intense, span of control must be kept small to achieve manageability and productivity. This is the case when Theory X is applied.

Span of control and the number of steps or layers in the command hierarchy exist in an inverse relation with effect on manageability and productivity. If an agency has each supervisor overseeing only a few subordinates, it will require many more layers of supervision. An increased span of control will produce a decrease in communication time and efficiency. This occurs because an increase in the hierarchy adds additional layers or links in the communication chain, and this produces delays and a decrease in communication transfer. The more drawn out the command–control chain, the more information is lost.

When does supervision need to be intense? Theory X scientific management and contingency models would recommend it with a workforce that has low skills and little motivation.

When does communication "line-loss" need to be kept at a minimum? Theory Y human relations and contingent models would advise it when criticality, responsiveness, discipline, or control are critical to managerial situations.

There is an inherent paradox to all of this: an abbreviated chain of command can produce a greater span of control but also can enhance internal communication. However, this is not guaranteed. A greater span of control can reduce the communication line-loss in two ways:

1. more face-to-face communications will be necessary
2. fewer transmission links will be required from the top down

A greater span of control also can reduce overall internal communications effectiveness by:

1. reducing the time a manager has with each subordinate
2. increasing the likelihood that a manager will miss someone

Management Theorists Consider the Three Models

Philip Selznick (1948, 1992) sees an organization as a social entity existing to accomplish an "agreed purpose through the allocation of functions and responsibilities" (1992, p. 114). The maintenance of the system is an implicit agreed purpose; hence, his five "imperatives" (1992, pp. 118–119):

1. The security of the organization as a whole in relation to the social forces in its environment.
2. The stability of lines of authority and communication.
3. The stability of informal relations within the organization.
4. The continuity of policy and of the sources of its determination.
5. A homogeneity of outlook with respect to the meaning and role of the organization.

The imperatives cross-cut the three models. However the criminal justice manager approaches the organization of his or her agency, these concerns must be met. It is the duty of the manager to select the appropriate organizational structure and the organizational model that will best enable the agency to meet its mission and responsibilities to the public.

LEARNING OBJECTIVES

Upon finishing this chapter, you should be able to do the following:

1. Identify the key features of a criminal justice bureaucracy.
2. Summarize the 11 principles of organization.
3. Describe command, communications, and control relationships on a criminal justice agency organizational chart.
4. Identify the key aspects of the division of labor and span of control.
5. Identify some of the problems and paradoxes inherent in applying the principles of organization.
6. Discuss the five imperatives of organization proposed by Philip Selznick.

IMPORTANT TERMS AND NAMES

- *agent*
- *apex*
- *attached*
- *bureaucracy*
- *chain of command*
- *"comb" arrangements*
- *detailed*
- *division of labor*
- *economies of scale*
- *functional divisions of labor*
- *hierarchy*
- *ideal type*
- *liaison*
- *middle line*
- *officer*
- *operating core*
- *operational control*
- *rank and file*
- *red tape*
- *sense of mission*
- *span of control*
- *spatial divisions of labor*
- *support staff*
- *techno-structure*
- *temporal divisions of labor*

References and Supplemental Sources

Fiedler, F. E. (1967). *A theory of leadership effectiveness.* New York: McGraw-Hill.

Fosdick, R. B. (1920). *American police systems.* New York: Century.

Fuld, L. F. (1910). *Police administration: A critical study of police organizations in the United States and abroad.* New York: Putnam.

Graper, E. D. (1921). *American police administration.* New York: Macmillan.

Gulick, L. (1937). Notes on the theory of organization. In: Gulick, L., & Urwick, L., (Eds.), *Papers on the science of administration.* New York: Institute of Public Administration.

Harris, M. B. (1936). *I knew them in prison.* New York: Viking.

Herzberg, F. (1968/1987). One more time: How do you motivate employees? *Harvard Business Review, 46*(1), 53–62. (reprinted in the *Harvard Business Review,* 65(5): 109–120.)

Horton, D. M., & Nielsen, G. R. (2005). *Walking George: The life of George John Beto and the rise of the modern Texas prison system.* Denton: University of North Texas Press.

Jaques, E. (1990). In praise of hierarchy. *Harvard Business Review, 68*(1), 127–134.

Lucko, P. M. (2007). Beto, George John. The Handbook of Texas Online. Retrieved from <http://www.tshaonline.org/handbook/online/articles/fbenm/>.

Luthans, F. (1976). *Introduction to management: A contingency approach*. New York: McGraw-Hill.

March, J. G., & Simon, H. A. (1958). *Organizations*. New York: Wiley.

Maslow, A. H. (1970). *Motivation and personality* (2nd ed.). New York: Harper & Row.

Mayo, E. (1933). *The human problems of an industrial civilization*. Cambridge, MA: Harvard University Press.

McCarthy, T. C. (1997). Correction's Katharine Bement Davis: New York City's suffragist commissioner. New York: New York City Department of Corrections. Retrieved from <http://www.correctionhistory.org/html/chronicl/kbd/kbd_15.html/>.

McGregor, D. (1960). *The human side of enterprise*. New York: McGraw-Hill.

Mintzberg, H. (1979). *The structure of organizations*. Englewood Cliffs, NJ: Prentice Hall.

Roethlisberger, F. J. (1941). *Management and MORALE*. Cambridge, MA: Harvard University Press.

Rogers, J. W. (2000). Mary Belle Harris: Warden and rehabilitation pioneer. *Women and Criminal Justice, 11*(4), 5–28.

Roth, M. (1997). *Fulfilling a mandate: A history of the Criminal Justice Center at Sam Houston State University*. Huntsville, TX: Sam Houston Press.

Selznick, P. (1948). Foundations of the theory of organization. *American Sociological Review, 13*(1), 25–35.

Selznick, P. (1992). Foundations of the theory of organization. In: Shafritz, J. M., & Ott, J. S. (Eds.), *Classics of organizational theory* (pp. 114–123) (3rd ed.). Pacific Grove, CA: Brooks/Cole.

Smith, A. (1776/1937). *The wealth of nations*. New York: Random House, Modern Library.

Smith, B. P. (1940). *Police systems in the United States*. New York: Harper.

Souryal, S. S. (1995). *Police organization and administration* (2nd ed.). Cincinnati: Anderson.

Spaulding, E. R. (1924). Experimental study of psychopathic delinquent women. *Journal of Nervous and Mental Disorders, 59*(4), 444.

Taylor, F. W. (1911/1967). *The principles of scientific management*. New York: Norton Library, Harper & Row.

Vanderbilt, A. T. (Ed.). (1949). *Minimum standards of judicial administration*. New York: The Law Center of New York University.

Vanderbilt, A. T. (1955). *The challenge of legal reform*. Princeton, NJ: Princeton University Press.

Vanderbilt, A. T., II (1976). *Changing law: A biography of Arthur T. Vanderbilt*. New Brunswick, NJ: Rutgers University Press.

Vollmer, A. (1936). *The police and modern society*. Berkeley: University of California Press.

Weber, M. (1922). In: Roth, G., & Wittich, C. (Eds.), *Economy and society* (2 vols). Berkeley, CA: University of California Press.

Wilson, J. Q. (1968). *Varieties of police behavior*. Cambridge, MA: Harvard University Press.

Wilson, J. Q. (1975). *Thinking about crime*. New York: Basic Books.

Wilson, J. Q. (1989). *Bureaucracy*. New York: Basic Books.

Wilson, O. W. (1950). *Police administration*. New York: McGraw-Hill.

Wilson, O. W. (1956). Bruce Smith. *Journal of Criminal Law, Criminology, and Police Science, 47*(2), 235–237.

Wilson, O. W., & McLaren, R. C. (1977). *Police administration* (4th ed.). New York: McGraw-Hill.

6

Decision-Making and Planning

Decision-making or "deciding" is the "D" in LODESTAR; this is different from the "D" in POSDCORB, which stands for "directing." Making decisions is a major managerial responsibility and will be significantly influenced by the leadership style of the manager. Type A managers are more likely to decide autocratically and give orders, direct subordinates, and expect those subordinates to comply. Type B managers are more likely to decide democratically and enter into discussions (reciprocal communication and joint study of the issue).

We will merge the study of deciding with "planning," the "P" of POSDCORB, noting that deciding and planning have many common features. Some authorities separate decision-making from planning, as does Joseph L. Massie (1987), but others (including me) disagree. A plan is a type of decision, and planning uses a decision-making process. As Massie (1987) points out, decision-making is a process involving three components:

1. choice—the manager considers options and alternatives.
2. thought—the manager exercises what Massie calls a conscious mental process.
3. purpose—the manager determines missions, goals, objectives, and end states. (p. 42)

Each of those three components also are present in planning. Massie (1987) identifies five steps to sound managerial decision-making, and these too are essential in good managerial planning:

1. understanding the situation
2. recognition of the right problem
3. identification and analysis of available alternatives
4. selection of the solution
5. organizational acceptance (pp. 42–45)

Decision-making is found at every process stage in the justice system, often with lower-level officials making critical decisions the whole organization must live with. Police officers in the field and correctional officers often make life-and-death decisions with little opportunity for deliberation, guidance, or option evaluation. In comparison, judges also make life-and-death decisions, but do so after a lengthy process of fact-gathering and deliberation, with input from prosecutors, defense attorneys, and even juries.

It is absolutely essential that criminal justice practitioners have and exercise discretion in the performance of their duties. **Discretion** is an expression of decision-making authority, and it exists throughout the entire justice system. For example, a police officer is expected to decide when to make an arrest and when to issue only a warning, when to use force and what level of force to use. A prosecutor must decide which cases to prosecute, what specific charges to bring, whether to accept or reject a plea bargain, and what sentence to recommend. Judges are expected to rule on motions, make verdicts, and sentence those who have been convicted. Corrections officials need to decide how to classify inmates, what treatment options to use with them; how to respond to indiscipline, escape attempts, and riots; and when to approve parole. However, these kinds of decisions are *operational decisions,* not *managerial decisions.*

James Q. Wilson (1989) notes that many Americans are uncomfortable with the discretionary powers of its civil servants; he is not. However, he is aware that one of the major problems of bureaucratic decision-making is the risk of **arbitrariness** (p. 326). He notes that there is a tension between equal treatment and responsiveness in decision-making. If everyone is treated exactly the same way, then individual needs, circumstances, and conditions will be ignored. If every decision appears to be unique and without precedent, then there will be no consistency and no predictability in the decision-making process.

Managerial Decision-Making

Managerial decisions are those that involve the mission, goals, objectives, policies, and end states desired for the organization. These decisions may modify or refine the mission, goals, and objectives, and most certainly will influence the policies that subsequently influence the operational decisions made by the workforce. Major figures in the development of planning and decision-making include Chester Barnard (*The Functions of the Executive,* 1938/1968), Herbert Simon (*Administrative Behavior,* 1957), Fred Luthans (*Introduction to Management: A Contingency Approach,* 1976), Chris Argyris (*Personality and Organization,* 1957), and Wendell French and Cecil Bell (*Organizational Development,* 1973).

From these experts, we learn that the manager must compromise rational, goal-oriented behavior with economically nonrational (but socially rational) requirements of employees and client populations. In their decision-making and implementation, modern criminal justice managers make exchanges with workers, and do not simply command them to perform. This is the transition from scientific management, which *directs,* to human relations, which *leads and negotiates.* As pointed out above, actors at all levels in the criminal justice organization are decision-makers, but managerial decision-makers are making policy for their agencies, not making operational decisions.

Managerial decision-making concerns include rationality, efficiency, and productivity. Good decision-making requires data collection, analysis, action planning, implementation, and evaluation.

Decision-Making Theory: There are four models of managerial decision-making:

1. rational choice
2. bureaucratic

3. decision process (decision-tree)
4. political

The traditional view of decision-making is that decisions are made following a **rational choice model** (Pfeffer, 1981), in which:

1. all alternatives are identified
2. advantages and disadvantages of each are itemized
3. projected costs, consequences, and outcomes are anticipated
4. the best option stands out from the others and is chosen

Yet Herbert Simon was quick to observe that this usually was not the way decisions are made. He looked at decision-making empirically, and observed that, "Few managers actually decided things by rational searches for alternative solutions for anticipated problems." Instead, they rely on "bounded rationality" and "satisficing," two terms that are associated with Simon's critical analysis of formal decision-making. **Bounded rationality** is rational choice that takes into account the cognitive limitations of both knowledge and cognitive capacity. **Satisficing** is Simon's term for the all too common managerial practice of treating as sufficient (*sufficing*) the first solution to emerge that will meet (*satisfy*) the necessary criteria for a solution, even if there might be other, better solutions that could be discovered by further study and consideration of the problem.

Rather than follow the rational-choice model faithfully, typically managers simply follow **programmed decisions.** These are the rituals, routines, and traditional practices of criminal justice agencies, which require minimal discretion and very little actual deciding but generally ensure organizational norm maintenance. The key managerial role in this model is establishing routines, and promulgating and maintaining the norms and values that sustain them. This is done using such premises as previous decisions, the preferences of supervisors, and preexisting **standard operating procedures** (SOPs), all of which supplant rational decision-making.

This leads Jeffrey Pfeffer to identify the second managerial decision model: the bureaucratic. Best explained by March and Simon (1958) and Cyert and March (1959), this approach tends to be low risk, but also unoriginal, and limits choices open to the decision-maker (Pfeffer, 1981). The bureaucratic model relies on the procedures and precedents of the past, as found in the much cherished rules of the organization. This is the famous "by-the-book" behavior of some managers. It assumes that the rules—that is, "the book"—were formulated by a rational decision process in the past, so they remain rational still. Not everyone would agree. As far back as the 1920s, Mary Parker Follett was identifying problems with predetermined decisions that were passed along to the workforce in the form of orders or rules (Follett, 1926). This led her to propose that managers not rely on orders but on the law of the situation—the recognition that situations are always evolving, so that rigid orders (the established rules of the organization) will be out of place much of the time.

The third approach uses a **decision-process model** and assumes that the outputs (the decisions) are products of multiple actors, each having input into the process. Pfeffer (1981) refers to this as "organized anarchy." **Decision trees** often are used to help the process, and there is an aspect of computer modeling implicit (e.g., If A, then B; if not A, then C). The Law Enforcement Assistance Administration (LEAA) flowchart depicted in Chapter 2 is an example of a decision tree. Contingency theory applies this decision-process model and fits well in modern police organizations (Zhao, Ren, & Lovrich, 2010, pp. 212–213), which have to adapt to ever-changing circumstances and new challenges.

The fourth model relies on *political power* and is commonly exemplified in the decisions made in an election year; otherwise, the use of an economic rational choice or bureaucratic model would find other courses of action to be preferable. The U.S. Congress and state legislatures change laws for many reasons—some rational, others ideological, and still others politically expedient. Once a political decision has been made by the legislature or a lawful executive order is issued by the president, governor, or mayor, the criminal justice executives and midlevel managers must make their decisions in harmony with those political policies.

Decision-Making: General Principles and External Planning Factors

Just as Tannenbaum and Schmidt (1958) identified different managerial leadership styles, there are corresponding decision-making styles. These and other factors will help determine how a decision is made. Reminiscent of the contingency models favored by Fred Fiedler (1967) and Fred Luthans (1976), and as exemplified in *The Managerial Grid* (Blake, 1964), a wise decision-maker will not adhere to just one approach but will consider several ways of coming to a decision. There are five key factors a manager should consider in selecting a managerial decision-making method.

1. What is the managerial style preferred by the decision-maker?
2. Time? Does the situation require quick action, or is there time for deliberation?
3. Significance and severity? How important or serious is the problem? How much effort does it justify?
4. Frequency? Will the problem arise again?
5. What are the ripple effects and outside consequences of the decision?

Theorists and experienced decision-makers adhere to different models and have different leadership styles. Some may prefer solo decision-making; others prefer group decision-making. It would seem that they agree on few things, but there is consensus on three points:

1. Come to a decision ("make the decision"; this is in keeping with Theory X).
2. Do not worry about the decision (it proves itself; somewhat laissez-faire).
3. Do not try to satisfy everyone. It can't be done (more in keeping with Theory X).

> **BOX 6.1 MEANS–END ANALYSIS AND THE MANAGERIAL DECISION-MAKING PROCESS**
>
> 1. Set the objective.
> 2. Identify obstacles.
> 3. Collect and analyze data.
> 4. Develop alternative solutions.
> 5. Select preferred alternatives.
> 6. Develop and implement a plan.
> 7. Evaluate results.

Criminal Justice Managerial Planning

Orlando W. Wilson (1950) and John P. Kenney (1959) were among the first to apply planning to police management. In court administration, Arthur Vanderbilt (1947) planned the overhaul of the New Jersey court system and saw that plan implemented. He then applied his experiences to advising courts nationally. Planning is an extension of the decision-making process. It is future-oriented decision-making in which a manager anticipates and visualizes what is coming and makes decisions based on that vision of the future. "A plan is a predetermined course of action" (Massie, 1987, p. 83). It consists of five distinct elements:

1. setting goals
2. searching for opportunities (data collection, forecasting, research and development activities)
3. formulating plans (program development)
4. setting targets (defining desired end states)
5. following up (pp. 84–85)

Long-, Intermediate-, or Short-Range Planning

Time is a factor in planning. Planning can be long-range, intermediate, or short-range (Kenney, 1959, pp. 15–16). There is no absolute definition of which is which, but as a general guide, long-range planning involves multiple operational cycles that are usually defined in terms of the budget cycle for an agency (e.g., in a state using a 2-year budget, the operational cycle is 2 years). An intermediate- or short-range plan involves one operational cycle or just part of one cycle. Typically a short-range plan is a response to an immediate problem or the one-time application of some new methods, procedures, or technologies. Planning a police response to a major public event, like a presidential visit to the city, would be a short-term plan. In court administration, implementing a new court procedure also would involve short-term planning. Preparing to train correctional officers in the use of a new communications system also would be short-term planning. An intermediate plan might develop, implement, and evaluate a comprehensive community-oriented policing program or a new correctional treatment program. Most strategic planning in criminal justice is long-range planning.

Strategic (Large-Scale) Planning

Strategic managerial planning was a key feature of large-scale military planning in the two World Wars. It first became popular in commercial management in the 1950s (Gilmore & Brandenburg, 1962), and was applied in the public sector in the late 1980s. The LEAA required comprehensive statewide strategic plans for states to become eligible for LEAA grants in the 1970s. In turn, the states required regions, counties, and cities to develop their own strategic plans to qualify for pass-through grants. The LEAA is long gone, but strategic planning has endured. It has become part of criminal justice management in localities across the United States, and urban planners have become a common feature of local government (Gordon, 2005). Newer federal criminal justice programs also called for strategic planning, including Community Oriented Policing (COP) programs (Cordner, 1997; Zhao, Thurman, & Ren, 2008). In criminal justice applications, strategic planning will involve the political leadership of the jurisdiction, the chief executives of the criminal justice agencies involved in the plan, and representation from community and client populations.

The plans can be either market-oriented (externally oriented) or centralized (internally oriented) approaches (Stewart & Garson, pp. 123–129). The type of approach is determined by whose interests, needs, and opinions are being considered. Large-scale strategic planning can be national, statewide, or community-wide in scope. It is broad in application, influencing the lives of many people and representing multiple agencies and client groups both within and outside the organization (Stewart & Garson, 1983, Chapter 6). Zhao, Thurman, and Ren (2008, pp. 20–23) have developed a four-part model for strategic planning in COP programs. It is derivative of the leadership style models discussed in Chapter 4. With dimensions of participation ("ranks involved") and "extent of application," their model reflects the contrast of hierarchical scientific management planning and more democratic, full-participation human relations planning in the implementation and continuation of COP programs. These are large-scale plans because they integrate efforts of the police with a wide range of community interests and agencies, both within criminal justice and beyond it.

In recent years we have observed a vivid example of strategic planning: the national responses to 9-11. In the months after the September 11, 2001, attack on the United States, the federal government, the states, localities, and private organizations were brought together to develop a national response to the threat of terrorism. Among the obvious products were the creation of the Department of Homeland Security (DHS), the passage of the USA PATRIOT Act (officially the Uniting and Strengthening America by Providing Appropriate Tools Required to Intercept and Obstruct Terrorism Act), and the undertaking of aggressive antiterror operations worldwide. These plans involved and integrated the efforts and resources of many entities—the Department of Defense

(DOD), including the Army, Navy, Marines, Air Force, Defense Intelligence Agency (DIA), and National Security Agency (NSA); the Department of Justice (DOJ), including the U.S. Marshal's Service; the Drug Enforcement Agency (DEA); the Federal Bureau of Investigation (FBI) (with its Joint Terrorism Task Force [JTTF]); the Department of Energy (DOE); the Central Intelligence Agency (CIA); the Centers for Disease Control and Prevention (CDC); and many others at both federal and state levels. Also involved in national security planning have been nongovernmental organizations (NGOs) such as the International Association of Chiefs of Police (IACP) and the International City/County Management Association (ICMA) (Oliver, 2007).

Small-Scale/Operational/Tactical Planning

Tactical or operational planning is used to develop a project or program, carry out some anticipated new activity, prepare for future developments, and so on. Operational or tactical planning is centered on the organization itself and involves implementation of tasks clearly associated with that organization. Other agencies or client populations may be impacted, but not in so significant a way as to disrupt their own continuing operations. For example, a police crackdown on some particular traffic violation may result in more traffic cases in court, but not so many more as to require special court responses. A court plan to improve case docketing will have a bearing on the schedules of witness programs, the prosecutor's office, and defense attorneys, but will not introduce any new burdens on them.

Forecasting is an important feature of planning. When forecasting, a manager makes certain informed, empirical assumptions about what the future is likely to bring. It uses several processes (Massie, 1987, pp. 87–88):

1. quantitative time-series analysis—using data on existing patterns to project future patterns
2. derived forecasts—using forecasts from similar situations as models for the one under consideration (e.g., How has another state achieved the same objectives our state aims to achieve?)
3. causal models—using mathematical models to express relationships among interactive variables
4. surveys of individual plans and attitudes—a survey of individuals can anticipate what they hope to achieve, and thus provide a model for where the whole organization should be moving (e.g., by asking how many of their employees want to continue their formal educations in the next 5 years, and in what specialties, management can develop coordinated staff-development training plans)
5. brainstorming—a group comes together to discuss options under some preagreed conditions, such as:
   a. no criticizing the ideas of others
   b. encouraging support for the ideas of others
   c. recording all comments for future consideration

6. Delphi method—RAND Corporation method using expert opinions collected independently by questionnaire
7. contingent forecasting scenarios—developing a likely narrative of how events might unfold, as in writing a novel or short story

Planning is absolutely necessary in certain situations. According to James Thompson (1967), plans are needed for:

1. Buffering (protection from environment with input/output structures)
2. Leveling (balancing the inputs and outputs to reduce fluctuations)
3. Adaptation (dealing with changes that cannot be leveled or buffered)
4. Rationing (restricting input or output to match capacity)

The Products of Planning

The types of decisions fall into three broad categories: (1) routine (assigning leaves, days off, etc.), (2) problem-solving—crisis, emergencies, and challenges, and (3) innovative future-oriented decisions. These will result in the following four products:

1. *Policy:* a guide for making decisions
2. *Rule:* a precise statement of what is required, with minimal discretion
3. *Procedure:* a detailed system of actions (steps) to be followed to accomplish a task
4. *Tasks:* specific actions to be taken to carry out the plan

Methods of Group Decision-Making: Cooperation and Consensus versus Competition

Group decision-making is thought to be better than making "individualized" decisions for several reasons (Shermer, 2004):

1. Groups have a "broader fund of knowledge"; that is, they have more experience collectively than any one manager is likely to possess on his or her own.
2. Groups are likely to identify far more alternatives.
3. Groups are likely to be more critical of alternatives than a solo manager.
4. Groups will take more risks, "think outside of the box" more readily, and be more creative (because the potential blame is shared).
5. Group decisions are more likely to be accepted when they are the product of multiple authors rather than a single author.

There are potential flaws in group decision-making. We are cautioned that: "Group decision making is rarely of as high quality as the decisions of the organization's most proficient member" (Stewart & Garson, 1983, p. 138). There are several reasons for this:

1. Group discussion inhibits some people.
2. There is a general desire to "get along" in a group setting.

3. Dominance by a few vocal opinion-setters can determine the outcome.
4. The desire to incorporate ideas from all participants in order to avoid leaving anyone out can produce unsatisfactory results. This infamous committee malaise is humorously exemplified by the camel: "The camel is a racehorse designed by a committee."

There are other potential problems to be considered:

1. *Personalities* within the decision group sometimes will clash, with disruptive results. Egos will clash when some members of the decision group seek to promote agendas and ideas in competition with others who hold strongly opposing views.
2. The *homogeneity versus heterogeneity* of the group can be a factor. Multiple individuals sharing the same viewpoint (a homogeneous group) will be far less likely to propose or consider a wide range of options.
3. The *setting* can either facilitate or retard deliberation. The talk circle usually will work better than other arrangements. It is important to avoid prominent seating (thrones) and cross-table barriers when free and open discussion is desired. A meeting in the senior manager's office will be dominated by him or her, whereas a meeting in a conference room used by all usually will encourage a freer flow of ideas.
4. The *group size* will influence the deliberations. Too small a group will limit ideas, and too many participants will be unmanageable, circumstantially limiting the opportunities for all to take part. An ideal group size is in the 5- to 12-person range; the actual number should reflect the interests to be represented in the deliberations. When the group must be large because of other considerations, either voting or parliamentary procedures should be used. There are, however, problems with them as well.

Democratic, Nondivisive Group Decision-Making

Voting and parliamentary procedures may be democratic, but often they are also competitive and divisive. Various alternatives to traditional voting methods have been offered (Dasgupta & Maskin, 2004). Two decision-making techniques using a mix of democratic principles and expertise are the *Delphi method* and the *nominal group technique.* Both are now widely used.

Delphi Method
Developed by the RAND Corporation in the 1950s, the Delphi method allows the manager the advantage of using many of the best minds in the country on an issue, technology, or area of expertise, without having to put them on the payroll for an extended period. The process includes the following:

1. Identify and enlist outside experts.
2. Administer questionnaires on the issue by mail asking:
    a. direction
    b. degree

    c. time frame
    d. likelihood
3. Aggregate results from survey and reedit questionnaire.
4. Resubmit revised questionnaire.
5. Repeat cycle until new responses decline to negligible level.
6. Arrange a face-to-face analysis session.
7. Define the explicit group consensus.

Nominal Group Technique

Developed by Andre L. Delbecq, Andrew H. Van De Ven, and David H. Gustafson (1975), the nominal group technique uses the expertise of those already in the organization. It is less costly than hiring dozens or hundreds of consultants, and it has the additional advantage of involving those who are or will be affected by the decisions reached.

1. Hold a face-to-face meeting of experts and involved in-house staff on the given problem.
2. Invite all participants to offer ideas on the issue.
3. List ideas on paper, one idea at a time, as an analyst records all.
4. After all ideas are recorded, each is discussed for:
    a. clarification,
    b. agreement, and
    c. disagreement.
5. Conduct anonymous balloting to rank order suggestions.
6. Lead a further discussion of rank-order results to eliminate duplication and to consolidate similar ideas, dropping low-priority, low-regard items.
7. Conduct anonymous final ranking, with average ranks calculated, to select the preferred solution.

Systems Management and Planning

Social planning models often have been used in criminal justice planning, reflecting the rise of "the systems management" philosophy and the rise of management by objectives (MBO) (Lynch & Lynch, 2005, Chapter 13). Recall that Souryal (1985, 1995) views "systems" as a school of thought in management science on a par with either scientific management or human relations.

    The growth of computer modeling has required a method for managerial planning that conforms to the "path models" of computer analysis. This reinforces the systems approach by indicating the concern for the system as an entire thing, rather than the particularizing of "task mission" planning.

BOX 6.2 MANAGEMENT DECISION-MAKING AND PLANNING MODELS AND STYLES

Different authors have presented various models and proposed differing styles used by decision-makers and planners. Klofas, Stojkovic, & Kalinich (1998, pp. 300–301) list the following:

Sequentialists use experience to select key information, then proceed to examine these in prioritized, sequential, and detailed fashion.

Ah, Yes! People amass a great body of information, infer a pattern, and then make a decision that unsystematically fits this pattern.

Simplifiers seek to reduce the problem to its simplest expression, then decide based on that simplification.

Ratifiers wait to see what others are thinking, then join the apparent majority.

Planners also have been classified according to their styles. Lynch and Lynch (2005, pp. 160–163) note that most try to create a balance of risk and concern for the system. Lynch and Lynch classify planners into one of four categories:

Purposeful: High concern for continuity of the system, yet willing to take risks (objective-oriented);

Traditional: High concern for continuity of the system and prefer to be low-risk (status quo–oriented);

Crisis: Low concern for the continuity of the system; unwilling to take risks, but forced into crisis problem-solving (beset by emergencies; not a planner but a reactor) (This is not the planner who anticipates crises and does what he or she can to avoid their disruptions.);

Entrepreneurial: Low concern for continuity of the system; willing to take risks (objective-oriented), willing to attempt exploration and speculation (action-oriented).

Program Planning

The key elements to program planning include:

1. Objective setting
2. Data collection—fully exploit "historical data," identify available resources and project requirements to be served, seek out working examples (models)
3. Simulation—mentally track each actor's role in the events sequentially (chronologically) (PERT/CPM [Program Evaluation and Review Technique/Critical Path Method] will illustrate), scenario-building
4. Circulation of the plan to interested parties—solicit suggestions
5. Synthesis of suggestions—especially those that are most critical and negative—these will best predict problems
6. Seeking approval for revised plan
7. Implementing plan
8. Revising continuously, even when implemented, to reflect new information and status reports, problems encountered, solved, and so on

---

BOX 6.3 ANALYTICAL DIMENSIONS FOR PLANNING PURPOSES

- goals
- functions
- administration and policy
- information systems and data requirements
- procedures and practices
- human-labor resources
- clients
- physical facilities
- cost and budgetary considerations

Problem Analysis

According to Lynch and Lynch (2005, pp. 168–171), there are five steps to **problem analysis:**

1. Recognize and identify the problems of the organization.
2. Separate the problems into their component areas, answering several key questions: Where? When? Who is most concerned? What is the extent, magnitude and seriousness of the problem? Are there any trends in evidence?
3. Prioritize by component area, and among components.
4. Select and analyze the priority problems in detail.
5. Test for true causes. What really is producing the problem? Avoid treating only the symptoms when the disease itself is left unremedied.

The armed services of the United States long ago realized the critical importance of detailed planning for complex operations. Beginning in 1917 during World War I, army staff officers were provided a manual to help them with performing their staff functions, including problem analysis and planning. The staff study format in Box 6.4 was developed for the manual to assist in problem analysis. Various editions and revisions of what

---

BOX 6.4 STAFF STUDY FORMAT

1. Statement of the problem or issue under study.
2. Assumptions, theories, and inferences being considered.
3. Summary of data and relevant facts (appendices may be attached).
4. Discussion of the options available.
5. Conclusions based on the assumptions and supported by the data.
6. Actions recommended for the agency.
7. Concurrences and nonconcurrences from others.
8. Appendices with detailed data.

BOX 6.5 MILITARY OR MANAGER–STAFF DECISION-MAKING PROCESS

The U.S. military has done complex operational planning and decision-making, involving thousands and even millions of persons, for much of its history. The armed services have developed a procedure for this, adapted here for criminal justice organizations doing large-scale planning and operational decision-making as the "manager–staff decision-making process."

1. Mission (Objective) Determined—by the manager or by the manager's superior.
2. Estimate of the Situation—initial estimate from information immediately available and/or from experience.
3. Planning Guidance—given by the manager to his or her staff (omitted if the manager is coming to his or her decision without staff input), including such elements as:
   a. Specified tasks contained within the general mission.
   b. Implied tasks essential to the mission.
   c. Preferences, options, possible course of action.
   d. Potential sources of information and data.
   e. Staff's functional organization—if not already delineated (who will work on what aspects of the planning).
   f. Timetables, deadlines, reports, and inputs requested.
4. Staff Estimates (staff work rising from the planning guidance [omitted if there is no staff]), uses the Staff Study (see Box 6.4):
   a. Problem statement
   b. Assumptions (derived from above)
   c. Facts Bearing on the Problem
   d. Discussion of Options
   e. Conclusions (original staff work)
   f. Actions Recommended
      See: the Staff Study (see Box 6.4)
5. Manager's Estimate/Decisions
   a. Mission
   b. Situation
   c. Courses of Action (options)
   d. Analysis of Opposing Courses of Action—factors to overcome
   e. Comparison of our Courses of Actions—the agency's options
   f. Decision/Recommendation
6. Preparation of Plans/Orders—done by either the manager himself/herself or by the staff:
   a. Situation Statement: opposition; assets
   b. Mission: what specifically is to be done
   c. Execution: the concept of the operation and submissions for each participant
   d. Support: material, services, personnel needs to sustain the activities
   e. Control/Coordination: supervisory activities
7. Approval of Plans/Orders by the manager (omitted if no staff work is involved).
8. Issuances of Plans/Orders: Communications
9. Supervision by the manager and managerial staff
10. Mission Completion—concluding step, confirming that the mission has been accomplished, crediting the contributions of participants, and usually including a follow-up report with lessons learned.

is known in the army as *FM-101-5* were prepared as the army faced other wars and periods of conflict—in 1940 for World War II, in 1954 and 1960 for the Cold War, in 1972 for Vietnam, and in 1984 and 1997 for contemporary global challenges including the current "War on Terror" (Military/Info, 2008). In these evolving manuals, a process for carrying out comprehensive large-scale planning and operational decision-making was developed that involves staff input and joint decision-making by the lead manager and his or her staff. This "military decision-making process" has been proven by the test of time. This is modified for nonmilitary applications and provided in Box 6.5 as the "manager–staff decision-making process."

Organizational Development

Organizational development is planned, organization-wide, long-term change. It applies principles of the behavioral sciences and requires changes in attitudes, behavior, and organizational structure to achieve greater individual and organizational effectiveness (French & Bell, 1999, pp. 1, 24). There are eight features of organizational development:

1. It is ongoing and dynamic, a continuous process.
2. It is applied behavioral/social sciences, using
   - psychology
   - sociology
   - economics
   - political science
   - business administration.
3. It is a reeducation process.
4. It is a "systems approach" that treats agency activities as interactive operations.
5. It is a rational process based on data acquisition evaluation and verification.
6. It is experienced-based.
7. It uses planning and decision-making processes such as means-ends analysis.
8. It uses work teams or task forces to achieve its implementation.

Forming the Work Teams

Task forces and **T-Groups** (also called *T-Teams* and *tiger teams)* are small working committees or training groups that study, make collective decisions, and implement action programs to effect major changes. Typically the T-Group leader is a "passive facilitator" and "resource person" who guides the group to help it find its own change solutions.

Management workshops are especially useful when outside consultants are employed to facilitate and control the process. A facilitator administers a questionnaire to the management group of the organization, asking them what their organization does well (getting the group thinking positively), what it can improve on, and what new things it should consider. The facilitator then will conduct follow-up interviews with key sub-managers to develop an agenda for the upcoming workshop. This agenda should be discussed with the senior manager to include his or her inputs. The workshop is scheduled, and the key decision-makers in the management team are brought together. Notes are taken, and a synthesis of contributions is prepared. These are shared in a report distributed afterward.

Retreats are similar to management workshops. The planners of the retreat take the key people away from the workplace to a relaxing setting where the key manager and staff can learn to interact constructively.

BOX 6.6 PROBLEMS IN MANAGERIAL DECISION-MAKING (A LITTLE HUMOR)

Dead Pony Principles of Management: The origins of this item have been lost, for it has been circulating on the Internet in one form or another for many years with the authorship long since deleted. The humorist who penned the original version was expressing the cynicism that surrounds the failures of modern management.

In the version shared here, we are informed that Dakota Amerind tribal wisdom says that when you discover you are riding a dead pony, the best strategy is to dismount. However, managers often try other strategies with dead ponies, including the following:

1. Buying a stronger whip.
2. Changing riders.
3. Saying "This is the way we always have ridden this pony."
4. Appointing a committee to study the pony.
5. Arranging to visit other sites to see how they ride dead ponies.
6. Increasing the standards to ride dead ponies.
7. Appointing a "tiger team" to revive the dead pony.
8. Creating a training session to increase our riding ability.
9. Comparing the state of dead ponies in today's environment.
10. Changing the requirements, declaring that "this pony is not dead."
11. Hiring contractors to ride the dead pony.
12. Harnessing several dead ponies together for increased speed.
13. Declaring that "no pony is too dead to beat."
14. Providing additional funding to increase the pony's performance.
15. Doing a cost-effectiveness study to see if contractors can ride the dead pony more cheaply.
16. Purchasing a product to make dead ponies run faster.
17. Declaring that the pony is "better, faster, and cheaper" dead.
18. Forming a quality circle to find uses for dead ponies.
19. Revisiting the performance requirements for ponies.
20. Saying this pony was procured with cost as an independent variable.
21. Promoting the dead pony to a supervisory position.

Summary

Mastering decision-making and planning is something of an art. Some managers excel at both; some have to work hard at them. Making decisions and planning ahead will be a chore faced by all criminal justice managers. It is important that the manager be flexible rather than taking up one style and rigidly sticking to it.

LEARNING OBJECTIVES

Upon finishing this chapter, you should be able to do the following:

1. Discuss the features of the four models of managerial decision-making: rational choice, bureaucratic, decision trees, and political.
2. Distinguish between operational decisions and managerial decisions.
3. Contrast long-range and short-range planning in terms of the planning cycles of criminal justice organizations.
4. Discuss the five key factors a manager should consider in selecting a managerial decision-making method.

IMPORTANT TERMS AND NAMES

- *arbitrariness*
- *bounded rationality*
- *decision-process model*
- *decision trees*
- *Delphi method*
- *discretion*
- *forecasting*
- *management workshops*
- *nominal group technique*
- *organizational development*
- *policy*
- *problem analysis*
- *procedure*
- *programmed decisions*
- *rational choice model*
- *retreats*
- *rule*
- *satisficing*
- *standard operating procedures (SOPs)*
- *T-Groups*
- *tasks*
- *task forces*

References and Supplemental Sources

Argyris, C. (1957). *Personality and organization.* New York: Harper Collins.

Barnard, C. I. (1938/1989). Economy of incentives. In: Ott, S. J. (Ed.), *Classic readings in organizational behavior.* Pacific Grove, CA: Brooks/Cole.

Barnard, C. I. (1938/1968). *The functions of the executive.* Cambridge, MA: President and Fellows of Harvard College (reprinted as 30th anniversary edition).

Blake, R. R. (1964). *The managerial grid: Key orientations for achieving production through people.* Houston, TX: Gulf.

Cordner, G. W. (1997). Community policing: Elements and effects. *Critical issues in policing.* In: Dunham, R. G., & Alpert, G. P. (Eds.), Prospect Heights, IL: Waveland Press (pp. 451–468).

Cyert, R. M., & March, J. G. (1959). *Modern organization theory.* New York: Wiley.

Dasgupta, P., & Maskin, E. (2004). The fairest vote of all. *Scientific American, 290*(3), 92–97.

Delbecq, A. L., Van de Ven, A. H., & Gustafson, D. H. (1975). *Group techniques for program planning: A guide to nominal group and Delphi Processes.* Glenview, IL: Scott, Foresman.

Fiedler, F. E. (1967). *A theory of leadership effectiveness.* New York: McGraw-Hill.

Follett, M. P. (1926). The giving of orders. *The scientific foundations of business administration.* In: Metcalf, H. C. et al., (Eds.), Baltimore, MD: Williams and Wilkins.

French, W. L., & Bell, C. H., Jr. (1973). *Organizational development.* Englewood Cliffs, NJ: Prentice Hall.

French, W. L., & Bell, C. H., Jr. (1999). *Organizational development* (6th ed.). Upper Saddle River, NJ: Prentice Hall.

Gilmore, F. F., & Brandenburg, R. G. (1962). The anatomy of corporate planning. *Harvard Business Review, 4*(6), 61–69.

Gordon, G. L. (2005). *Strategic planning for local government* (2nd ed.). Washington, DC: International City/County Management Association.

Harvey, J. B. (1974). The Abilene paradox: The management of agreement. *Organizational Dynamics, Summer,* 63–80.

Kenney, J. P. (1959). *Police management planning.* Springfield, IL: Thomas.

Klofas, J., Stojkovic, S., & Kalinich, D. (1998). *Criminal justice organizations: Administration and management* (2nd ed.). Belmont, CA: West-Wadsworth.

Luthans, F. (1976). *Introduction to management: A contingency approach.* New York: McGraw-Hill.

Lynch, R. G., & Lynch, S. (2005). *The police manager* (6th ed.). Newark, NJ: LexisNexis, Matthew Bender.

March, J. G., & Simon, H. A. (1958). *Organizations.* New York: Wiley.

Massie, J. L. (1987). *Essentials of management* (4th ed.). Englewood Cliffs, NJ: Prentice Hall.

Military/Info (2008). Staff operations. Plymouth, MN: Military/Info. Retrieved from <http://www.military-info.com/MPHOTO/p054.htm/>.

Oliver, W. M. (2007). *Homeland security for policing.* Upper Saddle River, NJ: Prentice Hall.

Pfeffer, J. (1981). *Power in organizations.* London: Pitman.

Shafritz, J. M., & Ott, J. S. (Eds.). (1996). *Classics of organizational theory* (3rd ed.). Pacific Grove, CA: Brooks/Cole.

Shermer, M. (2004). Common sense: Surprising new research that crowds are often smarter than individuals. *Scientific American, 291*(6), 38.

Simon, H. (1957). *Administrative Behavior: A study of decision-making processes in administrative organizations.* New York: The Free Press.

Souryal, S. S. (1985). *Police organization and administration*. Cincinnati: Pilgrimage/Anderson.

Souryal, S. S. (1995). *Police organization and administration* (2nd ed.). Cincinnati: Anderson.

Stewart, D., & Garson, G. D. (1983). *Organizational behavior and public management*. New York: Dekker.

Thompson, J. D. (1967). *Organizations in action: Social science bases of administrative theory*. New York: McGraw-Hill.

Thompson, J. D. (2003). *Organizations in action: Social science bases of administrative theory*. New Brunswick, NJ: Transaction (with a new preface by Mayer N. Zald and new introduction by W. Richard Scott).

Vanderbilt, A. T. (1947). *Minimum standards of judicial administration*. Washington, DC: American Bar Association.

Wildavsky, A. (1973). If planning is everything, maybe it's nothing. *Policy Sciences, 4*, 127–153.

Wilson, J. Q. (1989). *Bureaucracy*. New York: Basic Books.

Wilson, O. W. (1950). *Police administration*. New York: McGraw-Hill.

Zhao, J., Thurman, Q. C., & Ren, L. (2008). An examination of strategic planning in American law enforcement agencies: A national study. *Police Quarterly, 11*(1), 3–26.

Zhao, J., Ren, L., & Lovrich, N. (2010). Police organizational structures during the 1990s: An application of contingency theory. *Police Quarterly, 13*(2), 209–232.

7

Evaluating, Appraising, and Assessing Performance

The "E" in LODESTAR is for evaluating. Evaluation and the closely related concepts of *appraisal* and *assessment* are major managerial tasks, and often they are very troubling for the manager. The terms "evaluation," "appraisal," and "assessment" are often used interchangeably in the management literature and in criminal justice workplaces. **Assessment** focuses on the process of determining performance of individuals and organizations. Management theorists speak of tools and instruments used in the assessment process. Evaluation uses assessment processes to produce evaluations of individuals and work groups. Appraisal is the final aspect of the assessment–evaluation process. An **appraisal** is the score, rating, or ranking given an individual or organization. Because performance appraisals are the products of assessment and evaluation processes, the three are closely entwined, and one is difficult to distinguish from the other in practice. For the purposes of this chapter, the distinctions among them will not be developed further. Evaluation activities are needed both for individuals in the organization and for the organization as a whole, as well as for each of its operational subunits.

Individual Evaluation

Individual evaluation is sometimes referred to as "performance appraisal" (Phillips & McConnell, 1996: 183). It often involves managers and supervisors assigning ratings to subordinates. Individuals often are given ratings that may be compared with those of other coworkers. The chief criminal justice manager should develop an evaluation plan, if one does not already exist. If there is an existing evaluation plan, the manager should review it occasionally to determine whether it addresses the needs of the organization and its employees. An example of an evaluation plan is found in Box 7.1.

Managerial Issues in Personnel Evaluation
Content and Criteria of Evaluations

"You can't expect what you don't inspect" is the mantra of the police academy drill sergeant. Indeed, evaluation criteria ought to reflect that which is most important in the job

---

BOX 7.1 INDIVIDUAL PERFORMANCE-EVALUATION PLAN

1. The evaluation process and criteria used will be explained to and discussed with all new personnel upon reporting for employment, and annually thereafter.
2. The evaluation of each staff member will be prepared by the immediate supervisor of the employee.
3. All employees shall develop and submit to their supervisors an individual professional-development plan that will comply with the employees' job descriptions and the mission, goals, and objectives of the organization.
4. The individual professional development plan will be reviewed annually by the supervisor and updated as required.
5. All employees will be evaluated (annually, semiannually, quarterly).
6. Each supervisor preparing evaluations will be trained in evaluation techniques and standards and on the use of the evaluation instruments.
7. Each person evaluated shall be given a copy of the evaluation and will acknowledge receiving it in writing.
8. An evaluated employee will be provided an opportunity for submitting a rebuttal or appeal.
9. The organization shall have an evaluation appeals panel composed of experienced supervisory personnel of the agency.
10. The employee exercising the right to file an appeal will be given an opportunity to review all documents to be presented to the evaluation appeals panel.
11. The appeals panel shall prepare a statement of its findings and attach this to the original evaluation if that evaluation is upheld.
12. The appeals panel may direct that an inappropriate evaluation be revised and resubmitted to correct errors or other identified issues.
13. The evaluation-plan process will not discriminate on the basis of race, national origin, religion, marital status, sex, or disability.
14. The evaluation shall be filed with the official personnel records of the employee.
15. Individual evaluations, rebuttals, and appellate reports will be kept as permanent documents.

---

description of the employee. Clearly, evaluations should be based on job descriptions and the expectations of the job. For example, Orlando Wilson and Roy McLaren (1977) advised using the following categories in police evaluations:

- observance of work hours
- attendance
- grooming and dress
- compliance with rules
- safety practices
- public contacts
- suspect contacts
- employee contacts
- knowledge of work requirements

- work judgments
- planning and organizing abilities
- job skill level
- quality of work
- volume of acceptable work
- meeting deadlines
- accepts responsibility
- accepts direction
- accepts change
- effectiveness under stress
- appearance of work station
- operation and care of equipment
- work coordination
- initiative
- other additional factors specific to the officer's assignment or the needs of the agency
- supervisory factors (when appropriate):
  - scheduling and coordinating
  - training and instruction
  - effectiveness
  - evaluating subordinates
  - judgments and decisions
  - leadership
  - operational economy
  - supervisory control

Frequency of Evaluations

The frequency of performance appraisals is up to the manager. They can be as frequent as monthly or quarterly, but more often they are done annually. Novice and probationary employees may be subjected to more frequent evaluation during their probationary period. Veteran employees in highly professional organizations can be evaluated far less frequently. There also are one-time only "**critical incident**" evaluations (Phillips & McConnell, 1996: 191-192) and "**after-action reports**" which critique and evaluate performance in specific incidents and key events.

The Evaluator

The general rule is that the evaluation should be done by the supervisor who has direct control over the evaluated subordinate, as defined by the organizational chain of command. The person designated to prepare the evaluation is the evaluator or rater. Often, the next manager in the chain of command is designated as the endorser, whose responsibility is to see that the evaluation is timely, reasonable, and appropriate.

Shared or Secret?

When employee improvement is an objective in giving evaluations, the best policy is to share evaluations, in which the evaluator provides the evaluated party a copy of the evaluation. Often the evaluated person is given an opportunity to respond and even appeal.

Secret evaluations have their own time and place, such as special evaluations rendered to assist in making some kinds of highly sensitive personnel decisions. These may include selecting subordinates for further training or schooling; identifying persons who have the potential for advancement, greater leadership, and promotion; and identifying individuals for dismissal when reductions in the workforce are being contemplated.

Some managers prefer secret evaluations simply to avoid sharing their appraisals with the employee. There are several important purposes to evaluations, and most of these are not served by secrecy. Nevertheless, some criminal justice organizations still pursue secrecy practices.

Purposes of Individual Evaluations

Among the purposes for giving formal individual evaluations are:

1. assisting in individual development
2. encouraging and maintaining discipline
3. allocating promotions or compensation

Formats

Many formats are acceptable, and each has its distinct advantages and disadvantages (Phillips & McConnell, 1996: 186). Lists of desired traits followed by check-boxes or scores for each are popular. Some agencies prefer open-ended evaluations, in which the evaluator must comment on the performance in each performance area. Other agencies apply percentages, with 100% being ideal, or use grades such as are encountered in schools and universities. Some agencies used mixed formats, asking for information in several ways. As Figures 7.1 and 7.2 illustrate, the format of an evaluation can vary significantly.

Means of Assessment

Criminal justice managers will assess the work performance of subordinates in several ways:

1. regularly observing employees and having routine contact during work
2. visiting workplaces
3. conducting formal inspections
4. reviewing management reports
5. asking the workers to evaluate themselves
6. using performance testing, such as:
   a. scores from weapons qualification
   b. results of physical agility and fitness tests

Alexander Maconochie Correctional Center
Managerial Appraisal

Manager's Name: _____   _____
Manager's Unit : _____
Time Period : _____
Evaluation Date: _____   _____

1. ADMINISTRATION AND MANAGEMENT FUNCTIONS

Rate the unit manager on the performance factors using the performance definitions:

        1 = truly exceptional outstanding performance
        2 = routinely exceeds expectations
        3 = fully satisfactory
        4 = needs improvement
        5 = unsatisfactory

Performance Factor	Rating	Remarks and Explanations
Organizational Leadership		
Organization of Work		
Planning		
Decision Making		
Organizational Development		
Information Management		
Budgeting and Resource Allocation		

2. INTERPERSONAL SKILLS

Rate the unit manager on the performance factors using the performance definitions:

        1 = truly exceptional outstanding performance
        2 = routinely exceeds expectations
        3 = fully satisfactory
        4 = needs improvement
        5 = unsatisfactory

Performance Factor	Rating	Remarks and Explanations
Oral Communication		
Written Communication		
Coordination and Collaboration		
Supervisory Control		
Commitment to Equal Opportunity		
Staff Appraisal and Development		

3. INDIVIDUAL LEADERSHIP ATTRIBUTES

Rate the unit manager on the performance factors using the performance definitions:

        1 = truly exceptional outstanding performance
        2 = routinely exceeds expectations
        3 = fully satisfactory
        4 = needs improvement
        5 = unsatisfactory

Performance Factor	Rating	Remarks and Explanations
Mentoring of Subordinates		
Empowering Subordinates		
Team Building		
Professionalism		
Vision		
Self-Improvement		
Innovation		
Objectivity		
Credibility		
Flexibility		
Effort and Initiative		

4. OVERALL APPRAISAL (Please check one.)

_____ Exceptional And Outstanding
_____ Routinely Exceeds Expectations
_____ Fully Satisfactory
_____ Needs Improvement
_____ Unsatisfactory

What were the unit manager's performance highlights in the past year?
_____

What could be improved in the unit manager's performance in the next year?
_____

What should be the unit manager's new performance goals for the next year?
_____

_____ Date _____

Evaluator's Signature _____

Evaluated Manager's Signature _____

Date Evaluation Reviewed by the Evaluated Unit Manager: _____

FIGURE 7.1 Alexander Maconochie Correctional Center Managerial Appraisal.

Vanderbilt County District Court Clerical Employee Evaluation Form

Employee Name: _____

Employee Title: _____

Period Covered: _____

Date of Evaluation: _____

Days Absent in Rating Period: _____

	Excellent	Very Good	Satisfactory	Needs Improvement	Inadequate
1. Work Quality					
2. Technical Skills					
3. Reliability					
4. Initiative					
5. Versatility					
6. Efficiency					
7. Public Demeanor					
8. Punctuality					

General remarks on employee's performance (The rater must explain and justify all "excellent" and all "inadequate" scores given above):

Rater's goals for the employee in the coming year (These will be mutually discussed by the supervisor and employee, and will be based upon the employee's job description):

Name of Rater: _____   Signature of Rater: _____

Acknowledgement by Employee (signature): _____

    The Employee's signature above does not imply agreement with the evaluation received.

    The Employee may attach a one-page response to the ratings given if there is disagreement.

Date Acknowledged: _____   Response Attached: _____ yes _____ no

FIGURE 7.2 Vanderbilt County District Court Clerical Employee Evaluation Form.

   c. written or orally administered knowledge tests

   d. technical "hands-on" skills tests

The Stress of Personnel Evaluation

Individual evaluations can be highly traumatic events in employee–supervisor relations. Even an overall "good" evaluation can be disappointing to an employee who has a very high self-image. Some managers are quite adept at "damning with faint praise." All too often, evaluations are viewed as punitive, backward-looking, and regressive.

Management by Objectives (MBO)

MBO provides a useful, forward-looking, and personally enriching approach to individual performance evaluation. MBO can be defined as "a process whereby individual managers and employees identify goals and work toward their completion and evaluation within a specific work period" (Klofas, Stojkovic, & Kalinich, 1990, p. 96). The key is the "process" (Massie, 1987, pp. 124–125). The concept originated with Peter F. Drucker in *The Practice of Management* (1954, pp. 119, 121–122); it was popularized by George Odiorne in *Management by Objectives* (1965) and many others who were influenced by Drucker's concepts.

BOX 7.2 USING MBO WITH A SUBORDINATE

Step 1: The supervisor begins the process as a traditional scientific manager by preparing a comprehensive job description for the subordinate (or updates and uses one already on file). This is given to the subordinate employee who is instructed to:

Step 2: Identify the subordinate's work objectives and their measurement standards in writing. These objectives should include:

> Routine Objectives—The subordinate will express the job in his or her own terms, following the job description framework.
>
> Problem-Solving Objectives—These allow the subordinate to make observations and suggestions to improve the organization toward its goals.
>
> Innovative Objectives—These allow the subordinate to propose new ideas for the organization in which the employee wishes to take part.
>
> Personal Objectives—These allow the subordinate to express personal needs and ambitions as they relate to the job.

Step 3: The manager and subordinate employee spend some time together going over the objectives, creating a dialogue on common objectives. They should produce a common set of objectives on which they both agree and that both agree to use to evaluate the success of the subordinate.

Step 4: They put the revised objective statement aside and come back to it 6 months or a year later (whichever is the manager's policy) and the manager will review the objectives with the subordinate to assess the progress of the subordinate toward meeting the enumerated objectives.

Step 5: This review is used by the supervising manager as the basis for periodic individual evaluations. The supervisor will have the subordinate evaluate himself/herself against those objectives, rather than evaluating the employee unilaterally. Together they will agree on what has been achieved and what remains to be done. They prepare a summary report of the prior term's accomplishments and shortfalls and file it as the performance appraisal for that rated period.

Step 6: Together, the supervisor and the subordinate employee identify new and modified objectives for the next period. In essence, they return to Step 2 and start again.

Organizational Evaluation

As important as evaluation is for individuals, it also is a critical managerial activity to help identify ways to improve the entire organization. Statistics on agency performance are used as an essential measure of that agency's performance. Since the 1930s, police agencies have used the Uniform Crime Reports (UCR), prepared annually by the Federal Bureau of Investigation, to assess their success in dealing with the crime problem, making arrests, and clearing criminal cases. Prosecutors keep statistics on the number of cases presented to grand juries and brought to preliminary hearings and trials. They keep count of the number of cases plea-bargained and handled by various alternatives to adjudication. Many prosecutors publicize their conviction records. The courts track the number of cases heard and keep additional statistics on the number of days taken to bring cases to trial, on continuances, and on the number of decisions and sentences issued. Some courts also collect data on the fines levied and funds collected by the courts on behalf of the state and on behalf of crime victims and successful civil litigants. Correctional units keep track of data on the numbers of inmates in their custody; overcrowding; escapes; the average length of time served; participation in furlough, study, and work-release programs; discharge data; and the productivity of their correctional industries. Probation and parole agencies keep track of the number of clients under their supervision; successes and failures (recidivism rates); probation violations discovered; parole revocation hearings; and successful discharge from probation or parole supervision. All are appropriate measures of performance in the criminal justice system, and such managerial statistics typically are made public.

However, the interpretation of these statistics is complex. A police department may have low UCR statistics because it successfully prevents and suppresses more crime than other comparable police departments. However, low UCR statistics also could reflect a lack of public confidence in the local police, hence, their reluctance to call the police when criminally victimized. Some police departments have deliberately falsified UCR data to create a misleading impression of their performance. A high prosecutorial conviction rate can indicate stellar performance in court or pressure on indicted individuals to accept excessively lenient plea bargains to achieve convictions easily. The number of court decisions and verdicts does not speak to the quality or justice of those verdicts. Correctional data can be interpreted in multiple ways. Early release of unrehabilitated inmates may reduce overcrowding but does not improve public safety. High rates of failure of probation or parole may actually indicate very close supervision, while high rates of successful discharge may be explained by a lack of effort in supervising probationers and parolees and failure to detect their misconduct.

Moreover, there are other aspects of the organization that these managerial performance measures miss entirely. Organizational efficiency cannot be measured easily. Organizational standards of professionalism and integrity cannot be determined from such performance statistics. Whereas commercial managers can look to "the bottom line" of profitability, criminal justice agencies are not created to make profits. Criminal justice managers would be wise to develop and look to other measures of agency performance to augment the official statistics. Among the other aspects of a criminal justice agency performance that are especially useful in evaluating an organization are:

1. efficiency (cost-effectiveness) measures
2. absenteeism rates
3. turnover rates
4. measures of goal consensus and conflict

Using MBO with an Organization

MBO also can be used to evaluate entire work units or the whole organization. As Ronald Lynch applied MBO to criminal justice (1986, pp. 152–153, 161–169), it is the duty of the criminal justice manager to recognize the values preset for his or her agency by the community and the law, including the constitutional principles under which all American governments must operate. The manager must then articulate the mission statement that is assigned to his or her organization by the government and public processes. The manager then sets goals for the agency. These are abstract and long-term statements of what the organization ultimately hopes to achieve. However, it is not supposed that the agency will ever be completely successful in accomplishing its goals, including such ongoing statements as "preventing crime," "protecting the innocent," "identifying the guilty," and "achieving justice." The criminal justice manager then derives the objectives for the agency from such broad and abstract concepts. These objectives define the performance and results the agency hopes to achieve in the near future. These objectives relate to the goals, but they are reasonable, clear, and realistic and can be achieved in the near term. They are typically integrated into the organizational planning and budgeting cycle (which is usually annual). From the objectives, the criminal justice manager will develop projects and action plans. Evaluation follows the implementation of these projects and plans and must: (1) be based on measurable objectives, (2) have a detailed and practical evaluation design, (3) establish data-collection procedures, and (4) specify the data analysis methods to be used.

Pitfalls of MBO

MBO is not a panacea for all management ills. It cannot correct deep, systemic problems that can infect a criminal justice organization. For example, a corrupt agency will not acquire integrity by using MBO. Low levels of talent or training in the workforce will not become upgraded simply by using MBO with a pool of poorly selected, poorly prepared, or chronically underachieving employees. It also cannot be allowed to replace day-to-day operations. The participation of an entire organization all at one time can disrupt the work of the organization. Therefore, it is best to rotate MBO through each of the units of the larger organization over a lengthy evaluation cycle, returning to the first unit using MBO after all units have been so evaluated.

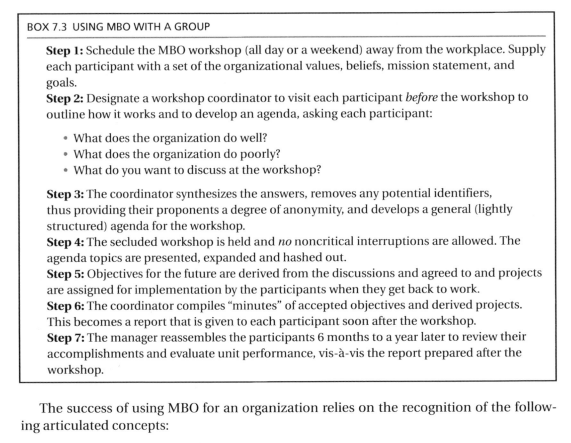

BOX 7.3 USING MBO WITH A GROUP

Step 1: Schedule the MBO workshop (all day or a weekend) away from the workplace. Supply each participant with a set of the organizational values, beliefs, mission statement, and goals.

Step 2: Designate a workshop coordinator to visit each participant *before* the workshop to outline how it works and to develop an agenda, asking each participant:

- What does the organization do well?
- What does the organization do poorly?
- What do you want to discuss at the workshop?

Step 3: The coordinator synthesizes the answers, removes any potential identifiers, thus providing their proponents a degree of anonymity, and develops a general (lightly structured) agenda for the workshop.

Step 4: The secluded workshop is held and *no* noncritical interruptions are allowed. The agenda topics are presented, expanded and hashed out.

Step 5: Objectives for the future are derived from the discussions and agreed to and projects are assigned for implementation by the participants when they get back to work.

Step 6: The coordinator compiles "minutes" of accepted objectives and derived projects. This becomes a report that is given to each participant soon after the workshop.

Step 7: The manager reassembles the participants 6 months to a year later to review their accomplishments and evaluate unit performance, vis-à-vis the report prepared after the workshop.

The success of using MBO for an organization relies on the recognition of the following articulated concepts:

- Mission
- Goals
- Objectives
- Action plans
- Project implementation
- Evaluation

Law Enforcement Accreditation

An organization also can be evaluated by an outside team of evaluators. In 1984, for the first time, a police department in the United States underwent accreditation under national standards of the Commission on Accreditation of Law Enforcement Agencies (CALEA). **CALEA** originally was sponsored by LEAA in the 1970s, but was created by a group of law enforcement professional organizations. Since 1984, hundreds of police agencies have been accredited by CALEA. To be accredited, an agency must meet high standards for recruiting, training, supervision, management, casework, administration, and accountability—all supported by written policies and actual practices.

Theodore Caplow on Personnel Issues

Theodore Caplow is an organizational sociologist who has examined in great depth the importance of employee morale in organizational assessment. He has concluded (1983) that organizational morale is high in the workforce when all or most of the 14 features presented in Box 7.5 are in evidence.

Morale is satisfaction with the organization and one's place in it. The turnover rate is one of the most obvious clues to gauging employee morale and is a key to organizational efficiency. An astute manager will know actual numbers and percentages of employees departing from the organization and its component units each year, but this information alone is not enough. There are many reasons for turnover. Some of these reasons do not reflect negatively on employee morale. Key questions that each manager should seek to answer for each employee separation are the proportions for:

1. nonorganizational reasons: death, serious illness, relocation of other family members, other family priorities, retirement eligibility, etc.
2. disciplinary reasons, to the advantage of the organization; for example, an employee fired for serious misconduct
3. efficiency or productivity reasons, to the advantage of the organization; for example: an employee fired or urged out for poor performance
4. external competitive reasons, other economic activities outside the current career field that draw the employees to seek new career opportunities; for example, a corrections officer quitting to take a sales job with a retail firm
5. internal competitive reasons, transfers to other organizations engaged in very similar activities; for example, a municipal police detective applying for and being hired by the FBI or DEA

BOX 7.4 THEODORE CAPLOW

Theodore Caplow is Commonwealth Professor Emeritus of Sociology at the University of Virginia, and he held a similar chair at Columbia University. He was president of the Tocqueville Society and served as the secretary of the American Sociological Association. He has authored or coauthored several major books, including *The Sociology of Work* (1954), *Two Against One: Coalitions in Triads* (1968), *Managing an Organization* (1983), *American Social Trends* (1991), and *The First Measured Century: An Illustrated Guide to Trends in America 1900–2000* (2001). He holds both Ph.D. and LL.D. degrees, and he is a highly regarded expert on management and the workplace.

FIGURE 7.3 Theodore Caplow. *PR Photo from PBS.*

BOX 7.5 THEODORE CAPLOW'S INDICATORS OF HIGH ORGANIZATIONAL MORALE

1. There are no cliques, and no groups are fearful of the boss.
2. Although minor infractions do occur, employees know and obey the organization's more important rules and regulations, and the violations that do occur do not impact on the organizational mission (discipline).
3. Employees stay with the organization (low turnover rate).
4. New employees are better qualified than those they replace (rising standards).
5. New employees are rapidly integrated into the informal networks of the organization.
6. Employees accept the goals of the organization (value and goal congruence).
7. Hiring, firing, promotion, and demotion decisions are usually unanimous or consensual.
8. Dismissals and demotions are rare and do not require complex, litigiously elaborate precautions and rules.
9. Supervisors know their subordinates and feel free to share that knowledge with those higher up, although evaluation documents are not taken seriously.
10. Pay and privileges are not major topics of discussion, and the existing distribution of benefits seems acceptable.
11. Organizational ceremonies and events are well attended.
12. Subordinate (midlevel) managers do not need to appeal to top management to maintain their authority.
13. Although conflicts occur, people who enter into them are apologetic and interested in resolving them in a fashion that reunites the organization.
14. Intervention by top management is welcomed when a conflict does occur.

There is an increasing degree of importance in each of the five reasons. If most employee separations are for the first two reasons, then the manager does not have significant evidence of a morale problem. However, reasons 3 through 5 signal the existence of progressively more serious problems.

Cost–Benefit Analysis

Assessment of decisions can use **cost–benefit analysis,** a utilitarian concept with its origins in the early 19th century (although it was not called that then). Jeremy Bentham spoke of it as his "felicific" calculus or **hedonistic calculus.** In more modern managerial slang, it is spoken of as "running the numbers" or "numbers crunching."

A cost–benefit analysis is a process that identifies, quantifies, and adds together all the positive factors of a decision, activity, or ongoing process to calculate the benefits. Then the analysis identifies, quantifies, and sums up all the negative factors to determine the costs. The two are then compared, and the difference between the two summations reveals whether the decision, activity, or process is favorable. The secret to doing cost–benefit analysis correctly is including all the actual costs and determining them realistically, as well as properly and accurately calculating the benefits. Fudging the numbers will bias the results and negate the value of doing the analysis.

Cost–benefit analysis is information-based. It must be done systematically. It is the link between the planning and decision-making processes and the budgeting and allocation processes of the criminal justice organization. It is closely integrated into the Program Planning and Budgeting System (PPBS) and Zero-Based Budgeting (ZBB) systems, which will be covered in Chapter 10.

Change in Organizations

One of the principle purposes of evaluation is to effect meaningful, directional change within the workforce (changing individuals) and within the whole organization (changing the organization). It is a striving for improvement. Bringing about purposeful, orderly change is a key managerial responsibility—so much so, that the "transformational" leadership role (Tichy & Ulrich, 1984) has been identified for special mention.

Justice agency managers have been called on to effect numerous, major changes in policy, practice, and technology in the years since the LEAA encouraged widespread innovation and reform across the criminal justice system. However, the intervention of the federal government and the infusion of massive amounts of federal funding were only part of the story. The attitude of the criminal justice manager toward change has been critical in bringing about the developments that have been the hallmark of the past generation. Warren Bennis (1966) observed that managers can bring about purposeful change by fostering (quoted in Ott, 1989, p. 584):

1. joint effort: the manager can offer freedom of choice within the change process by sharing information, goals, and situational data
2. a spirit of inquiry: the manager can foster favorable attitudes toward new information and experience, especially by sharing all data
3. relationship-building: the manager can involve the people to be affected by the change by mutual interaction, allowing voluntary participation and allowing all parties equal influence

Freedom of Choice

By interesting those involved in the change and giving them input into the decision-making, the personnel become agents of the change by choice. This recalls Mary Parker Follett's advice on giving and taking orders: "One person should not give orders to another person, but both should agree to take their orders from the situation" (Follett, 1926/1989, p. 259).

New Information and Experience

Many people usually fear change, but also enjoy variety and new experiences. Changes can be packaged as positive attractions rather than as fearful episodes. Sending old hands to a computer seminar in a resort city, thus mixing change with pleasure, can make the transition to change pleasant. Identifying the change agents of the organization in a very positive light can encourage participation in the change process.

Involvement

Involvement is akin to freedom of choice—bringing those most involved in the consequences of the change into the initiation of the change. By inviting those who will be impacted most by the changes into the planning process and implementation activities, the criminal justice manager will "co-opt" them, and by doing so, make them agents in the change process. Philip Selznick contributed the sociological analysis of co-optation as a managerial device. **Co-optation** is the process whereby the management of an organization absorbs the aims of the workers (Selznick, 1948; quoted in Shafritz & Ott, 1992, p. 120): "Co-optation is the process of absorbing new elements into the leadership or policy-determining structure of an organization as a means of averting threats to its stability or existence."

Kinds of Change

Problem-solving and innovative decision-making produces decisions that are intended to yield organizational changes when implemented. Evaluation and assessment activities identify areas where change is needed to produce a better-performing individual or organization, and later in the change process, to measure the success of the implementation of the intended changes. Change comes in many forms (Bennis, 1966, pp. 81–94).

Natural change involves no deliberation and no goal-setting and exists independently of the presence or absence of hierarchical arrangements. It occurs in three basic patterns: the *straight line,* following a trend in a consistent fashion, either maintaining a steady state, rising, or falling; the *rise-plateau-crash,* in which some feature or technological application rapidly achieves acceptance, stabilizes, and then drops off when a new feature or technology arises to replace it; and the *cyclic* (oscillating), in which frequencies will rise, then fall, only to rise again, in repetitive cycles. Natural change is not easily managed and is not relevant to this section. It will be discussed again in Chapter 12, however, when the futures will be discussed.

Planned change ideally occurs with mutual goal-setting, an equalization of power between change agents and those being changed, and deliberateness of process. It is one of the most important reasons for undertaking organizational evaluation. This kind of change is the responsibility of criminal justice managers. Arising from the assessment and appraisal processes of the evaluation function, planned change is undertaken to improve the agency over its prior state.

> **Indoctrination** also occurs with mutual goal-setting, and is deliberate, but the change agent dominates in the power balance.
> **Coercive change** also is deliberate, but lacks mutuality, and has an imbalanced power ratio in favor of the change agent.

Technocratic change does not involve goal-setting (or does not have goal-setting as a prime aspect). It is information-based and identifies sources of problems with the implicit assumption that their identification will lead to their elimination via some form of actual or social engineering.

Interactional change arises from the normal interaction of people in social relationships. It includes mutual goal-setting and equal power distribution, but no conscious deliberation.

Socialization change is modeled on the hierarchical parent–child and teacher–student relationship, as expressed in training and supervised on-the-job training (OJT). (This will be discussed in more detail in Chapter 9.)

Emulative change also occurs in hierarchical relationships, wherein subordinates seek to pattern themselves on successful superiors.

Resisting Change

Both personal (individual) and organizational sources may resist change (Klofas, Stojkovic, & Kalinich, 1990, p. 285, Table 12-1). The criminal justice manager needs to accept resistance to change as a normal reaction to new ideas. Such resistance should not be interpreted as disloyalty or distrust of the leader, but it is a managerial problem the manager must work to overcome if positive changes are to be set in place. Therefore, it is important to understand the sources of resistance to change, both rational and emotional, and then to consider strategies that will help overcome them.

Change and Conflict

Although change is inevitable, it also often leads us into conflict. Even if we have a near-perfect working situation, natural changes in worker maturity, goal fulfillment, organizational needs, new technologies, and so on will bring about conflict.

General **conflict theorists** like Ralf Dahrendorf (1959) and Austin Turk (1969) have shown how change naturally leads into conflict. They begin with four logical "conflict" assumptions:

1. Social change occurs everywhere.
2. Dissent and conflict are everywhere in a society.
3. Every element contributes to disintegration and change.
4. Coercion of some by others is everywhere.

Austin Turk's approach to understanding change and conflict is both complex and abstract:

- Each of us has different perceptions and understandings.
- Our disagreements lead to conflicts.
- Each of us promotes one's own concepts.
- Conflict also occurs over scarce resources.

BOX 7.6 RESISTANCE TO ORGANIZATIONAL CHANGE

Personal sources:
1. misunderstanding
2. failure to see need
3. fear
4. status and power loss
5. no involvement in change
6. habit
7. vested interest in status quo
8. group norms counter to change
9. threat to existing social network
10. conflict between personal and organizational objectives

Organizational sources:
1. reward system and reward structures
2. rivalry and conflict
3. "sunk costs"—prior investment
4. balance of power shifts
5. organizational climate
6. poor introduction to change
7. past failures with changes
8. structural rigidity
9. conflict between personal and organizational objectives

There are many quite reasonable reasons to resist change that the "transformational leader" must overcome or address (Tichy & Ulrich, quoted in Ott, 1989, pp. 346–347, Table 1).

Source: Lists adapted from Klofas, Stojkovic, and Kalinich (1990, Table 12-1).

- Alliances with co-believers are forged.
- Conflict becomes institutionalized.
- Political domination and economic exploitation follows from these institutionalized alliances.
- Social power is the key leverage.
- Group membership produces shared experiences and views.
- Human interaction is dynamic and changing, leading to even more conflict.
- "Good" is acceptance of the institutionalized co-beliefs of the dominant coalition.
- "Wrong" is any counterbelief.
- Serious counterbeliefs can be classified as "deviant" or "criminal."

Intervention to manage conflict involves two processes: involvement in the sequence of events (consciousness-raising and interaction management) and structure-altering conditions in the organization (selection and training, context modification). What can be modified?

BOX 7.7 REASONS TO RESIST ORGANIZATIONAL CHANGE

Habit and Inertia—The current workers have mastered the old ways and are comfortable with them.

"Sunk Costs"—Prior investments in the old ways, old equipment, and previous training all will be lost when the new system is implemented.

Effort and Resources—The old ways were reduced to the most efficient process by trial-and-error and practice; a change will require retraining, learning new ways, acquiring new equipment, and using more resources.

Fear and Anxiety—Change introduces unknowns, and these are as often feared until accepted.

Pride and Traditional Conservative Values—Our sincere convictions about the propriety of the old ways are invalidated when their replacement occurs; the old decisions, policies and procedures are made to seem wrong.

Sense of Lost Power—The veteran members of the organization are made equal with the new people, and this undermines the advantages of seniority.

Self-Interest—How will the change benefit the resister? If there is nothing to gain at a personal level, why should a rational employee support change?

Conflict—Change evokes conflict.

Suspicion—There are questions about the value of the change to the organization; most veterans in an organization have been through change cycles before and can recall their many failures.

A Genuine Awareness That Some Change Is Folly—"I was to learn later in life that we tend to meet any new situation by reorganizing, and a wonderful method it can be for creating the illusion of progress, while producing confusion, inefficiency, and demoralization." Petronius Arbiter, ca. c.e. 60, *The Satyricon*.

The folk expression, "If it ain't broke, don't fix it," is another expression of the folly of making some ill-considered changes. In addition, some things simply cannot be changed for the better. As Reinhold Niebuhr said in the "Serenity Prayer," "God grant me the serenity to accept things I cannot change, courage to change the things I can, and wisdom to know the difference."

- working personality
- informal rules
- constituent pressures
- interest competition
- power and status
- organizational policy

Ronald Lynch categorizes the sources of conflict as either emotional or rational, and gives examples for emotional conflict—defensive attitudes, group loyalty, self-image, face-saving, and interpersonal factors. Conflicts arise from sources that are both emotional and rational—not either/or as Lynch implies (1986, p. 214)—so we cannot, as Lynch suggests, "distinguish between rational and emotional elements in each major disagreement." He

---

BOX 7.8 COMMON FEATURES OF ORGANIZATIONS THAT CAN ACCEPT CHANGE

1. High complexity in professional training
2. High decentralization of power
3. Low formalization
4. Low stratification in terms of rewards distribution
5. Emphasis on quality over volume productivity
6. Low emphasis on efficiency versus product or service quality
7. High job satisfaction levels

Source: List adapted from Klofas, Stojkovic, and Kalinich, 1990, pp. 287–288.

BOX 7.9 APPLICATION OF CHANGE STRATEGIES

1. modifying task structure
2. balancing reward–punishment relationships
3. decision centralization and decentralization balance
4. providing achievement emphasis
5. providing training and development emphasis
6. security versus risk balance
7. favoring openness versus defensiveness
8. promoting status and morale
9. providing recognition and feedback
10. having organizational competence and flexibility

Source: List adapted from Klofas, Stojkovic, and Kalinich, 1990, p. 295.

---

places "values" in the rational category, but excessive attachment to one's values is emotional. A defensive attitude may be perfectly rational, but can lead to a pseudo-paranoid state that clearly is emotional. Group loyalty also is rational; we need our alliances and affinity groups, but some attachments can be excessive. Self-image is a perfectly valid rational concern, but it also can become an obsession. Face-saving can become an obsession, but one's reputation and image are rationally valuable attributes for one's career. It is always rational to maintain good interpersonal relations, but balance is the key.

Excessive group loyalty can lead to cliques and the subversion of the interests of the organization. What Lynch seems to have rediscovered is the ancient Greek adage, "nothing in excess." By focusing on the rational aspects, rather than the sources, of an item in dispute, some change-based conflicts can be resolved. Lynch counsels (1986, p. 17):

1. Deal in principles, rather than details.
2. Determine criteria against which judgment is to be made.
3. Experiment, not debate with alternatives.
4. Apply rational decision-making processes.

Kurt Lewin wrote that the process of effecting change involves a three-step procedure (quoted in Ott, 1989, pp. 546–547): (1) **unfreezing:** to "break open the shell of complacency and self-righteousness, it is sometimes necessary to bring about deliberately an emotional stir-up." (p. 547); (2) **moving or changing:** making the change-oriented decisions and beginning the process of implementation; and (3) **refreezing:** allowing the new ways to become established as replacement habits.

Summary

Evaluation and its related concepts of assessment and appraisal are essential managerial functions. They are needed to pursue good personnel practices and for organizational development, the bringing about of planned change within the criminal justice organization. Evaluation uses many tools and sources of data under the control of the manager. These data sources identify what things are going well and what needs to be changed to improve the individual employee or the whole organization. Change encounters resistance, and the wise criminal justice manager needs to understand this resistance in order to overcome it.

LEARNING OBJECTIVES

Upon finishing this chapter, you should be able to do the following:

1. Distinguish between individual and organizational evaluation.
2. Discuss the data elements appropriate to an individual evaluation.
3. Identify sources of managerial information that can be used as criminal justice agency performance measures.
4. Describe ways of using MBO in both individual and organizational evaluation.
5. Identify sources of resistance to organizational change.
6. Identify features of a criminal justice agency that are favorable to change.

IMPORTANT TERMS AND NAMES

- *appraisal*
- *assessment*
- *CALEA*
- *coercive change*
- *conflict theorists*
- *co-optation*
- *cost–benefit analysis*
- *emulative change*
- *endorser*
- *evaluator*

- *hedonistic calculus*
- *indoctrination*
- *interactional change*
- *MBO*
- *moving or changing*
- *performance appraisal*
- *rater*
- *refreezing*
- *secret evaluations*
- *shared evaluations*
- *socialization change*
- *"sunk costs"*
- *technocratic change*
- *turnover rate*
- *unfreezing*

References and Supplemental Sources

Bennis, W. G. (1966). *Changing organizations.* New York: McGraw-Hill.

Caplow, T. (1954). *The sociology of work.* Minneapolis: University of Minnesota Press.

Caplow, T. (1968). *Two against one: Coalitions in triads.* Upper Saddle River, NJ: Prentice Hall.

Caplow, T. (1983). *Managing an organization* (2nd ed.). New York: Holt, Rinehart and Winston.

Caplow, T. (1991). *American social trends.* New York: Harcourt Brace Jovanovich.

Caplow, T., Hicks, L., & Wattenberg, B. (2001). *The first measured century: An illustrated guide to trends in America 1900–2000.* Washington, DC: American Enterprise Institute Press.

Dahrendorf, R. (1959). *Class and class conflict in industrial society.* Stanford, CA: Stanford University Press.

Drucker, P. F. (1954). *The practice of management.* New York: HarperCollins, HarperBusiness.

Follett, M. P. (1926). The giving of orders. In: Metcalf, H. C. (Ed.), *The scientific foundations of business administration.* Baltimore: Williams & Wilkins.

Follett, M. P. (1926/1989). The giving of orders. In: Ott, J. S. (Ed.), *Classic readings in organizational behavior.* Pacific Grove, A: Brooks/Cole.

Klofas, J., Stojkovic, S., & Kalinich, D. (1990). *Criminal justice organizations: Administration and management.* Pacific Grove, CA: Brooks/Cole.

Lewin, K. (1989). Group decision and social change. In: Ott, J. S. (Ed.), *Classic readings in organizational behavior* (pp. 543–548). Pacific Grove, CA: Brooks/Cole.

Lynch, R. G. (1986). *The police manager: Professional leadership skills* (3rd ed.). New York: Random House.

Massie, J. L. (1987). *Essentials of management* (4th ed.). Englewood Cliffs, NJ: Prentice Hall.

Odiorne, G. (1965). *Management by objectives: A system of managerial leadership.* New York: Pitman.

Ott, J. S. (1989). *Classic readings in organizational behavior.* Pacific Grove, CA: Brooks/Cole.

Phillips, R. L., & McConnell, C. R. (1996). *The effective corrections manager.* Gaithersburg, MD: Aspen.

Selznick, P. (1948). Foundations of the theory of organization. *American Sociological Review, 13*(1), 25–35.

Selznick, P. (1992). Foundations of the theory of organization. In Shafritz, J. M., & Ott, J. S. (Eds.), *Classics of organizational theory* (pp. 114–123) (3rd ed.). Pacific Grove, CA: Brooks/Cole.

Tichy, N. M., & Ulrich, D. O. (1984). The leadership challenge—A call for the transformational leader. *Sloan Management Review, 26*(Fall), 59–68.

Turk, A. (1969). *Criminality and legal order.* Chicago: Rand McNally.

Wilson, O. W., & McLaren, R. C. (1977). *Police administration* (4th ed.). New York: McGraw-Hill.

8

Staffing and Personnel Issues

The "S" in both LODESTAR and in POSDCORB stands for "staffing," one of the major managerial responsibilities of a criminal justice official. Staffing involves hiring agency employees, then fostering their career development, protecting their employment rights, disciplining them, and promoting them. Most criminal justice staffing actions are covered by civil service rules, but there are some exceptions. In most states, elected criminal justice officials are exempt from some or all of the civil rights laws and regulations, as are many of their personal appointees. This divided approach was one of the recommendations made by Woodrow Wilson in his seminal 1887 article on public administration. Prior to the 1880s, most criminal justice staffing actions were not covered by civil service laws and practices but were in the domain of **patronage appointments,** that is, appointments in whole or in large measure made because of one's affiliation with a victorious political party or candidate.

Historical Developments in Public Personnel Practices

In the United States, the manner in which people have been selected for public service and the ways they have experienced their careers have undergone significant changes since 1789. Frederick C. Mosher (1967, pp. 53–95) proposed that five distinct eras can be defined and delineated by major events in American political history. In this text, a similar approach will be taken, but some minor differences between Mosher's typology and the one used here are appropriate.

In this text, "Government by Gentlemen" will be discussed as the **Jeffersonian ideal** (1789–1829). Thomas Jefferson clearly influenced the manner in which both the states and the new federal government selected people for public service positions. People were selected for government employment based on Jeffersonian assumptions about *noblesse*

BOX 8.1 FREDERICK C. MOSHER'S ERAS IN CIVIL SERVICE CONCEPTS

Government by Gentlemen, 1789–1829
Government by the Common Man, 1829–1883
Government by the Good, 1883–1906
Government by the Efficient, 1906–1937
Government by Administrators, 1937–1955

BOX 8.2 FREDERICK CAMP "FRITZ" MOSHER (1913–1990)

This giant of the academic world was editor of the *Public Administration Review* between 1953 and 1956 and was on the faculties of Syracuse University, the University of Bologna, UC–Berkeley, and the University of Virginia. He also was grounded in the reality of public service. He was a veteran of the Army Air Corps, worked for the Tennessee Valley Authority, the City of Los Angeles, the U.S. Department of State, and the United Nations Relief and Rehabilitation Agency (New York Times, 1990) and has been described as the "quintessential practitioner scholar" by Stephenson and Plant (1991, p. 97).

He was the author of several important books and numerous articles. In *Program Budgeting in Theory and Practice*, he anticipated the contemporary debates about government budgets and programs and revealed how the adoption of new

FIGURE 8.1 Frederick Mosher. *Photo courtesy of Special Collections, University of Virginia Library.*

programs drives budgets (Mosher, 1954). He was an advocate of replying on applied research over subjective opinion in policy-making (1956). His book, *Democracy and the Public Service*, 1967, 1982), is the classic text on the historical development of the civil service and public administration in the United States. His ideas provide the basis of this chapter. He was a strong advocate for public employees and wrote (1986, p. 4):

> *When one works for government, his or her efforts are exerted not alone for self and family, but for others in the community, in the society. This kind of idealism has been a prime motivator in the development of this field from its self-conscious beginning in the early days of Luther Gulick and his colleagues.*

---

oblige (which suggests that a burden of responsibility comes with noble ancestry and privilege) and the concept of fitness of character based on a good family background, educational attainment, social status, and patriotic military or political service during the revolution (Thompson, 1991, p. 1). In the federal service, another consideration was added: representation in federal hiring among the states approximately proportional to a state's population. Thomas Jefferson's concept of government officials as public servants, with an emphasis on service, was paramount. Most people who accepted employment in the state or federal governments did so because they felt a duty to serve rather than seeing it as a path to economic reward. Indeed, many already were successful in private careers and enterprises before accepting their government appointments.

"Government by the Common Man" was an expression of Jacksonian egalitarianism (1829–1883). From Andrew Jackson's assumption of the presidency in 1829 through the passage of the Pendleton Act in 1883, the prime criterion for being appointed to public service was political loyalty. Jackson saw education and opportunity as being the keys to suitability for public service and equality of performance. He believed that all men were equal in capacity, so anyone properly educated could serve successfully in government if given the chance. Therefore, in his view, political loyalty was an appropriate precondition for selection. Thus, he was committed to a loyalty-based patronage system for selecting men to serve in government. His critics called it a "spoils system," drawing on the expression, "to the victors belong the spoils of war." Jackson was opposed to lifelong civil service tenure. Yet his invitation to the "common man" to join and serve in government inadvertently led to the development of government employment as a career choice. The people chosen for patronage appointments were not the wealthy elite gentlemen chosen for government office under the Jeffersonian ideal. For this new breed of appointees, government employment was a move up. By the standards of the day, it paid well and was far more pleasant work than might otherwise be available to an ordinary laborer. It was very important to such people that they keep their patrons in office as the means of retaining their jobs. This "patronage system" also had advantages for the public and our two-party political system (Sorauf, 1960, p. 28). Patronage was useful for:

1. maintaining an active party organization
2. promoting intraparty cohesion
3. attracting voters and supporters
4. financing the party and candidates
5. procuring favorable government action
6. creating party discipline in policymaking

The period of *Reformist Merit Selection* (1883–1930) merges Mosher's "Government by the Good" (1883–1906) and "Government by the Efficient" (1906–1937). The year 1883 marks the passage of the Pendleton Act, the first federal **civil service law,** which held that "appointment or promotion shall be given to the man best fitted to discharge the duties of the position, and such fitness shall be ascertained by open, fair, honest, impartial, competitive examination" (as quoted by Paul P. Van Riper [1958] from the 1882 report of U.S. Senate Committee on Civil Service and Retrenchment) (Thompson, 1991, p. 7). Although patronage did not go away with the Pendleton Act, this legislation marked the beginning of the decline in patronage selection of public servants. The original civil service law protected only lower-level federal appointees and did not apply to the states. The states copied it, though, and the number of federal employees covered by it expanded over the following decades, until hiring under civil service rules became the primary means of securing government employment at every level.

Applying Woodrow Wilson's political reform ideas (1887) and Frederick Taylor's ideas on efficiency (1911), plus contributions by other social, governmental, and managerial reformers such as Theodore Roosevelt (1897), civil service rules applied assumptions of merit criteria for screening prospective workers, while also looking into the moral character of prospects. The "rule of three" was pronounced, under which a person would be

BOX 8.3 THEODORE ROOSEVELT: CRIMINAL JUSTICE MANAGER

Before Theodore Roosevelt, Jr. (1858–1919) became president in 1901, and even before he led the Rough Riders against San Juan Hill in Cuba during the Spanish–American War of 1898, he was a member of the National Civil Service Commission (1889–1895) and a vocal advocate of civil service reform (Roosevelt, 1897, p. 135). He was named president of the Police Board for the City of New York in 1895 and undertook the reform of the NYPD, which was then notoriously corrupt (1897, p. 162). Under his administration, hiring standards were raised and the police acquired new crime-fighting techniques; rewarded the integrity, efficiency, and heroism of its officers; and instituted formal firearms training. The department increased arrests, and New York enjoyed a decline in crime (1897, pp. 182–187).

FIGURE 8.2 Theodore Roosevelt, 1904 *Library of Congress, Prints & Photographs Division, photograph by Pach Brothers, LC-USZ62-13026.*

hired from the top-three scorers on the civil service test. Once on the job, political neutrality was expected. Discharge could occur only for misconduct or poor performance, and never for political reasons. At the federal level, the Congress began giving the executive direction on hiring processes and criteria, giving rise to **Ackerman's question** (Van Riper, 1958, 1991, p. 12). Amos T. Ackerman, who was President Ulysses S. Grant's Attorney General, raised the constitutional question of how much influence the legislative branch should have in the **contracting process** whereby the executive branch selects its preferred workforce. Prior to the Pendleton Act, this was exclusively an executive function, but today it is one shared by all three branches.

As Ackerman's question suggests, not everyone was happy with filling public service positions under civil service laws. Even today, some criminal justice positions are filled outside of the civil service. Sheriffs, most of whom are elected in partisan campaigns, to this day continue to hire and promote their deputies under a patronage and mixed patronage–civil service selection process. Many state judges, clerks of court, coroners, and prosecutors are still elected, and often the prosecutors and chief clerks of court can appoint and promote their assistants as patronage hires rather than under civil service rules. In the federal courts, judges are chosen by a complex political process of presidential appointment with senatorial advice and consent. Federal prosecutors, known as U.S.

Attorneys, are patronage appointees to this day. The chief U.S. marshals also are patronage appointees of the president. Even when civil service rules apply, there are still critics of civil service and some exceptions. Raymond Fosdick (1920), one of the leading police theorists of the early 20th century, was completely committed to police reform throughout all of his professional life, yet he wrote:

> *A far better balance between civil service protection and effective leadership can be achieved than has been reached up to the present. In our endeavors to eliminate the spoils system we have swung too far toward rigidity, and a rational approach is needed to a compromise which will protect the police force from the politician without robbing the police executive of initiative and leadership. (p. 292)*

Fosdick still wanted civil service selection, but with a probationary period and the elimination of promotion solely by examination. Fosdick advocated the use of the Boston promotional system, whereby the police commissioner nominated a list of eligible officers for promotion. Civil service tests were administered to all of the nominees to ensure that their intelligence, knowledge, and general capacity were sufficient for promotion. All of those who passed the tests could then be promoted (1920, p. 294). He also favored police training schools (pp. 293–298) and improved police discipline:

> *The question of discipline is the final factor in regard to which current civil service procedure needs radical modification. There is no chance for progressive improvement in a police department if the hands of the responsible executive are tied in his dealings with his men. . . . To divide responsibility with a civil service commission, a mayor, a court, or any other authority, is to sow the seed of demoralization and to make real success impossible for any administrator, no matter how able. (pp. 296–297)*

Civil service protections had an unintended consequence for criminal justice employment: the rise of public service unions. This was an era of rapidly expanding organization of industrial unions. Observing their success, police unions were organized early in the 20th century and were gaining popularity until 1919. In 1918, police officers in Cincinnati successfully went on strike for 3 days. In New York that same year, union negotiations won pay increases in the face of a strike threat. When the Boston police did the same in 1919, the city declined to negotiate and the police were warned that they would be dismissed for misconduct if they did go on strike (Richardson, 1974, pp. 110–120). They did strike and the city and state retaliated, barring the striking officers from any future public service employment. The strikers were replaced, and the union was broken. Massachusetts and other states passed laws prohibiting public service unions and strikes, making them criminal acts in some cases. Union growth in criminal justice was dealt a major setback from which it would not recover for many decades.

BOX 8.4 FEATURES OF CIVIL SERVICE REFORM

Sam Souryal (1995) identified these seven key civil service reforms, exemplified in the Pendleton Act of 1883.

1. merit hiring with objective standards
2. competitive examinations for employee selection
3. probationary employment preceding tenure
4. veterans to be given legal preference
5. freedom from political contribution solicitations
6. annual reports required of government agencies
7. creation of the federal Civil Service Commission

Mosher selected 1937 to delineate the end of government by the efficient. This coincided with Luther Gulick's POSDCORB paper. In criminal justice, though, the year 1930 is a better separation point. In 1930, the Federal Bureau of Investigation began to collect data for the Uniform Crime Reports, and the Wickersham Commission was conducting its hearings into American criminal justice practices. The recommendations of those hearings were to have a profound influence on all aspects of criminal justice and included recommendations on improved personnel practices for the entire criminal justice system.

Professionalism and Managerial Emphasis (1930–1973)

In this era, public personnel managers applied the ideas of Max Weber (1922) on proper bureaucratic arrangements, Luther Gulick on public administration (1937), the Wickersham Commission reports, and the efforts of then-President Herbert Hoover and others on improving governmental efficiency. They continued to apply the ideas of scientific management, while also seeking to apply the best practices of progressive personnel management: intensive formal training and education (e.g., certificate training programs, police academies, masters of public administration degree programs, etc.) and a growing emphasis on what has been called **credentialism**—having the right credentials, transcripts, and documents to demonstrate one's rational–legal competence for a job.

The National Committee on Law Observation and Enforcement, better known as the Wickersham Commission, was established in 1929 by President Herbert Hoover. George W. Wickersham (1858–1936) headed the commission, which was tasked with making recommendations for criminal justice public policy. Although the emphasis was on national alcohol prohibition, the Commission consulted experts in many areas and prepared several reports on their findings, including the final Wickersham report (National Committee on Law Observance and Enforcement, 1931). Primarily written by August Vollmer, the report recommended many managerial reforms. Sam Souryal (1995) has identified six personnel-management reforms suggested by the Wickersham Commission.

1. Police leaders should be selected for their experience and demonstrated competence.
2. Personnel should be selected who have met intelligence and fitness standards.

3. Adequate salaries should be provided for police and other criminal justice officials.
4. An 8-hour work day, with vacations, sick leave, pensions, and other remuneration and compensation, should be provided
5. Efforts should be undertaken to isolate politics and other corrupting influences from law enforcement.
6. Training should be offered prior to independent employment.

The next major national study of criminal justice was the 1967 U.S. President's Commission on Law Enforcement and Administration of Justice. It released nine Task Force reports plus *The Challenge of Crime in a Free Society* (U.S. President's Commission on Law Enforcement and Administration of Justice, 1967a), which called for the creation of the Law Enforcement Assistance Administration (LEAA) to provide federal assistance to state and local criminal justice programs and agencies. Its *Task Force Report: The Police* (U.S. President's Commission on Law Enforcement and Administration of Justice, 1967b) offered more managerial and personnel reforms. Three recommended personnel reforms were not included in the reform recommendations of earlier eras:

1. state-set minimum training and selection standards
2. minority affirmative action recruitment
3. implementation of career-development programs

Many critics of civil service practices have emerged in recent decades, objecting to what the civil service has become. E. S. Savas and Sigmund G. Ginsburg (1973) identify the most commonly noted flaws of the system:

1. There is no scientific evidence to show that the entrance examinations really are related to on-the-job performance.
2. The rule-of-three eliminates other, potentially very well-qualified applicants.
3. Tenure for life is almost assured, regardless of the quality of work output after the probationary period.
4. Dismissal is exceptionally difficult, even with cause.
5. There is little opportunity for job growth within the bureaucracy.
6. Promotions usually come within units, so they are not truly open and competitive.
7. Performance may be secondary to examination results in gaining promotions.
8. Salary increases are automatic and not usually performance-based.
9. Midlevel managers may belong to the same unions as their subordinates, and thus they are not as likely to be acting in the interests of the organizational management.
10. Union influence is significant in politics, so the net effect is workers influencing legislators who order about upper-level managers.

While the general thrust of civil service systems and their rules has been to insulate public servants from excessive political influence, not every administration seeks a politically neutral civil service. When President Richard Nixon came to office, he was determined to rid his administration of midlevel managers loyal to the programs and priorities of the Kennedy–Johnson period. This gave rise to the **Malek Manual,** whose rule was "You cannot achieve management, policy or program control unless you have established political control" (Thompson, 1991, p. 58). Section III-3 is the most devious, suggesting ways of ridding the government of its protected civil servants:

a. elimination:
   a-1. frontal assault
   a-2. transfer technique
   a-3. special assignment technique
b. layering
c. shifting responsibilities and isolation
d. new activities

The **special assignment technique** made the unwelcome worker into a "traveling salesman" for his or her agency, sent to remote locations and kept away from his or her normal duties. Transfers were to undesirable assignments and locations with the intention of convincing the employee to resign or retire. The Malek Manual also contained advice on how to confront bureaucratic countermeasures. Observing how well the Republicans were able to frustrate the aims of the existing civil service, when James Earl Carter became president in 1977, he and the Congress joined in a venture of strengthening and streamlining civil service protections (Campbell, 1978, 1991), leading to the Civil Service Reform Act of 1978. Following that, the National Academy of Public Administration developed its "functional model" (Thompson, 1991, pp. 173–174) with standards for each of the key personnel-management responsibilities:

1. recruiting and examining
2. classification
3. merit standards for:
   a. merit protection
   b. merit pay
   c. EEO [equal employment opportunity]
   d. training
   e. performance appraisal
   f. incentive awards
4. labor-management relations
5. adverse actions
6. program evaluation

The Civil Rights Era and Equal Opportunity (1973–Present)

Major victories of the civil rights struggle were achieved between 1954, when the Supreme Court's *Brown v. Board of Education* decision refuted the validity and justice of the doctrine of "separate but equal," and 1964, when the U.S. Congress passed the Civil Rights Act of 1964. But it was not until the Equal Employment Opportunity Act of 1972, as amended in 1973, that civil rights law applied unambiguously to state and local units of government. With the 1973 amendment, all civil rights protections from earlier laws had to apply to public service occupations. The struggle to achieve full civil rights, to do away with unconstitutional bias and prejudice, and to provide true equality of opportunity to all Americans, regardless of race, ethnicity, sex, religion, political preference and ideology, or physical handicap still goes on, but the moral high ground of **equality of opportunity** (an equal distribution of government jobs, promotions, and similar advantages) was established in 1964 and brought to criminal justice agencies in 1973. Oddly enough, it was during the presidency of Richard M. Nixon, a Republican, that the Equal Employment Opportunity Act of 1972 was passed and the federal government took the lead in achieving affirmative action (Yuill, 2006).

Affirmative Action

Today's struggles over civil rights issues involve how far to carry programs to achieve affirmative action. Affirmative action programs precede the initial success of the civil rights struggle by a full decade, though. The first affirmative action program in federal personnel law involves *veterans preference*. **Veterans preference** was part of the civil service reforms of the 1880s. The current federal policies became law in 1944, as the nation, still heavily involved in World War II, was thinking ahead to what would happen when our combat veterans returned home to find their jobs taken by those who had not served in the armed services. In the federal civil service and in many of the states as well, preferential hiring privileges were given to veterans, and an even greater priority was given to hiring those who suffered war wounds.

Discrimination against persons based on sex, race, ethnicity, religious belief, age, and disabilities that can be accommodated has been outlawed. Affirmative action programs have been created to encourage greater workplace participation by persons previously denied or given only limited access to public service careers.

The Americans with Disabilities Act (ADA) protects the interests of potential public service workers with handicaps that can be overcome with reasonable accommodations. Determining what is a reasonable accommodation is decided situationally, reflecting the demands of the employment and the limitations imposed by the disability. The Equal Employment Opportunity Commission (EEOC) provides a forum for helping resolve questions of reasonableness (Colbridge, 2000: 15).

Frank J. Thompson (1991, p. 3) identifies five basic values in competition with each other in civil service systems:

1. agency competence
2. individual merit
3. political responsiveness
4. social equity
5. employee rights

Over time, one or another will rise to prominence as the others decline in significance, but all five are retained. Only the priority order shifts.

Scientific Management and Personnel Practices

Frederick Winslow Taylor, in *The Principles of Scientific Management* (1911/1967), presented four basic principles on the application of managerial science to the design of work and the selection of workers. The essentials of his principles of scientific management are:

1. develop a science for each element of a man's work
2. scientifically select and then train, teach, and develop the workman
3. cooperate with the men so as to ensure all of the work [is] being done in accordance with the principles of the science
4. divide the work and the responsibility between management and the workmen (pp. 36–37)

From Taylor's first point comes the now common practice of having a detailed job description for each position in an organization. Ideally, the written **job description** lists all the routine and major responsibilities of the position and is prepared from a careful study of what the worker should be able to do once successfully trained for the position. The *position advertisement* becomes a useful tool in that part of the second principle referring to scientifically selecting the workers. When a vacancy occurs, a criminal justice manager must prepare an advertisement for this job. It is common practice to omit all reference to salary scales. The affirmative action plan probably will require that it include a note to the effect of: "Our agency is an equal opportunity employer." It is up to the manager to select the educational criteria, physical standards (eyesight, height, weight, age, sex, health, and other physical limitations, if any), prior skills or experience, or other preliminary limitations associated with the job. The efficient criminal justice manager will use the advertisement to prescreen the applicant pool, but the screening criteria must be empirically valid and nondiscriminatory. Theodore Caplow (1983) made the following recommendations regarding the recruiting process:

1. Identify what required qualifications are essential
2. Consider a few candidates, as few as possible
3. Ensure the candidates understand their duties (provide an accurate job description)
   a. Ensure that the hiring manager understands it
   b. Ensure that coworkers and supervisors of the new employee understand it
4. Study the candidates closely
   a. Review their biographies and résumé carefully
   b. Check their official records
   c. Test for their essential aptitudes and abilities
   d. Contact their references
   e. Assess their attitude
5. Be prompt in making the selection (pp. 118–123)

The second of Taylor's principles involves the selection of the right worker for the job and providing that newly selected worker with the proper training needed to master the job. Ideally, the selection criteria should be based on the job description, to match prospective workers' existing talents, interests, and abilities to the requirements of the job. Taylor knew, however, that having the general aptitude and ability to do a job does not necessarily mean having the specific, detailed knowledge of the way the work is done in a specific agency. The latter requires formal training, **on-the-job training (OJT),** and work experience.

Taylor and other scientific managers knew also that simply having qualified workers did not ensure quality work output. That led to his third and fourth principles. The worker had to be supervised and his or her efforts integrated and coordinated with the efforts of others. This was one of the jobs of the manager.

Programs for Affirmative Action

As noted, the first program in modern federal law to seek to achieve an affirmative action purpose was the Veterans Preference Act of 1944, which was meant to help returning veterans, especially those with war wounds, find jobs on their return from the war. It added points to the civil service tests of returning veterans and additional points to those who were wounded or disabled as a result of their war service. The Equal Pay Act of 1963 required equal pay for equal work, making it unlawful to have different pay scales for men and women or for people of different races or ethnic groups (Stewart & Garson, 1983, p. 242). The Civil Rights Act of 1964 (Stewart & Garson, 1983, p. 238) made discrimination based on race, ethnicity, national origin, religion, sex, and political preference unlawful in public accommodation. The Age Discrimination in Employment Act of 1967 (Stewart & Garson, 1983, p. 244) protects the rights of older workers. Presidential Executive Orders 11246 and 11373 (Stewart & Garson, 1983, p. 246) created contracting quotas and denied contracts to organizations that discriminate. The Equal Employment Opportunity Act of 1972, with the 1973 amendment that applied it to state and local units of government, prohibited discrimination in hiring and other personnel practices. The Rehabilitation Act of 1973 (Stewart & Garson, 1983, p. 247) and the Americans with Disabilities Act of 1990 require reasonable accommodations for handicapped people seeking employment as well as those currently employed.

In 1994, the Congress revised the law on veterans' rights and employment preference with the passage of the Uniformed Services Employment and Reemployment Rights Act (USERRA). Like its 1944 predecessor, USERRA guarantees reemployment of veterans who left civilian occupations to perform military service. The federal law does not obligate employers to pay workers for their time in federal military service, but private employers and states can do so. USERRA requires employers to reinstate those taking military leave without loss of seniority or promotional eligibility in the same or similar duties they had prior to military service. Military leave can be for short periods of training, such as weekend training drills (known as inactive duty training), or extended periods of activation (mobilization and deployment) lasting many months. The military service can be voluntary or compulsory. One does not need to have been in the military prior to his or her nonmilitary employment, which means that an employee can join the armed services after being hired by a criminal justice agency and seek military leave for initial military training. There are severe civil penalties for supervisors, employers, and organizations that punish their military members in violation of these reemployment and military leave rights.

The Terminology of Affirmative Action

Affirmative action programs use a variety of abbreviations that everyone involved in criminal justice staffing needs to know:

AA: Affirmative Action
BFOQ: Bona Fide Occupational Qualification
EEO: Equal Employment Opportunity
EEOC: Equal Employment Opportunity Commission
OFCCP: Office of Federal Contract Compliance Programs

Compliance with Civil Rights Laws

The EEOC and the OFCCP have been exerting their influence on public agencies and local and state units of government by a combination of "carrot" and "stick." If a public agency or institution does not comply, it can get the stick, that is, be sued in federal courts for denying citizens equal access or opportunity. More often, however, the carrot is offered. Local and state units of government and nongovernmental public service agencies and institutions can qualify for federal funds only if they practice equality of employment opportunity and make strides to effect affirmative action programs. If discrimination is present, a cutoff of federal aid is threatened.

The Role of the Courts

The U.S. Supreme Court has taken the leadership role in defining civil rights in recent decades. In a series of decisions, the court has sent confusing and apparently contradictory signals to public service employers. In *Griggs vs. Duke Power* (1971), the Court applied statistical evidence to establish the practice of racial exclusion, even when hard evidence of an employer "intentionally engag[ing] in unlawful employment practice" was not demonstrated.

In a 1986 case, the U.S. Supreme Court also allowed to stand a voluntary plan of redress favoring African-American Cleveland firefighters through promotion quotas. The workers' union had disagreed with the city's affirmative action plan, arguing that no clear evidence of discrimination existed in the policies the quota plan replaced, and no victims of deliberate discrimination could be identified. Please see the appendix for more information. In 1984, in the case of *Firefighters v. Stotts*, the U.S. Supreme Court allowed the seniority plans of Memphis, Tennessee, firefighters to take precedence over affirmative action plans when those seniority plans had been shown to be untainted by racial or other prejudicial exclusions. Historically, the Supreme Court had been opposed to accepting statistical evidence alone, or accepting involuntary affirmative action programs without identifiable victims coming forward to show how they had been harmed by past practices. The Court did not disagree with the Cleveland firefighters union, but saw that in its history the city had not achieved equal opportunity in hiring and promotions. Some critics of affirmative action have interpreted these rulings as having settled this civil rights issue and that affirmative action programs are needed only where evidence of racial or other prejudicial exclusions can be found (Eastland, 1996), but affirmative action plans still govern most civil service employment practices in criminal justice agencies.

Federal courts and political leaders remain divided on whether their goal simply should be providing "equality of opportunity" or achieving the more far-reaching objective of **"equality of result,"** which measures success based on results rather than opportunities. Diversity and representativeness in the criminal justice workforce are worthwhile goals that few critics of affirmative action actually oppose (Edelman, Fuller, & Mara-Drita, 2001; Yates, 1994). More often it is the methods used to achieve affirmative action that have troubled its critics (Hammerman, 1988; Livingston, 1979; Loury, 1997; Moore, 2001).

Many proponents of EEO/AA programs see good as determined by "outcome" or "equality of result." This is a consequentialist line of reasoning, although not necessarily utilitarian (fairness in application might not alter the "number" in "the greatest good for the greatest number"). Opponents of continuing EEO/AA programs often see good as being determined by providing the equality of opportunity, created by the rules themselves, even if the desired outcome—an equal distribution of government jobs, promotions, or similar advantages—is not achieved. If the opportunities are equally accessible, no biased criteria are permitted, and only merit, talent, and motivation are used as the selection criteria, then fairness is achieved. This is deontological, nonconsequential reasoning. The critics are especially opposed to the use of quotas for minority hiring in the absence of deliberate discrimination. Quotas are inherently unfair to the categories of people being excluded.

Some also make use of the distinction between being **fully qualified** and being the **best qualified.** For example, if seeking the "fully qualified," when minimum passing scores are established, everyone who exceeds the minimum can be viewed as equally qualified for selection or promotion, even though some have passed with higher scores than others. If the "fully qualified" standard is being applied, then this needs to be made clear from the onset.

Unfortunately, subjectivist reasoning can sometimes disguise itself as an ethical argument. "Equality of opportunity" arguments can be used to mask covert racism or sexism. For instance, a black partisan could demand equality of result simply because he or she has a racial bias for his or her own kind—a pattern of pro-minority, anti-majority racism.

Where Will Affirmative Action Take Us Next?

A new civil rights issue was raised and hotly debated in the 1980s, that of **comparable worth**—equal pay for work of equal value. The issue has to do with salary differentials for positions that are similar (i.e., requiring similar credentials), but that have been classified as different. In the past, women working as correctional officers were called "matrons" and were paid less than men who were called "jailers" or "guards," yet all had essentially the same duties. Proponents of comparable worth, including many feminists, see this as an unresolved civil rights question (Gold, 1983; Hill & Killingsworth, 1989; Paul, 1989; Remick, 1984). For the most part, however, criminal justice agencies have not had a recent history of differential pay for similar positions. Examples that have existed in the past, such as the matron-versus-guard distinction, have generally been eliminated.

More conservative voices claim that affirmative action has gone too far and has evolved into a distasteful form of reverse discrimination against white males. These critics often resist all formal quotas for minority hiring and promotion and oppose using statistical evidence in the absence of hard evidence of actual discrimination (Eastland, 1996).

Employee Turnover

One of the major concerns of any criminal justice manager is staff turnover. Turnover involves the departure of experienced personnel and their replacement with new employees who usually are less experienced (Orrick, 2005; Wright, 1993). There are both positive and negative aspects to turnover. Agencies often benefit from "new blood" with fresh perspectives and recently acquired skills and competencies that older employees may lack. But the criminal justice organization also loses experience and maturity. There are significant costs involved in the hiring and training of new employees (Minor, Wells, Angel, & Matz, 2011, p. 73). Some turnover is normal, as individuals retire or seek better career opportunities in other careers or in different agencies (Kiekbusch, Price, & Thesis, 2003; Lambert, 2001; Wright, 1993).

When turnover is high and is a function of job dissatisfaction, then it is a diagnostic measure of problems within the organization (Byrd, Cochran, Silverman, & Blout, 2000; Camp, 1994; Jacobs & Grear, 1977; Lambert & Hogan, 2009; Stohr, Self, & Lovrich, 1992). A study of police turnover in Australia and New Zealand revealed that female officers resigned at higher rates than male officers in the 25-to-39-year age group (Lynch & Tuckey, 2008), often giving up on police work altogether. Similar patterns are thought to exist in the United States.

Police agencies spend great sums of money on recruiting, selecting, and training new employees, often because they lose experienced officers they would prefer to retain. A North Carolina study reported that police agencies there experienced a 14 percent turnover rate in patrol positions and that the average tenure for a new officer is only 33 months (Orrick, 2005). Veteran police officers routinely leave smaller, lower-paying departments to take positions in better-paying agencies.

Turnover in corrections is exceptionally high, especially in the first few years of employment. Slade and Vogel found that encouraging correctional employee participation in decision-making helped reduce stress and turnover (1977). Most such cases involve corrections officers simply leaving corrections altogether or shifting from correctional custodial positions to probation or parole work. The federal prison system also draws many employees from lower-paying state and local correctional positions.

Sample Personnel Policies

Most criminal justice agencies operate under state personnel laws. As long as an agency complies with those laws, it has some discretion to develop personnel benefits packages. The Minnesota Council of Nonprofits has offered some excellent suggestions for nonprofit personnel policies (2007). Their recommendations start with the assumption that the organization is committed "to fair, clearly stated and supportive relationships between the organization and its staff." It is the responsibility of the organization to administer personnel programs that comply with all federal, state, and local laws and personnel regulations.

Employee Classification

Employees are classified as either "regular" or "temporary." Regular employees are those hired without a specific termination date. Temporary employees are those whose position is for a short term. Full-time employees also are classified as either exempt or nonexempt, according to provisions of the Fair Labor Standards Act (FLSA). Nonexempt employees are protected by the FLSA; exempt employees are not. Full-time employees earning hourly wages, typically working about 2,000 hours per year, and eligible for employee fringe benefits, are covered by the FLSA. Those classified as nonexempt have to be paid at least the minimum wage and extra overtime pay if they work more than the allowable maximum of hours per week, usually 40 hours in a single week (University of Louisville, Human Resources, 2007). Employees who work rotating shifts and other unusual schedules, averaging 40 hours per week over the work year, also may be excluded from overtime pay. Those on contract to be paid a fixed salary and those classified as managerial employees generally are exempt from FLSA and are not covered by its protections. Most civil service hires and entry-level police, corrections, and court officials are nonexempt, while many senior criminal justice managers are exempt. Upon hiring, a new employee should be told his or her status under FLSA.

Affirmative Action

A criminal justice agency is required to provide equal employment opportunity for all persons regardless of race, color, religion, national origin, marital status, political affiliation, disability, sex, or age. Affirmative action programs apply to all personnel practices, including, but not limited to, recruiting, hiring, placement, promotion, demotion, transfer, training, compensation, benefits, layoff, recall, and termination.

Recruitment Procedures

A criminal justice agency is expected to recruit, hire, and assign applicants on the basis of their relative knowledge, skills, and abilities. The decision to employ an applicant should be based on an individual's qualification for the particular position, along with other requisite job skills. Employment qualifications should be specified in the job description. When a position is vacant, the personnel manager or chief executive will generally prepare a job announcement stating the position's responsibilities and advertise the position for a reasonable length of time.

Compensation and Benefits

Criminal justice agency employees receive a salary and benefits as established in advance for their position. Agencies can provide salary supplements for education, relevant prior experience, and special skills such as foreign language abilities. At the time of hire, new employees will receive a letter of appointment along with a job description, an enumeration of salary and benefits, and a copy of the agency's personnel policies. Larger criminal justice agencies usually provide medical care, disability income, life insurance, and retirement programs for their employees. Often this is governed by state law or local personnel policies.

Work, Leave, and Holiday Schedules

The agency establishes work schedules, and when 24-hour, 7-day-a-week staffing is required, shift assignments may be required. Official holidays as designated by the state or the federal government should be followed when possible, and when employees must work on holidays because of staffing needs, *compensatory leave* days or *overtime pay* usually will be provided.

Antiharassment Policy

Workplace harassment is any unwanted attention or action by someone in the workplace that creates or contributes to an intimidating, hostile, or offensive work environment, including sexual harassment. The criminal justice manager must establish and publicize agency procedures for reporting and dealing with this issue. An investigation of each complaint will take place, protecting the rights of all people involved. If there appears to be substance to the complaint, the agency must take steps to resolve the problem. This may include verbal or written reprimand, suspension, or termination. No retaliation can be directed toward an employee who has, in good faith, reported an incident of suspected harassment.

Substance Abuse

Employees of a criminal justice agency are in especially sensitive positions regarding unlawful substance abuse. Those needing help with substance-abuse problems should be encouraged to seek treatment. The agency will need to determine whether such an employee should be placed on leave, suspended, or terminated because of the problem.

Performance Reviews

Newly hired employees should have at least one evaluation during their probationary period. A schedule for periodic personnel reviews should be established by the agency chief executive, and the content of the evaluation should be revealed in advance.

Prior Employment References

Criminal justice agencies should have a policy of seeking information on their prospective employees, including prior work locations, job titles, supervisors' names, dates of all prior employment, and reasons given for leaving. The agency also should ask for references and should contact those references, conduct criminal background investigations, and investigate the applicants' financial and credit information. A criminal justice agency needs to avoid hiring people with serious prior employment problems or histories of criminality and substance abuse and those whose debts and history of financial difficulty could impact negatively on their performance.

Termination

A criminal justice employee should tender a resignation in writing well in advance of the effective date of the resignation. The agency should have a policy with regard to the use of or payment for any accrued annual leave. Typically employees are not compensated for any unused sick leave at the time of resignation. "Dismissal for cause" may occur because of serious inappropriate or criminal behavior or a history of unsatisfactory performance. Temporary and long-term layoffs may occur because of fiscal limitations or mission changes. Typically those laid off are given priority when hiring resumes.

Employee Appeals and Grievance Procedures

An employee **appeal procedure** provides a means for employees to resolve their workplace concerns with management. An employee should be able to file a grievance or an appeal for an unfavorable personnel action without risk of retaliation. A grievance or an appeal is appropriate when there is an alleged misapplication of agency personnel policies or a violation of employment law. Should there be some substance to the grievance or appeal, the agency should offer a mechanism for resolving disputes to resolve the issue. Usually an appeal or grievance initially will be submitted to an immediate supervisor, but if the issue involves that supervisor, an alternative complaint procedure should be in place. Upon investigation, a written response should be given to the employee.

Union Membership and Collective Bargaining

Criminal justice employees are allowed to form associations that can represent them in negotiations with their managers. However, some states limit these negotiations, some do not recognize public service unions, and most prohibit one common tactic of labor unions: the strike. Criminal justice worker unions are governed by the labor laws in their states. The South and Southwest have not been supportive of public service organized labor, while the Northern, Midwestern, and Pacific Coast states typically model their laws and boards after the practices found in the federal National Labor Relations Act of 1935. Where a union is allowed to organize criminal justice system employees, the union organizers usually must win the support of a majority of those they seek to represent. The criminal justice manager and the union then may negotiate the terms and conditions of employment and enter into a contract. When labor disputes arise, the parties will use a grievance procedure to resolve them. If the matter is not resolved, they then will send the dispute to binding arbitration, where a neutral third party will review the competing claims and render a decision. Where a union exists, criminal justice employees do not have to take part in union activities. However, some states allow closed shops. In a **closed shop,** all covered employees must be members. Some of these states collect union dues from active and passive members alike as a payroll deduction. Other states require public service employment under the rules of an **open shop,** whereby workers do not have to be members but usually acquire the same benefits arising from union negotiations.

Work Products and Files

All supplies, materials, and work products of a criminal justice agency employee remain the property of the agency after resignation, discharge, or layoff of that employee. The employee may retain some personal files, but confidential work files and other documents shall remain with the agency.

Consultant Fees, Honoraria, and Gifts

Criminal justice agency employees are encouraged to participate in a variety of community and professional activities. When such activities are part of an employee's regular duties and responsibilities, consultant fees, honoraria, and gifts should be reported to the agency and may be claimed by the agency. To avoid actual conflict of interest, or the appearance thereof, any employee who engages in any compensated activity related to agency programs and activities must have approval from a supervisor or more senior agency manager.

> BOX 8.5 LEAVE OPTIONS FOR CRIMINAL JUSTICE AGENCIES
>
> **Annual Leave (Vacation):** Annual leave is provided to all full-time employees, usually based on the length of time employed by the agency. Annual leave often starts with each individual's anniversary date with the agency or by calendar or fiscal year, with proration for partial-year employment. Some agencies will allow leave to be carried over from one year to the next, but in others unused leave will be forfeited.
>
> **Special and Compassionate Leave:** Special leaves of absence, usually without pay, may be granted to an employee because of highly unusual personal, family, or career situations. Examples include a death or serious, life-threatening illness or injury in their immediate family, such as of a mother, father, sister, brother, spouse, child, grandparent, or grandchild.
>
> **Parental Leave:** Parental leave assists new parents by permitting leave, usually unpaid, for the birth or adoption of a child.
>
> **School Conference and Activities Leave:** Some criminal justice agencies will permit employees time off or nonpaid leave to attend school activities when such activities must be scheduled during working hours. In other agencies, vacation leave or compensatory time will be used for such activities.
>
> **Sick Leave:** Criminal justice agencies will provide leave for health needs, usually paid time off. In some agencies, this sick leave may be accumulated and carried over from one year to the next.
>
> **Blood, Organ, and Bone-Marrow Donor Leave:** Some criminal justice agencies will give their employees time off to donate blood, organs, or bone marrow. Others will allow their employees to apply sick leave or ordinary leave for such purposes.
>
> **Jury Duty Leave:** Typically criminal justice system employees will not be seated on juries, but they still will need to answer jury calls. Many criminal justice agencies will pay an employee who is performing jury duty.
>
> **Voting Leave:** A few criminal justice agencies will grant their employees brief periods off during the working day to vote in elections when voting hours fall within regularly scheduled work time. This is especially appropriate when their agencies require long work shifts that may conflict with voting hours. For example, 10- or 12-hour shifts are required by some police and correctional agencies.
>
> **Military Leave:** Federal law guarantees that reserve or national guard duty, including extended call-ups, shall be considered as excused leaves of absence, but criminal justice agencies are not obligated to pay service members called to military duty. Employees called up for extended active duty must be allowed a leave of absence to meet their military responsibilities, regardless of the length of their absence. Upon release from active duty, the employee is entitled to be reinstated in the same job formerly held, with the same duties, level of pay, and benefits and seniority that would have accrued had the service member not been on active military duty. Typically, most employee benefits do not accumulate during military leave. Some criminal justice agencies will allow one of the following options related to their pay:
>
> *The employee may use accumulated vacation time and thereby retain both military pay and the criminal justice agency wages.*
>
> *The employee may take unpaid leave from the criminal justice agency and thus will be required to subsist only on military pay.*
>
> *A few agencies will continue an employee's criminal justice pay, or make up the difference between the criminal justice pay and military pay during some part of their absence, usually only for a limited time, without requiring the forfeiture of any vacation time.*

Summary

Staffing and personnel issues are a major responsibility of a criminal justice manager. Staffing involves hiring agency employees, then fostering their career development, protecting their employment rights, disciplining them, and promoting them. A knowledge of civil service rules and equal employment opportunity law is essential.

LEARNING OBJECTIVES

Upon finishing this chapter, you should be able to do the following:

1. Identify the key features of the five eras of public service in the United States.
2. Understand both the positive and the negative aspects of the patronage system for criminal justice hiring.
3. Identify the seven key civil service reforms exemplified in the Pendleton Act.
4. Identify key legislation and court rulings bringing about the "civil rights" revolution in criminal justice hiring.
5. Know the following commonly used abbreviations:
   - AA: Affirmative Action
   - BFOQ: Bona Fide Occupational Qualification
   - EEO: Equal Employment Opportunity
   - EEOC: Equal Employment Opportunity Commission
   - OFCCP: Office of Federal Contract Compliance Programs

IMPORTANT TERMS AND NAMES

- *Ackerman's question*
- *appeal procedure*
- *best qualified*
- *civil service law*
- *closed shop*
- *comparable worth*
- *contracting process*
- *credentialism*
- *employee classification*
- *equality of opportunity*
- *equality of result*
- *exempt*
- *fitness of character*
- *fully qualified*
- *Jacksonian egalitarianism*
- *Jeffersonian ideal*

- *job description*
- *Malek Manual*
- *noblesse oblige*
- *nonexempt*
- *on-the-job training (OJT)*
- *open shop*
- *patronage appointments*
- *special assignment technique*
- *spoils system*
- *staffing*
- *turnover*
- *veterans preference*
- *workplace harassment*

References and Supplemental Sources

Byrd, T. G., Cochran, J. K., Silverman, I. J., & Blout, W. R. (2000). Behind bars: An assessment of the effects of job satisfaction, job-related stress, and anxiety on jail employees' inclinations to quit. *Journal of Crime and Justice, 23,* 69–93.

Brown v. Board of Education of Topeka, 347 U.S. 483 (1954).

Camp, S. D. (1994). Assessing the effects of organizational commitment and job satisfaction on turnover: An event history approach. *The Prison Journal, 74,* 279–305.

Campbell, A. K. (1978). *Civil service reform.* Washington, DC: Government Printing Office. U.S. House Committee on Post Office and Civil Service

Campbell, A. K. (1991). Testimony on civil service reform and organization. In: Thompson, F. J. (Ed.), *Classics of public personnel policy* (pp. 82–104) (2nd Ed.). Pacific Grove, CA: Brooks/Cole.

Caplow, T. (1983). *Managing an Organization* (2nd ed.). New York: Holt, Rinehart, and Winston.

Colbridge, T. D. (2000). Prohibited discrimination under the Americans with Disabilities Act. *FBI Law Enforcement Bulletin, 69*(12), 14–21.

Eastland, T. (1996). *Ending affirmative action: The case for colorblind justice.* New York: Basic Books.

Edelman, L. B., Fuller, S. R., & Mara-Drita, I. (2001). Diversity rhetoric and the managerialization of law. *American Journal of Sociology, 106*(6), 1589–1641.

Firefighters v. City of Cleveland, 478 U.S. 501 (1986).

Firefighters v. Stotts, 467 U.S. 561 (1984).

Fosdick, R. B. (1920). *American police systems.* New York: Century.

Gold, M. E. (1983). *A dialogue on comparable worth.* Ithaca, NY: ILR Press/Cornell University.

Griggs vs. Duke Power, 401 U.S. 424 (1971).

Gulick, L. (1937). Notes on the theory of organization. In: Gulick, L., & Urwick, L. (Eds.), *Papers on the science of administration.* New York: Institute of Public Administration.

Hill, M. A., & Killingsworth, M. R. (1989). *Comparable worth: Analyses and evidence.* Ithaca, NY: ILR Press/Cornell University.

Hammerman, H (1988). Affirmative-action stalemate: A second perspective. *Public Interest, 93*(Fall), 130–134.

Jacobs, J. B., & Grear, M. P. (1977). Drop outs and rejects: An analysis of the prison guard's revolving door. *Criminal Justice Review, 2*, 57–70.

Kiekbusch, R., Price, W., & Thesis, J. (2003). Turnover predictions: Causes of employee turnover in sheriff-operated jails. *Criminal Justice Studies, 16*, 67–76.

Lambert, E. G. (2001). To stay or to quit: A review of the literature on correctional staff turnover. *American Journal of Criminal Justice, 26*, 61–76.

Lambert, E. G., & Hogan, N. (2009). The importance of job satisfaction and organizational commitment in shaping turnover intent: A test of a causal model. *Criminal Justice Review, 34*, 96–118.

Livingston, J. C. (1979). *Fair game? Inequality and affirmative action.* San Francisco: Freeman.

Loury, G. C. (1997). How to mend affirmative action. *Public Interest, 127*(Spring), 33–43.

Lynch, J. E., & Tuckey, M. (2008). The police turnover problem: Fact or fiction?. *Policing: An International Journal of Police Strategies & Management, 31*(1), 6–18.

Minnesota Council of Nonprofits (2007). Sample personnel policies. *How to start a nonprofit: Templates and samples.* Retrieved from <http://www.mncn.org/info/template_hr.htm/>

Minor, K. I., Wells, J. B., Angel, E., & Matz, A. K. (2011). Predictors of early job turnover among juvenile correctional faculty staff. *Criminal Justice Review, 36*(1), 58–75.

Moore, E. W. (2001). Emerging legal constraints on affirmative action in police agencies and how to adapt to them. *Journal of Criminal Justice, 29*(1), 11–19.

Mosher, F. C. (1954). *Program budgeting in theory and practice, with particular reference to the U.S. Department of the Army.* Washington, DC: Public Administration Service.

Mosher, F. C. (1967). *Democracy and the public service.* New York: Oxford University Press.

Mosher, F. C. (1982). *Democracy and the public service* (2nd ed.). New York: Oxford University Press.

Mosher, F. C. (1986) The public service: Its condition and its prospects. Remarks prepared for the national convention of American Society of Public Administration (ASPA), 14 April 1986. Quoted in Stephenson and Plant (1991, p. 112).

National Committee on Law Observance and Enforcement [Wickersham Commission] (1931). *Report on the enforcement of the prohibition laws of the United States.* Retrieved from <http://www.druglibrary.org/schaffer/library/studies/wick/wick3.html/>.

New York Times (1990, May 24). Frederick C. Mosher: Government expert and teacher was 76. *New York Times.* Retrieved from <http://www.nytimes.com/1990/05/24/obituaries/frederick-c-mosher-government-expert-and-teacher-was-76.html/>.

Orrick, D. (2005). Police turnover. *The Police Chief, 72*(9) Retrieved from <http://www.policechiefmagazine.org/magazine/index.cfm?fuseaction=display_arch&article_id=697&issue_id=92005/>.

Paul, E. F. (1989). *Equity and gender: The comparable worth debate.* New Brunswick, NJ: Transaction.

Remick, H. (1984). *Comparable worth and wage discrimination.* Philadelphia: Temple University Press.

Richardson, J. F. (1974). *Urban police in the United States.* Port Washington, NY: Kennikat Press, National University Publications.

Roosevelt, T. (1897). *American ideals and other essays social and political.* New York: Knickerbocker Press, Putnam.

Savas, E. S., & Ginsburg, S. G. (1973). The civil service: A meritless system? *The Public Interest, 32*(Summer), 70–85.

Slade, R. N., & Vogel, R. E. (1997). Participative management and correctional personnel: A study of the perceived atmosphere for participation in correctional decision making and its impact on employee stress and thoughts about quitting. *Journal of Criminal Justice, 25*, 397–408.

Sorauf, F. J. (1960). The silent revolution in patronage. *Public Administration Review, 20*(1), 28–34.

Souryal, S. S. (1995). *Police organization and administration* (2nd ed.). Cincinnati: Anderson.

Stephenson, M. O., Jr., & Plant, J. F. (1991). The legacy of Frederick C. Mosher. *Public Administration Review, 51*(2), 97–113.

Stewart, D., & Garson, G. D. (1983). *Organizational behavior and public management.* New York: Marcel Dekker.

Stohr, M. K., Self, R. L., & Lovrich, N. P. (1992). Staff turnover in new generation jails: An investigation of its causes and prevention. *Journal of Criminal Justice, 20*(5), 455–478.

Taylor, F. W. (1911/1967). *The principles of scientific management.* New York: Norton Library, Harper & Row.

Thompson, F. J. (1991). *Classics of public personnel policy* ((2nd ed.)). Pacific Grove, CA: Brooks/Cole.

University of Louisville, Human Resources, *What does it mean to be an "exempt" or "nonexempt" employee?* Louisville, Kentucky: University of Louisville. Retrieved from <http://louisville.edu/hr/payroll/faq/what-does-it-mean-to-be-an-exempt-or-nonex-empt-employee.html/>.

U.S. President's Commission on Law Enforcement and Administration of Justice, *The challenge of crime in a free society.* Washington, DC: Government Printing Office.

U. S. President's Commission on Law Enforcement and Administration of Justice, *Task force report: The police.* Washington, DC: Government Printing Office.

Van Riper, P. P. (1958). *History of the United States Civil Service.* New York: Harper & Row.

Van Riper, P. P. (1991). Americanizing a foreign invention: The Pendleton Act of 1883. In: Thompson, F. J. (Ed.), *Classics of public personnel policy* (pp. 6–16) (2nd ed.). Pacific Grove, CA: Brooks/Cole.

Weber, M. (1922). In: Roth, G., & Wittich , C. (Eds.), *Economy and society* (2 vols.). Berkeley, CA: University of California Press.

Wilson, W. (1887). The study of administration. *Political Science Quarterly, 2*(2), 197–222.

Wright, T. A. (1993). Correctional employee turnover: A longitudinal study. *Journal of Criminal Justice, 21,* 131–142.

Yates, S. (1994). *Civil wrongs: What went wrong with affirmative action?* San Francisco, CA: ICS Press.

Yuill, K. L. (2006). *Richard Nixon and the rise of affirmative action: The pursuit of equality in an era of limits.* Lanham, MD: Rowman & Littlefield.

9

Training and Education for Criminal Justice

The "T" in LODESTAR stands for "training." Although there was no "T" in POSDCORB, Luther Gulick (1937) was aware of the importance of training as part of the staffing function. Frederick Taylor (1911) also stressed the importance of training new employees, making it a component of one of his four principles. Neither man, however, gave much attention to continuing education and in-service training, both of which occupy much of the time and a considerable part of the budgets of criminal justice agencies. Clearly, the training function has grown in importance since the period between Taylor's (1911) and Gulick's (1937) major articles on staffing. "Failure-to-train" lawsuits (Ross, 2000, pp. 330–331) have provided much of the impetus behind making current, correct, and comprehensive training a major managerial responsibility.

A History of Criminal Justice Training and Education

In 1900, police academies were virtually nonexistent. Many states permitted the election or appointment of prosecutors and judges who had not attended law school. Few correctional officers received any training at all. Most people undertaking employment in criminal justice agencies were expected to learn on the job, with the talents and skills they had prior to being hired, appointed, or elected. In just one century, all this changed dramatically.

Buffalo had a police training program in 1871, but it was discontinued soon after it opened. In 1886, Cincinnati established a program of police instruction that endured (Richardson, 1974, p. 12). Few other cities followed in the 19th century, but more police academies were established early in the 20th century. Most police were trained on the street, under the mentorship of a veteran partner. No training curriculum was established, and police officers often went on duty before being trained; they were issued a uniform, gun, and badge with little or no guidance on how to use them. Not until 1895 did the New York Police Department begin to require pistol practice for its officers (Roosevelt, 1897, p. 185).

Leonhard F. Fuld wrote *Police Administration* (1909), the first textbook on how to be a police manager. With an audience of prospective police managers, it offered his experience-based prescriptions on how to run a police agency. Coming in the era of social reform, the book was reform-oriented, and Fuld was both critical of existing personnel practices and an advocate for civil service improvements. He supported police training, the lateral entry of highly qualified, university-educated nonpolice managers into police executive positions (as opposed to selecting police managers from the ranks), and was a strong advocate of improved line supervision by police sergeants and midlevel management captains as the keys to better policing.

However, criminal justice education, other than in law, was virtually nonexistent in the 19th century, and Fuld's book had a very limited potential audience. As the "new ideas" man of American law enforcement practice, August Vollmer sought to change that. Under Vollmer's influence, San Jose State College offered the first degree program in law enforcement studies (Walker, 1977, p. 136), the forerunner to today's criminal justice and criminology degree programs.

Vollmer and his supporters also sought improved police training for officers and police managers already hired. In that time, few cities and no states required formal training of police recruits. Police academies were established in a few of the more progressive cities, but their curricula were ill-defined. Promotion in most police agencies was from the ranks, and little or no supervisory or managerial instruction was available. The pro-education reformers within the American police establishment sought to change all of this. They lobbied for training academies for recruits, midcareer supervision courses, and managerial education. (President's Commission on Law Enforcement and Administration of Justice, 1967a, 1967b, 1967c).

Judges, prosecutors, and defense attorneys were allowed to hold offices and practice law without law degrees in the first half of the 19th century, but by the 1880s, many states were requiring at least passage of a state bar examination. The practice of "reading law" in an apprenticeship with a veteran lawyer has lasted, and seven states still permitted it at the start of the 21st century (MacDonald, 2003).

Previously, we discussed the contributions of Frederick Taylor and the application of his four principles of scientific management (1911, pp. 36–37) to the design of work and the selection of workers. The second of these was to "scientifically select and then train, teach, and develop the workman." A formal training plan, based on the job description, was a necessary feature. The training plan first recognizes the skills and education the new worker should bring to the job, and then outlines the on-the-job and specialized occupational training program that the criminal justice agency will require and provide for the new employee. This will specify the general kinds of training to be given, who will provide the required training to the new employee, and how the training will be acquired. The roles of the supervisor, a training academy, or a specialized workshop or course will be included.

A training plan can include three major approaches to preparing the new employee for his or her initial work in the organization: **on-the-job training, in-house training,** and **contracted-out training.** Each has both advantages and disadvantages for the organization. Managers must choose among these to determine which is best for their organization.

Corrections training applied Taylor's principles, but many correctional agencies had lagged behind other parts of the criminal justice system in setting appropriately demanding entry and training requirements until the middle of the 20th century (Johnson, Wolfe, & Jones, 2008). The President's Commission on Law Enforcement and Administration of Justice (1967b) recommended both formal training and higher educational standards for correctional officers in its *Task Force Report: Corrections*. With

BOX 9.1 THREE WAYS TO TRAIN

ADVANTAGES	**DISADVANTAGES**
On-the-Job (OJT)	
It is the least expensive means of training.	Supervisors may not be good trainers.
It is done under existing supervisors, thus better acquainting trainees and the supervisors for whom they will work.	Supervisors may not know the most progressive and innovative methods in the field.
The trainee is available for work while training. It takes place in a totally realistic setting that replicates actual work situations and environment.	It can be hard to find sufficient training time in a busy work environment.
	Training continually is interrupted by the actual work of the agency.
There is time flexibility, with continuous training opportunities provided over an extended duration.	The work and training pace may be too fast for a new worker.
	Generally it takes longer than formal training.
	Unapproved practices, rather than formally approved policies, may be taught or shown.
In-House	
It acquaints new employees with additional organizational staff members, rather than just the immediate supervisors.	It is provided in a less realistic environment.
It can provide training on and familiarization with activities conducted in other departments of the agency beyond the immediate workplace.	In-house trainers usually have other responsibilities in the organization and rarely are totally qualified as trainers.
	It takes trainers away from their other, principle duties.
It is usually quicker than OJT. Time exclusively for training is provided. Trainers are well acquainted with agency requirements, peculiarities, eccentricities, and unique situations.	The trainee is not available for productive labor while in training.
	In-house trainers may not be acquainted with the most progressive and innovative methods in the field.
Contracted-Out	
Presumably, the trainers are totally professional and experienced in their subject areas.	It is the most expensive means of training.
It can provide training on and familiarization with activities conducted beyond the immediate workplace and in similar agencies, ideally including the most progressive and innovative methods in the field.	Trainers may not be knowledgeable about the agency's requirements, peculiarities, eccentricities, and unique situations.
It offers the most efficient use of agency labor and time: only the trainees participate; thus, it does not obligate the time and effort of supervisors or in-house trainers.	Scheduling inflexibility is common; programs are offered when the training contractor is ready and available, not necessarily when the agency needs the training.
Time exclusively for training is provided.	Workers often are sent "away" from the agency when in training and are not available for productive labor while in training.
It is usually quicker than OJT.	

the development of the rehabilitative ideal in corrections, which focuses on effecting change in the character, attitudes, and behavior of convicted offenders, it became necessary for correctional institutions and programs to employ college-educated teachers, social workers, counselors, and correctional psychologists. These programs could not be managed by high school graduates or those with even less education. By the time the various reports of the National Advisory Commission on Criminal Justice Standards and Goals were published in 1973, the federal government was calling on the states to undertake studies of what education and training should be required for criminal justice occupations, to work with colleges and universities to provide appropriate educational programs for criminal justice professionals, to develop curricula, and to coordinate their offerings with criminal justice managers and federal recommendations to ensure that their programs would be relevant. Knowledge and skill requirements for criminal justice hiring, initial, and in-service training were recommended, and incentives for upgrading the training and education of existing employees were suggested. Evaluation of training and educational efforts was advised (National Advisory Commission, 1973, pp. 168–169). The Law Enforcement Assistance Administration (LEAA) of the U.S. Department of Justice created an Office of Criminal Justice Education and Training, sponsored a major study of police education and training (Sherman and the National Advisory Commission on Higher Education for Police Officers, 1978), and funded many educational and training programs in the 1970s (Foster, Magers, & Mullikin, 2007, pp. 125–130). To help the states pay for these new programs, LEAA grants were authorized for new training centers and programs, for the creation of new criminal justice educational programs in colleges, and for tuition assistance through the Law Enforcement Education Program.

The *Law Enforcement Education Program (LEEP)* was a short-lived program that paid the tuition of full-time employees of the criminal justice system to attend college-level criminal justice programs. In the 1970s, tens of thousands of service police, correctional, juvenile justice, and other criminal justice employees were able to attend college and earn associate's, bachelor's, and even master's degrees in criminal justice or other related academic disciplines. The funding ended with the budget cuts imposed by the Carter administration, but criminal justice employees already in criminal justice educational programs were eligible to finish their degrees, so that LEEP funds continued to flow into the early 1980s. Many thought that the decade-long effort to improve the educational level of criminal justice practitioners would collapse with the end of LEEP support for criminal justice education, but that did not prove to be the case. Fewer in-service criminal justice practitioners were in college classrooms after 1980, but the appeal of criminal justice education was attracting preservice students who were thinking about criminal justice careers. Most of the college criminal justice programs created at community colleges, 4-year colleges, and universities continue to offer their courses to another generation of students.

College Education for Criminal Justice

The results of LEEP raised some important criminal justice policy questions. How much education is necessary to qualify for a criminal justice occupation? Do you need a high school diploma, an associate of arts (AA) or associate of applied sciences (AAS) degree, a bachelor of science (BS) or bachelor of arts (BA) degree, or even more formal education to perform well in a criminal justice occupation? The debate has continued since the 1970s. Certainly, more education, especially that which is focused on one's career choice, is a good thing to have (Mayo, 2006, 2008), but the jury is still out on the question of its necessity.

In Europe, college-level educational requirements for police and correctional managers have a long history (Pagon, Virjent-Novak, Djuric, & Lobnikar, 1996; Stead, 1988). In France, for example, special colleges exist to prepare police officers for command positions in the *Police Nationale*. Germany has created a German Police Leadership University (*Deutsche Hochschule der Polizei*), which offers a master's in public administration (Birkenstock, 2005). In the Netherlands, collegiate police academies offer both bachelor's and master's degrees and meet educational accreditation criteria approved by the Ministry of Education. The college curriculum is keyed to the professional competencies that police officers are expected to acquire, with four main categories: professional, contextual, social, and individual (Peeters, 2009, p. 48).

The professional competencies involve education, training, and skill acquisition at the core of the profession, so that the student learns the essential duties of the office. Contextual competencies promote organizational and procedural learning, so the student learns how the organization operates. Social competencies introduce the student-officer to the diverse social and cultural environment in which policing operates. Individual competencies involve the personal development of the officer-candidate, preparing the student for entry onto a successful career path (Peeters, 2009, p. 49).

Professional degrees are needed for some public service occupations: An assistant district attorney or a judge is expected to have a law degree. Several states require social workers working in corrections to have a master of social work (MSW) degree. A senior planner might be required to have a graduate degree in an academic discipline related to planning. Many of those holding line positions in criminal justice agencies should have some post–high school education, and certainly supervisors and managers would benefit from a college education. Other criminal justice organization positions easily can be filled by persons with much less education. Skilled laborers, janitorial staff, receptionists, security guards, and many others can perform quite well having only a high school education, and perhaps even less.

It is obvious that the position itself determines the education prerequisites. A criminal justice manager must make a realistic assessment of the requirements of the job and must be aware of what each level of education is likely to provide toward meeting those requirements. What can a high school graduate reasonably be expected to do? What knowledge, skills, and talents may be associated with the diploma? What about a specialized AAS or other 2-year college degree? Or a generalist BA or BS coupled with a major in a traditional liberal arts academic discipline in a technical field or applied science? Or should candidates acquire a bachelor degree in criminal justice or criminology? In most cases, a master's degree is not needed for an entry-level position in law enforcement, corrections, or court administration, but it would be an asset in correctional and juvenile justice counseling occupations, especially if the degree is in social work, counseling, or applied psychology.

The master of public administration (MPA) is an excellent and valuable credential for a person who is already in a criminal justice field and is preparing to advance into a managerial position, or who already holds such a position and is seeking to rise further.

What should the education of a criminal justice professional include? The appropriate education for someone in public service has been an open question for more than 2,000 years. Plato expressed his opinions on this matter in *The Republic*, citing the ideas of Socrates, an advocate of what we now refer to as the "liberal arts education" ideal:

> *Our best guardians will be a select band, those who are of the right temper and thoroughly trained; fierce to foes but gentle to friends. ... The known are friends, the unknown foes—knowledge begets gentleness.*
>
> *So our guardians must be trained to knowledge; we must educate them. Music and gymnastics, our national intellectual and physical training, must be taught. Literature comes first, ...*

On this issue, too, there is some debate. What are the purposes of a liberal arts education? Would not a professional preparatory education be superior? Training, both at entry and while in service, will provide the technical skills needed on the job, so technical and professional curricula will be duplicated if also taken in college. A broader education in the liberal arts, as suggested by Plato 2,400 years ago, therefore, has greater advantages. The technical and professional skills of this decade will someday be as obsolete as those acquired in the 1970s and 1980s are now, but the skills learned in the liberal arts will endure. In criminal justice occupations in the United States, excellent communications skills, the ability to comprehend a foreign language (especially Spanish), and the skills to deal with mathematical applications will be far more important by the time one is in mid-career in the 2020s than will be having mastered the crime scene technologies, correctional procedures, or court administrative practices of today.

While even 20 years ago a majority of the surveyed police departments informally gave preference to college-educated applicants, the overwhelming majority of police agencies formally require only a high school diploma or its general educational development (GED) test equivalent. Only 13.7 percent of surveyed law enforcement agencies in a Police Executive Research Forum (PERF) study (Carter, Sapp, & Stephens, 1989, p. xvii) had a formal college entry requirement, and those that did usually required a 2-year AA/AAS degree or 60 hours of college education. A slight majority (54.1%) reported that their hiring efforts were oriented toward recruiting college students, but only 6.6 percent targeted college students as their primary or exclusive applicant pool (Carter, Sapp, & Stephens, 1989, p. xix).

Determining Training and Education Needs

Some federal agencies, states, counties, and municipalities set minimal educational requirements for their new criminal justice employees. Educational credentials above the minimum can be required by the agency, however. A criminal justice manager often will have the authority to set these. This can be done formally, by including these requirements in the advertised employment criteria for a position, or informally, by giving preference to candidates with more education.

Given the education that a potential criminal justice agency employee brings to the job, what training is necessary to make that employee into a fully functioning staff member? Frederick Taylor clearly believed that training was an essential requirement for the newly hired, because there would be skills and knowledge needed on the job that even the very well-qualified applicant for the position would not be likely to possess (1911, pp. 36–37). The criminal justice manager needs to determine what these are and include them in the agency training plan. How should criminal justice training be acquired? Three major approaches can be used: (1) *on-the-job training (OJT)* under normal supervisors, (2) *in-house training,* with staff providing training, and (3) *contracted-out training programs* using specialists. There are distinct advantages and disadvantages to each that a criminal justice manager needs to consider (see Box 9.1).

Selecting the approach to be taken to training is a major managerial responsibility. Time, cost, instructional requirements, and available qualified instructors are all factors to be considered. So is litigation. **"Failure to train" liability lawsuits,** which allege that there was a "deliberate indifference" to proper training, are a real risk to criminal justice agencies, and both police and corrections agencies have found themselves in court to answer for their training failures (Ross, 2000, pp. 330–331). The absence of training in key performance areas—and incorrect or inadequate training in those areas—often will be cited to demonstrate an agency's negligence in such lawsuits.

Continuing In-Service Training and Education

Formal training should not end with the conclusion of the formal probationary period. Ideally, it will continue as long as the employee works for the agency. However, the character of the training and education will change as the employee climbs the organizational ladder. Some of that training and education will be self-acquired, as advancement-oriented individuals seek to better themselves with further training courses and participation in programs that grant college degrees.

Continuing Education Seminars

Some education after being hired is provided by the agencies directly or by the professional organizations affiliated with them. The American Bar Association has a long record of providing training seminars for practicing member attorneys, in and out of public practice. The American Correctional Association actively supports continuing education of its membership. The International Association of Chiefs of Police provides many seminars and training sessions for police managers and specialists.

This is true even in areas where high education criteria are the norm for entry. Judges in some states are required to take courses on judgeship before taking the bench, but now some are even engaging in advanced study of the judiciary (Green, 1987) to help them grow in their key roles.

College Education

During the golden years of the LEAA, criminal justice professionals had federal funding for college courses through the LEEP program. Thousands of police, courts, corrections, and other justice-system employees either returned to college or began college programs for the first time. Average police educational attainment advanced substantially, so that a majority of police officers were college-educated, usually in fields and majors related to their work, by the end of the program in the early 1980s.

Graduate Studies

In 1950, there were virtually no graduate programs specifically in criminal justice or criminology. Criminal justice courses often were offered in sociology, political science, and public administration graduate programs. Since the 1970s, though, an increasing number of universities have been offering graduate-level criminal justice programs (Frost & Clear, 2007). Doctoral programs now exist at some of America's finest universities.

There now is an Association of Doctoral Programs in Criminology and Criminal Justice (2008), whose members are the universities offering a doctoral program in criminal justice and criminology. The members meet in conjunction with the American Society of Criminology to conduct annual surveys of doctoral programs activities and promote the advanced study of crime and criminal justice.

There are a number of institutes and centers providing graduate-level courses for in-service criminal justice managers. Police managers enroll in various police institutes—among the oldest and best are the FBI Academy and its University of Virginia graduate program at Quantico, Virginia, the Southern Police Institute of the University of Louisville, and the Traffic Institute of Northwestern University. The federal government sponsors the John B. Pickett Fellowships in Criminal Justice Policy and Management at the John F. Kennedy School of Government at Harvard University for a select few, leading to the MPA degree (National Institute of Justice, 1993, 1995). The University of Virginia offers a master of laws in collaboration with the Appellate Judges Conference of the American Bar Association to sitting judges via a summer program (Green, 1987). The federal government has a Federal Executive Institute for its upper-level managers (including those in criminal justice) who are competing for "super-grade" status in the federal government. These and other programs provide advanced in-service educational opportunities to criminal justice professionals.

Fitting into the Organization
Chris Argyris and the Immaturity–Maturity Theory

In his book, *Personality and Organization*, Chris Argyris (1957) sought to examine the worker as part of a dynamic "system" of personal and organizational growth and

BOX 9.2 DOCTORAL PROGRAMS IN CRIMINOLOGY AND CRIMINAL JUSTICE, 2010

American University
Arizona State University–West Campus
California State University—Fresno and University of California Joint Program
Florida International University
Florida State University
George Mason University
Georgia State University
Indiana University
Indiana University of Pennsylvania
John Jay College of Criminal Justice
Michigan State University
North Dakota State University
Northeastern University
Old Dominion University
Pennsylvania State University
Prairie View A&M University
Rutgers University–Newark
Sam Houston State University
Simon Fraser University
State University of New York at Albany
Temple University
Texas Southern University
Texas State University–San Marcos
University of Arkansas–Little Rock
University of California–Irvine
University of Central Florida
University of Cincinnati
University of Delaware
University of Florida
University of Illinois at Chicago
University of Louisville
University of Maryland
University of Missouri–St. Louis
University of Montreal
University of Nebraska–Omaha
University of North Dakota
University of Pennsylvania
University of South Carolina
University of South Florida
University of Southern Mississippi
University of Texas–Dallas
Washington State University

Sources: Association of Doctoral Programs in Criminology and Criminal Justice (2008, 2010; Frost & Clear (2007); Georgia State University (2010); Stafford, M. C. (personal communication, August 30, 2010).

BOX 9.3 CHRIS ARGYRIS AND THE IMMATURITY–MATURITY THEORY

1. From: Passive—takes orders
   To: Active—offers suggestions and ideas
2. From: Dependent—waits for instruction
   To: Independent—works from own initiative
3. From: Limited (self-restricted) behavior
   To: Diversified behavior—experiments
4. From: Shallow interest—ignores policies and politics
   To: Deeper interest—concerned with office politics and issues
5. From: Limited-time perspective (here and now)
   To: Long-term perspective (past and future)
6. From: Subordinate
   To: Superior (seniority)
7. From: Not self-aware—has a weak sense of workplace identity
   To: Self-aware—has a well-defined sense of place in the agency

---

development. The "systems theory" and "systems analysis" arose as an attempt to recon-cile the extremes of the individual-oriented human relations focus with the needs of the organization—the exclusive concern of the scientific management advocates. The point raised by the systems advocates is that the individual finds identity and satisfaction as part of a social entity, and that can be his or her work group if the work environment pro-motes integration of one's identity with the organizational goals.

Taking ideas already popularized in educational psychology, also known as develop-mental psychology, especially the work of Jean Piaget in France on the development of intellectual maturity and reasoning in children, Argyris used a similar developmental approach to describe the progressive maturity of an employee. Argyris saw this process as gradual, continuous, and approximately sequential.

Occupational Socialization

"Occupational socialization is the process by which a person acquires the values, atti-tudes, and behaviors of an ongoing occupational social system" (Klofas, Stojkovic, & Kalinich, 1990, p. 150). It is described as a continuous process, both intentional and unin-tentional, both legal and illegitimate, and typically stable and persistent. Often informal occupational socialization will have more influence on a new criminal justice employee than will his or her formal training (Ott 1989).

The role of personality also needs to be considered. For decades there has been a sus-picion that some occupations attract different personality types. As for the police per-sonality question (Klofas, Stojkovic, & Kalinich, 1990, pp. 151–152), the evidence is not completely clear. We are aware, though, that those who wish to become police are some-how different from those who want to become social workers, librarians, teachers, minis-ters, or accountants.

There is much stronger evidence that the job contributes to the creation of an officer's **working personality.** This concept was contributed to the study of policing by sociologist Jerome Skolnick (1966, p. 42), and applied socialization concepts used earlier by Howard S. Becker and Anselm L. Straus (1956). Socialization into the "fraternal organization" of policing, lawyering, or judging is another explanation. There are three stages to the process: the anticipatory stage, the formal stage, and the informal stage.

The *anticipatory stage* involves what the potential applicant perceives the organization to be like. It is the image the agency projects to outsiders. For most criminal justice occupations, this is created by the mass communications media, especially entertainment programs on television.

The *formal stage* (training) includes both entry-level and in-service training. Herbert Kaufman examined the role of post-entry training in preparing men to become forest rangers (1960, 1991), a specialized form of law enforcement. Kaufman states that post-entry training creates the capacity—by which he means the skills, knowledge, and factual premises—to facilitate adherence to the work norms of the organization. The training will not necessarily develop the will to do so, however.

The *informal stage* (peer-group and coworkers' influences) is also critical. This was addressed in the article, "Banana Time: Job Satisfaction and Informal Interaction," written by Donald F. Roy in 1959 (Roy, 1989). In this article, he asked which has more influence on workers: the formal policies and the managers or the informal work groups and their "play"?

Factors influencing socialization include an "organizational culture" as discussed by Shafritz and Ott (1992, p. 482): "a strong organizational culture literally controls organizational behavior." The formal rules and authority systems do not control the worker as much as the cultural norms, values, beliefs, and assumptions of the coworkers—the organizational culture. This can be defined in terms of six features identified by Edgar H. Schein (1992, p. 492):

1. observed behavioral regularities
2. social and productivity norms
3. dominant values (and ideologies) expressed
4. philosophy
5. informal rules and "the ropes"
6. the social climate and layout of the workspace

Symbolic Management

Schein goes further, discussing the levels of culture that include what he refers to as artifacts, values, and basic underlying assumptions. These features are all symbolic measures that a manager can manipulate. **Symbolic management** includes the interpretations of events in an organization, which are often more important than the events themselves. Because ambiguity and uncertainty are common to most organizations, they preclude rational problem-solving and decision-making. Thus, symbolic meanings and ritual actions gain weight beyond their "rational" content. The symbols of the organization, such as logos, flags, lapel pins, and so on, are important to the management of the organization (Shafritz & Ott, 1992, pp. 484–485).

To study and comprehend workplace socialization, the organizational observer needs to examine (Klofas, Stojkovic, & Kalinich, 1990, p. 154, Figure 7-1):

- organizational factors
- attributes of the person
- interpersonal factors
- role-building process

    1. role expectations—preconceived notions
    2. role senders—communication put out about the role
    3. received role—messages received on the role
    4. role behavior—the actions of the receiver

Police Socialization

Police socialization now begins with a police academy. There are four variations of police academy training, when considered on two variables: a *residential* versus a *commuter* program, and a *collegiate* versus a *paramilitary* curriculum. **Residential academies** once were very common, but they are costly to manage, and fewer cities and states now provide full residential academies. More often, there are **commuter academies,** at which cadets commute to the academy from home or from temporary lodgings provided for them off-campus.

A **paramilitary curriculum** is structured similarly to a professional military force; a **collegiate curriculum** has more of the atmosphere of a college. The manner in which a police cadet is trained initially will vary the intensity of the formal socialization process. A paramilitary curriculum presented in a residential setting is the most intense. These often require the cadet to wear uniforms at all or most times, require military drill and daily physical fitness training, and are modeled on military boot camps and basic training programs. The cadets are boarded in barracks or dormitories at the academy and have meals together. A commuter program with a collegiate curriculum is the least intense. In some of these, uniforms are not required. Most training is given in a classroom setting, study is done individually, and the cadet is not removed from daily contact with family and friends. In between, in terms of socialization intensity, are the other two options: the paramilitary commuter academy and the residential collegiate academy.

When police cadets finish their academy experience, they are often assigned to a "field training officer" (FTO), a veteran officer selected to serve as a mentor to the new officer. The FTO concept differs from the old OJT approach of attaching a new officer to a veteran in that the FTOs are given training to become trainers and usually do their work from a curriculum of skills they are expected to teach to the new officers and then

---

BOX 9.4 THE FABLE OF THE MOTH, THE SCREEN, THE LIGHT BULB, AND THE PRESSURE COOKER

Once upon a time there was a moth who was irresistibly attracted to a glowing light bulb in the night. But each time the moth attempted to reach this object of desire, the moth encountered a fine mesh screen barring the way. After much effort the moth finally found a way past the screen and joyfully embraced the glowing orb. To the moth's shock and surprise, the embrace was a very painful and traumatic experience. Letting go of the hot bulb, wings burned by the heat, the moth dropped into a pot sitting below the bulb. Before the moth could escape, a tight lid was placed on the pot and the poor moth discovered that it was now in a pressure cooker. The moth's infatuation with the light bulb was over, but it was trapped in a place where it was very unhappy indeed. The moth endured but was never again the same.

The *Moth* represents the characteristics of potential police applicants. The work traditionally attracts Euro-Americans more so than other races and ethnicities, and males disproportionately, people from the lower middle class, laboring, blue-collar families, people who are generally idealistic, seeking job security, but also interested in glamour, excitement, outdoor work, and variety. The alleged attraction of authoritarian, coercive personalities to police work does not appear to be true.

The *Screens* are those factors used to select police recruits and eliminate police "wannabes." Some of the things keeping some "moths" from law enforcement include: (1) educational requirements, generally only a high school diploma; (2) residence, usually police must live in the same political jurisdiction or a closely adjacent one; (3) testing, including written examinations and oral interviews, usually conforming to civil service standards, sometimes including psychological testing; (4) age, usually falling within the 21-to-35-year range; (5) character and prior record, a felony conviction usually will disqualify one, but minor traffic violations and minor offenses (misdemeanors) usually do not. Most departments require a background investigation. Testing for drug use seems to be finding a place in police screening, with court decisions generally supporting testing. Some debate is now going on about whether individuals with a history of drug use in the past should be hired. Many agencies will hire former users who no longer experiment with controlled substances.

The *Lightbulb* stands for those factors drawing people to police work. The features of police careers that draw people include the image of glamour, excitement, outdoor work, and variety associated with police work. It also offers modest benefits, about on par with entry skilled blue-collar trades, and more job security than is associated with most such trades. The media have given police work most of its "glamour" image; the reality of the job is quite a bit duller. Many more people are not moths, but are like the butterflies who find the light bulb to be of little interest or appeal.

The *Pressure Cooker* is what happens to the people entering police careers. Peer socialization, traumatic on-the-job experiences, job stress, the overt hostility of some segments of the public, bad press, the temptations of corruption, and exposure to the cynicism of more veteran peers all contribute to the development of the police officer's "working personality" (Skolnick, 1966).

observe them perform. In the OJT system, the veteran simply had the new officer "tag along" as the veteran officer performed his or her duties.

After finishing field training, officers enter an occupational culture that is unique. Policing is a very insular culture, and police officers tend to socialize with other officers.

The uniform causes officers to stand out in public, and citizens, seeing the uniform, treat them differently than they do other people. There is a strong belief among officers that the average citizen cannot understand the nature of the job. John Van Maanen (1974) states that officer's view themselves as doing the "dirty work" of society. This leads to many officers resenting the public and in many cases a closing of ranks. In the worst of circumstances, this culture creates a "blue wall of silence" that covers up corrupt and unethical behavior. In the best of circumstances, it brings esprit de corps and a support-ive environment. With the trend toward community-oriented policing in recent decades, police managers have emphasized a reconnection with the community and the citizenry to deal with the resentments that Van Maanen discusses.

Socialization in the Courts

Kenneth Peak discusses the training of judges and court administrators, observing that "judges now must train to take the bench" (1998, p. 177). There is a National Judicial College in Reno, Nevada, and an advanced judicial institute at the College of William and Mary. The National Center for State Courts' Institute of Court Management was cre-ated in 1970 to train court administrators, not all of whom are actually judges. The center continues to provide seminars and online learning for judges (National Center for State Courts, 2008). Court clerks generally learn on the job, but increasingly more state-run court administration offices provide formal training. Many assistant clerks of court are hired from the graduates of paralegal studies programs offered at community colleges, training institutes, and colleges and universities.

Socialization in Corrections

The attractions of a career in correction include steady pay and job security. Applicants for positions as correctional officers rarely have much advance knowledge of the job's features prior to applying (Peak, 1998, p. 250). Some images of correctional work may have been acquired from popular culture, especially film and television. One of the vir-tues of a college criminal justice education is that students considering a corrections career have a more realistic image of what to expect in their future work.

Since the influence of the LEAA, there has been an increase in the use of academy training for custodial correctional officers. Often training is initiated after employment has begun, especially for local jailers. High rates of turnover are common in custodial corrections, resulting in much of the workforce being inexperienced. Better-educated custodial correctional officers often have higher levels of job dissatisfaction than their less well educated peers, especially if they do not rise rapidly into managerial or admin-istrative positions (Peak, 1998, p. 251). Fortunately, promotion is rapid in correctional work, and those with more education and good leadership and communications skills can expect to advance quickly. The use of the FTO concept is infrequent in this field, and many correctional FTOs are poorly prepared for their roles as mentors for new correctional officers. Informal socialization includes experiences of mistrust and lack of confidence in their peers and manager. The inmates also play a role in the training and socialization of new guards.

Probation and parole officers are more commonly college-educated and often are recruited from police departments and custodial corrections units. So they enter their careers with greater experience and maturity. The very nature of probation and parole supervision within the larger community allows officers greater independence and autonomy. A laissez-faire management style often is used by probation and parole managers (Peak, 1998, p. 267). Therefore, organizational socialization factors are less intensive than in custodial correctional settings.

General Socialization Strategies

Media images are very important in producing the initial perceptions of new police and corrections officers. Changing those media messages is beyond the capacity of criminal justice managers, but is a function that criminal justice educators can undertake (Freeman, 2000). More appropriate recruitment and selection standards also can help modify the socialization experience, molding it into one that is both more realistic and more favorable. New employees must lose their misconceptions about the job, learn what is really involved in their employment, and come to accept their work roles in harmony with the rules and needs of the organization. These are the concepts of unfreezing, remolding, and refreezing that Kurt Lewin (1989) identified as the steps in the change process a new worker will undergo (Souryal, 1995, pp. 128–129). A criminal justice manager can use these concepts to the advantage of the agency but needs to pay close attention to:

- job qualifications of new officers
- psychological assessment of recruits
- training of both new officers and veteran officers
- using workplace socialization to a managerial advantage

This can be done by developing and using most of six socialization strategies:

1. collective socialization strategy (training in and as a group)
2. individual socialization strategy (apprenticeship)
3. sequential socialization strategy (training stages)
4. serial socialization strategy (veterans train rookies)
5. divestiture socialization strategy (stripping away an old identity)
6. investiture socialization strategy (accepting and establishing a new identity)

Summary

Developing appropriate standards for training and education are two major requirements of the modern criminal justice manager. To a degree, recruiting better-educated officers will help. Once new employees are chosen, they need to be given initial training, and as they advance in their careers they need to acquire additional in-service education. A mix of OJT, in-house, and contracted-out training should be considered by the criminal justice manager to provide training. Additional higher education will help with career advancement. Formal education and training are only a part of the process. The job itself helps share the working personality of the staff, and peer-based organizational socialization also is important in the development of a criminal justice employee.

LEARNING OBJECTIVES

Upon finishing this chapter, you should be able to do the following:

1. Discuss the rising standards for education and criminal justice training in each of the major areas of criminal justice employment.
2. Debate the question of the competitive merits of a technical-professional versus a liberal arts preservice education for new criminal justice employees.
3. Discuss the relative merits and disadvantages of the three means of providing in-service training: OJT, in-house, and contracted-out training.
4. Explain Chris Argyris's immaturity–maturity theory in terms of criminal justice employee socialization.
5. Explain the three stages in criminal justice employee socialization: anticipatory, formal, and informal.
6. Discuss a criminal justice manager's socialization strategy options.
7. Know the meanings of the following commonly used abbreviations: AA, AAS, BA, BS, FTO, GED, LEAA, LEEP, MPA, MSW, OJT, and PERF.

IMPORTANT TERMS AND NAMES

- *collegiate curriculum*
- *commuter academies*
- *"failure-to-train" liability lawsuits*
- *occupational socialization*
- *paramilitary curriculum*
- *rehabilitative ideal*
- *residential academies*
- *symbolic management*
- *training plan*
- *working personality*

References and Supplemental Sources

Argyris, C. (1957). *Personality and organization*. New York: Harper & Row.

Association of Doctoral Programs in Criminology and Criminal Justice (2010). *ADPCCJ*. Huntsville, TX: College of Criminal Justice, Sam Houston State University. Retrieved from <http://www.adpccj.org/>.

Association of Doctoral Programs in Criminology and Criminal Justice, *Association of doctoral programs in criminology and criminal justice 2010 survey report*. Huntsville, TX: College of Criminal Justice, Sam Houston State University. Retrieved from <http://www.adpccj.com/surveys.html/>.

Becker, H. S., & Straus, A. L. (1956). Careers, personality and adult socialization. *American Journal of Sociology, 62*(3), 253–263.

Birkenstock, W. (2005). Curriculum des Masterstudiengangs "Public administration—Police management," Münster Polizei Führungsakademie. Cited in Peeters (2009). See also, Deutschen Hochschule der Polizei, retrieved from <http://www.dhpol.de/en/hochschule/index.php/>.

Carter, D. L., Sapp, A. D., & Stephens, D. W. (1989). *The state of police education: Policy directions for the 21st century.* Washington, DC: Police Executive Research Forum.

Foster, J. P., Magers, J. S., & Mullikin., J. (2007). Observations and reflections on the evolution of crime-related higher education. *Journal of Criminal Justice Education, 18*(1), 123–136.

Frost, N. A., & Clear, T. R. (2007). Doctoral education in criminology and criminal justice. *Journal of Criminal Justice Education, 18*(1), 35–52.

Fuld, L. F. (1909). *Police administration: A critical study of police organizations in the United States and abroad.* New York: Putnam.

Georgia State University. (2010). *Doctor of Philosophy (Ph.D.).* Atlanta: Department of Criminal Justice, Georgia State University. Retrieved from <http://chhs.gsu.edu/cj/phd.asp/>.

Green, L. M. (1987, January/February). From courtroom to classroom. *UVA Alumni News*, 24–25.

Gulick, L. (1937). Notes on the theory of organization. In: Gulick, L., & Urwick, L. (Eds.), *Papers on the science of administration.* New York: Institute of Public Administration.

Johnson, H. A., Wolfe, N. T., & Jones, M. (2008). *History of criminal justice* (4th ed.). Newark, NJ: LexisNexis Matthew Bender.

Kaufman, H. (1960). *The forest ranger.* Baltimore: John Hopkins University Press.

Kaufman, H. (1991). Developing the will and capacity to conform. In: Thompson, F. J. (Ed.), *Classics of public personnel policy* (pp. 212–214) (2nd ed.). Pacific Grove, CA: Brooks/Cole.

Klofas, J., Stojkovic, S., & Kalinich, D. (1990). *Criminal justice organizations: Administration and management.* Pacific Grove, CA: Brooks/Cole.

Lewin, K. (1989). Group decision and social change. In: Ott, J. S. (Ed.), *Classic readings in organizational behavior* (pp. 543–548). Pacific Grove, CA: Brooks/Cole.

MacDonald, G. J. (2003, June 3). The self-made lawyer. *Christian Science Monitor On-Line.* Retrieved from <http://www.csmonitor.com/2003/0603/p13s01-lecs.html/>.

Mayo, L. (2006). College education and policing. *Police Chief, 73*(8). Retrieved from <http://policechiefmagazine.org/magazine/index.cfm?fuseaction = display_arch&article_id = 955&issue_id = 82006/>.

Mayo, L. (2008). Support for college degree requirements: The big picture. *Police Chief On Line.* Retrieved from <http://www.policechiefonline.com/magazine/index.cfm?fuseaction = display&article_id = 959&issue_id = 82006/>.

National Center for State Courts. (2008). *Welcome to the National Center for State Courts.* Retrieved from <http://www.ncsconline.org/>

National Institute of Justice. (1993). *John B. Pickett fellowships in criminal justice policy and management.* Washington, DC: Author.

National Institute of Justice. (1995). *John B. Pickett fellowships in criminal justice policy and management.* Washington, DC: Author.

Ott, J. S. (1989). *Classic readings in organizational behavior.* Pacific Grove, CA: Brooks/Cole.

Pagon, M., Virjent-Novak, B., Djuric, M., & Lobnikar, B. (1996). European systems of police education and training: *Policing in Central and Eastern Europe.* Ljubljana, Slovenia: College of Police and Security Studies.

Peak, K. J. (1998). *Justice administration: Police, courts, and corrections management* (2nd ed.). Upper Saddle River, NJ: Prentice Hall.

Peeters, H. (2009). Ten ways to blend academic learning within professional police training. *Policing, 4*(1), 47–55.

Plato (1941). *The Republic,* translation by Benjamin Jowett. New York: Modern Library.

Richardson, J. F. (1974). *Urban police in the United States.* Port Washington, NY: Kennikat Press, National University Publications.

Roosevelt, T. (1897). *American ideals and other essays social and political.* New York: Knickerbocker Press, Putnam.

Ross, D. L. (2000). Correctional administration and section 1983 liability issues. In: DuPont-Morales, M. A., Hooper, M., & Schmidt, J. H. (Eds.), *Handbook of criminal justice administration* (pp. 317–342). New York: Marcel Dekker.

Roy, D. F. (1989). Banana time: Job satisfaction and informal interaction. In: Ott, J. S. (Ed.), *Classic readings in organizational behavior* (pp. 163–182). Pacific Grove, CA: Brooks/Cole.

Schein, E. H. (1992). Defining organizational culture. In: Shafritz, J. M., & Ott, J. S. (Eds.), *Classics of organizational theory* (pp. 490–502) (3rd ed.). Pacific Grove, CA: Brooks/Cole.

Shafritz, J. M., & Ott, J. S. (1992). *Classics of organizational theory* (3rd ed.). Pacific Grove, CA: Brooks/Cole.

Sherman, L. W., and The National Advisory Commission on Higher Education for Police Officers (1978), *The quality of police education.* San Francisco: Jossey-Bass.

Skolnick, J. H. (1966). *Justice without trial: Law enforcement in democratic society.* New York: Wiley.

Souryal, S. S. (1995). *Police organization and administration* (2nd ed.). Cincinnati: Anderson.

Stead, P. J. (1988). *Structure of education and police careers in Europe and America.* Rockville, MD: National Institute of Justice/National Criminal Justice Reference Service.

Taylor, F. W. (1911). *Principles of scientific management.* New York: Norton Library, Harper & Row.

U.S. President's Commission on Law Enforcement and Administration of Justice (1967a). *The challenge of crime in a free society.* Washington, DC: Government Printing Office.

U. S. President's Commission on Law Enforcement and Administration of Justice (1967b). *Task force report: Corrections.* Washington, DC: Government Printing Office.

U.S. President's Commission on Law Enforcement and Administration of Justice (1967c). *Task force report: The police.* Washington, DC: Government Printing Office.

Van Maanen, J. (1974). Kinsmen in repose: Occupational perspectives of patrolmen. In: Kappeler, V. E. (Ed.), *The police and society: Touchstone readings.* Long Grove, IL: Waveland Press.

Walker, S. (1977). *A critical history of police reform.* Lexington, MA: Lexington Books.

10 ⠿

Allocating Key Organizational Resources

In LODESTAR, the "A" stands for "allocating." A manager is called on to manage not just the staff of the organization but also vital organizational resources, such as *time, funds, equipment,* and *facilities.* The allocation function of the manager involves assigning these key assets to individuals and units within the organization in a manner most closely suited to advancing the mission, goals, and objectives of the organization. There is a great deal of competition—even open conflict—within an organization for the scarce resources of each organization. As Douglas Yates, Jr. (1985, 1989) points out, the personal resources of the manager are required to discourage or control this kind of conflict, those personal resources being:

- personal managerial authority
- coercive power and force
- persuasion
- rewards
- personal style
- bargaining techniques
- negotiating and mediating skills
- coalition-building approaches
- allocation strategies for the benefits, material rewards, and punishments (1989, pp. 500–501)

Time Allocation

After people and money, time is the next most precious resource a manager has to work with. In some ways, it is the most valuable, for lost time never truly can be replaced. Often a task that should have been done at one point does not have the same consequences if done later. The folk adage about the foolishness of "closing the barn door after the horse has gone" illustrates the point. Timing can be critical.

Many criminal justice agencies need to conduct operations 24 hours a day, 7 days a week, including all holidays. This adds to the time-management demands a criminal justice manager must meet. Reflecting their 24-hour-a-day operations, many criminal justice agencies use shifts, and essentially become three suborganizations with entirely different staff members on duty at different times of the day. Whatever these shift teams are called—be they midnight, daylight, and twilight or first, second, and third—a criminal justice manager faces additional challenges with continuous operations (Shiftwork Solutions, 2003). Some agencies will have **rotating shifts,** and others will have **fixed shifts.**

If shift rotation is the option the manager selects, a **rotation plan** will have to be developed that shows how the shifts will change. There are many options to consider in shift rotation. There is a debate in the research literature about the merits of shifting forward or shifting back, slow or quick rotations, partial rotations (some staff on fixed shifts, others rotating), and even oscillating shifts, in which one shift is fixed and the other two swap work hours (Shiftwork Solutions, 2005).

Time-Management Tools

A number of techniques for time management have been developed. Among them are the **Gantt chart,** developed by Henry L. Gantt (1861–1919), a contemporary and colleague of Frederick Taylor (Massie, 1987, pp. 17, 24), and a prolific author of books and articles on management in the early decades of the 20th century (Gantt, 1903, 1916/1973, 1919). The Gantt chart is a form of bar chart in which each task is given a horizontal line scaled to reflect how long that task should require. Time thus is depicted graphically (Massie, 1987, p. 149). There were earlier attempts to manage time graphically, including the **"harmonogram"** of Karol Adamiecki (Marsh, 1975).

Karol Adamiecki (1866–1933) was a Polish engineer and cofounder, in 1925, of the Polish Institute of Scientific Management. He is credited with developing the prototype of the Gantt chart. Adamiecki called it a "harmonograf," and others called it a "harmonogram."

Reading and Using a Gantt Chart

Regardless of the contribution of Adamiecki, it was Henry Gantt, an American engineer, who introduced his version of the chart to American managers to use as a graphic device to aid in scheduling and monitoring the progress of complex projects.

The chart is a scheduling tool that illustrates time in a linear graphic format. Today a Gantt chart can be developed using Microsoft Project, Microsoft Excel, or specialized software expressly written to produce Gantt charts such as SmartDraw® and MatchWare.® However, in Gantt's day, one would be prepared on graph paper.

The horizontal axis represents time, and the vertical axis lists the key components of the project. Equally spaced horizontal bars in the chart represent time units (the hours or days or weeks or months) needed to complete each component of the project. The criminal justice manager using a Gantt chart will break down the project into discretely defined pieces and list them in approximate chronological order on the left margin (vertical axis) of the chart.

BOX 10.1 ADVANTAGES AND DISADVANTAGES OF SHIFT ROTATION

ADVANTAGES	DISADVANTAGES

Rotating Shifts

Skills are balanced on every shift. Because all crews take equal turns at covering the undesirable shifts (weekends and nights), there is no incentive for all of the senior, more skilled workers to pool together on a single crew.

All workers are given equal exposure to the day shift. As crews rotate through their turn on day shift, they are exposed to managers, engineers, vendors, and company support personnel.

Training assets can be consolidated. Because all employees rotate through day shifts, there is no need to duplicate training efforts on all shifts.

Product uniformity goes up. As a result of equal training, equal exposure to support and management, and equal skills, all crews will perform in a much more uniform manner.

Employees prefer fixed shifts. About 90 percent of all shift workers prefer fixed shifts to rotating shifts.

Unbalanced workloads are difficult to manage with rotating shifts. If the work to be done on different shifts differs greatly, there may be a problem with essentially identical crews being assigned to the work.

It is generally more difficult for the body to adjust to rotating shifts. Slowing down the rotation rate can mitigate this.

Fixed Shifts

On a fixed-shift schedule, each crew comes into work at about the same time every day they are scheduled to work. Some variations include a rotation between days off during the week and varying shift lengths.

Employees prefer fixed shifts. The reasons for this vary. Senior people want to get (and stay) on day shift. Junior employees like the idea of eventually being able to get to a favorite shift. And most people simply want the stability of always knowing when they do not have to be at work—allowing them to better plan their family and social lives.

Unbalanced workloads can be more easily matched. If the workload is lighter on the night shift or if it requires different skills, it is a simple matter to create a crew that matches that specific condition.

Recruiting new employees becomes more difficult. After a brief training period, new hires are generally assigned to the least desirable shifts. Often it is many years before they can get transferred to the shift they want.

Different shifts become different companies. As the disparities between the crews (skills, seniority, morale, etc.) grow, the crews themselves will become more independent of each other. This can affect productivity, safety, quality, attrition, and other performance measures.

Source: Adapted from Shiftwork Solutions (2005).

Figure 10.1 shows a plan that assumes a total of 49 weeks of work, but the program only runs from mid-January to the end of August, about 32 weeks. The value of a Gantt chart is that it illustrates what tasks can be undertaken concurrently, and also indicates which participants are involved in implementing the plan at any moment. For example,

\multicolumn{14}{l}{Vollmer City Police Department (VCPD) Community-Oriented Policing (COP) Initiative}
Event	Participants	Task	Start	End	Weeks	Jan	Feb	Mar	Apr	May	Jun	Jul	Aug
---	---	---	---	---	---	---	---	---	---	---	---	---	---
1	Contractor	prepares draft of community concerns survey, briefs Chief and conducts survey	1/15	1/29	2	[---							
2	Contractor and Chief	analyze input from community surveys to design VCPD COP plan	2/1	2/8	1		[-]						
3	Chief and community leaders	meet to create neighborhood partnerships and secure more community input for COP	2/14	2/28	2		[--]						
4	VCPD Training Division and Contractor	prepare training plan and develop lesson modules for the VCPD trial COP program	2/8	3/10	4		[-----	--]					
5	Chief and City Manager and CityCouncil	approve and fund the implementation of VCPD trial COP program	2/15	2/15	1		[]						
6	VCPD supervisors and Personnel Director	recruit, interview and select COP cadre within VCPD	2/15	3/12	4		[----	--]					
7	Contractor, VCPD managers and key city leaders	conduct the VCPD COP training program for new cadre on site	3/16	3/31	2			[----]					
8	VCPD PIO and Chief	prepare press releases and hold press conferences on new trial COP program	3/16	3/31	2			[----]					
9	VCPD Operations Division & Chief	open COP-neighborhood kiosks around Vollmer City	4/1	4/8	1				[--]				
10	Chief, Operations Division, and new COP cadre	initiate trial COP program and deploy staff to kiosks	4/1	7/31	13				[--------	---------	---------	--------]	
11	Chief, COP cadre and Operations Division	collect data on VCPD trial COP program efforts and kiosk activities	4/15	8/15	15					[---	---------	---------	----]	
12	Chief and City Manager	evaluate trial COP program and kiosk activities data to revise program as needed	8/16	8/30	2								[---]

FIGURE 10.1 Sample Gantt Chart for Community-Oriented Policing Program.

on February 15, the plan will require the efforts of the Chief of Police, the City Manager, the City Council, the contractor hired to help design the plan, the staff of the Vollmer City Police Department (VCPD) Training Division, the VCPD supervisors, and the VCPD Personnel Director.

A more careful consideration of the plan will reveal that some tasks must be concluded successfully before other tasks can be initiated. For example, the training cannot proceed until the training plan and lesson modules are completed and the community-oriented policing (COP) cadre are chosen. This interdependency of tasks can be discovered using a simple Gantt chart, but such interdependence and the consequences of delays in much more complex projects are not as easy to identify using a Gantt chart. This led to the development of other graphic representation tools for time management, including the Critical Path Method (CPM) and Program Evaluation and Review Technique (PERT).

Network Analysis with CPM and PERT

Network analysis was the next graphic time-management approach to be developed. It provided a better way to illustrate the more complex interdependency of tasks in large-scale projects. In the 1950s, two very similar versions were developed essentially in parallel: the **Critical Path Method (CPM)** and the **Program Evaluation and Review Technique (PERT).** Today CPM and PERT have been blended into a common technique, the one

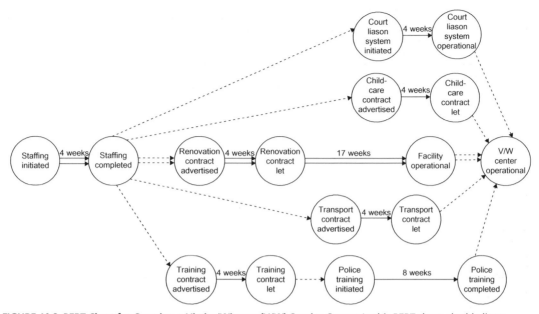

FIGURE 10.2 PERT Chart for Opening a Victim/Witness (V/W) Service Center. In this PERT chart, double lines designate the critical path. *Source: Reprinted by permission of Waveland Press, Inc., from Sylvia, Ronald D., Kathleen M. Sylvia, and Elizabeth M. Gunn. Program Planning and Evaluation for the Public Manager, 2nd ed. Prospect Heights, IL: Waveland Press, Inc., 1997. All rights reserved.*

illustrated in the **PERT chart** in Figure 10.2. Various criminal justice and public service applications have been offered (Clayton, 1980; Sylvia, Sylvia, & Gunn, 1997).

Network analysis uses the concepts of *events* and *activities*. An **event** typically is the accomplishment of a task, and an **activity** is the performance of a task. Events will occur at a moment in time, while activities require time to be accomplished (they have duration). CPM/PERT recognizes that some events must be accomplished prior to the beginning of some activities.

The CPM/PERT technique allows a manager to represent this interaction of events and activities graphically, recognizing that there are **leader events** and **follower events.** They are linked together with **activity arrows,** which are connected into **pathways.** The pathway that actually determines how long a project will take is designated the **critical path.**

Some of the leader events must be done on schedule in order to avoid delaying a complex task. Others can be delayed for various durations without upsetting the project time table. The amount of time in which an event can occur without producing a delay for subsequent events is its **float time.** Some float time can be expended with absolutely no consequences on subsequent events **(free float),** while other float time consumes later available float time (**interfering float**). A manager can schedule work most efficiently by computing each of these and setting work-event completion times to reflect these floats. The PERT chart also allows a criminal justice manager to calculate the impact of any delays in events on the final completion of a project or on intermediate activities and events. The basic principle is that any change that adds to any activity on the critical path will produce a corresponding delay in the time needed to complete the entire project.

Today, computer programs can do all the complex calculations of float times and all the intermediate computations required to prepare a PERT chart. Complex tasks, involving hundreds of people and performing hundreds of interrelated activities, can be coordinated by using such a chart, with the optimal use of time. Learning how to compute CPM/PERT equations is not necessary in this day and age, but learning how to read a PERT chart is a basic skill a criminal justice manager will need to acquire.

Allocating Equipment and Facilities

The facilities and equipment of an organization are part of its physical environment. They create the capacities of and restraints on the organization. Reflecting the importance of equipment and facilities, the capital budget of an organization often is kept separate from the operational budget. Unfortunately, it is often the capital budget that gets cut, which leaves the organizational aspects without their essential physical environment support base. The physical plant of an organization is important to the overall ability of the organization to perform its mission.

Even before Charles Babbage, whose contributions on the applications of advanced technologies to improved management were mentioned in Chapter 3, leaders in business, industry, and public service saw the advantages that equipment and facilities can provide to advancing organizational objectives. Since the 1980s, the computer has become the instrument of influence, as the telephone was some 70 years earlier and the telegraph before that. In law enforcement, the automobile changed the nature of police patrol from the 1930s foot-patrol approach to the fully motorized police of the 1960s.

Facilities and equipment can also be used as incentives or rewards for performance. The "best office" can be assigned to the best worker as a reward. New desks and furnishings can be used to uplift morale. A company car is a major perk for some employees, and especially fitting for those who have to be available "on call." Similarly, facilities and equipment can be used to improve agency morale. Paint and new carpet can make a sterile workplace feel cozy. An agency that lacks the resources to have their offices refurbished can allocate a day to improvements, with the agency buying only the paints and materials to make the improvements and the employees supplying the labor. Such an exercise can improve agency morale and commitment to the agency. The labor donated by the workers to make improvements in the facilities becomes a basis for greater personal involvement, an emotional investment in the place.

Facilities and equipment can promote positive change in an organization. When outdated ways are yielding a performance deficit or there is an attitude problem toward the work, new equipment and facilities can provide a means to overcome these problems. For example, the acquisition of advanced probationer monitoring devices can enhance the overall productivity of a probation office, reduce the labors of probation officers, keep better track of probationers, and improve the overall mission of probation services in the community. New equipment and new or rehabilitated facilities also can improve agency morale.

Providing advanced facilities and equipment can improve performance. Better equipment and facilities can result in improved work quality when used properly, but often agencies will become slaves to their equipment and facilities—old technologies retard them; new technologies overwhelm them. Sometimes people rely excessively on technological solutions, often ignoring older, simpler, and more reliable methods. In some offices, when "the computer is down," all work stops because people have become overly dependent on the technology. It is a managerial responsibility to see that this does not happen.

A criminal justice manager is responsible for the allocation of the equipment and facilities available to his or her agency. The manager can further allocate equipment and facilities, either using formulas or on a case-by-case basis, to support agency operations. The equipment and facilities at the disposal of each agency reflects each agency's mission, size, and circumstances. A fictionalized example based on real examples is provided in Box 10.2.

Assignments to preferred duties and provision of better equipment, better offices, new furniture, and so on, are perquisites (**perks**) that a manager can use as rewards and incentives. This aspect of the allocation function is an important managerial power, but in some cases it has to be diluted by union agreements and seniority systems. When such limitations are absent or do not specifically apply, however, then such allocations are the rewards that can enhance the power, authority, and esteem of the manager who wisely distributes them.

BOX 10.2 ALLOCATION OF "PLUM" ASSIGNMENTS

The Vanderbilt County Sheriff's Department has both four-wheel, rough-terrain vehicles and several power boats to provide patrol and protective services in and around the Fosdick Mountain resort areas, many of which can be accessed only by rough forest trails, and on Lake Peel, a popular summer vacation area in the county. The Vanderbilt County Sheriff has learned that assigning deputies to lake patrol duty in the late Spring through the Fall is considered a **plum assignment** and has made selection for lake duty a reward for excellent performance by his deputies.

The Chief of Police in Vollmer City has nothing to compare with lake duty, but does assign new police cruisers to officers with accident-free driving records as a reward for their good safety records. Getting one of the oldest police cars is a subtle but clearly noticed acknowledgment that the officer has not been careful with his or her previous police vehicle. The Chief also is considering rewarding his most community-oriented officers (i.e., those with the fewest complaints filed against them by the public and those receiving the most favorable letters from the public) by offering them assignments to the COP kiosks in the city commercial center and shopping malls and other community-oriented–policing assignments.

The capital facilities given to an agency are valuable public assets for which the agency manager must provide care and maintenance. While no one expects the warden of the Alexander Maconochie Correctional Center to actually make repairs to buildings and equipment at the prison, it is expected that he will ensure that his middle managers will see to having it done. The police vehicles of the Vollmer City Police Department need routine oil changes and occasional repairs. The chief is not the one who will be changing oil and replacing oil filters, but it is the chief who is responsible for seeing that it is done. So an additional allocational duty of a criminal justice manager is providing the funds, time, and personnel to attend to such important maintenance functions.

Fiscal Management and Funding Sources in Public Service

Appropriated Funds

A legislative body can allocate an agency either a total sum ("cap") or dictate detailed expenditures by category ("line items"). Agencies either can submit budget proposals to their legislatures or respond to allocations given to them. It is common for the two to occur at the same time. For example, an agency proposes a budget to its legislative body; the legislature provides some part of it; the agency then prepares a revised budget to use the funds actually provided. Money voted to an agency or program by a legislative body, or allocated to it under legal rules, usually from tax collections, fines, forfeitures, or user fees, is known as its **appropriation**. Greg Caldeira and Andrew Cowart (1980) studied congressional appropriations from 1935 to 1975 and observed that federal expenditures on criminal justice reflected changing crime rates. However, a 2009 article by Nancy Marion and William Oliver came to different conclusions. With official crime rates in a long-term decline since the 1970s, congressional expenditures on crime control now reflect a more symbolic expression of congressional support for crime fighting policies.

Tax Revenues

Most appropriations for government agencies come from taxes levied against income, property, services, or commercial transactions. Taxes collected for public purposes are not especially popular in the United States, and many jurisdictions seek other ways of funding essential public services.

Fines and Forfeitures

Fines and forfeitures are funding sources readily available to criminal justice agencies. Under federal or state law or via local ordinances, agencies can be authorized to collect fines and seize property that can be sold to raise additional revenues. In compliance with laws or regulations, these fines and forfeiture revenues either are retained by the agency to continue its operations or are turned over to the government treasury or fiscal agency. Court assessments known as **court costs** are not "fines" in a legal sense but are actually **user fees.** Agencies must follow laws, rules, and guidelines for the expenditure of such funds; the general rule is that these funds may be used only for purposes approved in advance by the funding jurisdiction. The actual expenditures are subject to periodic audit.

User Fees

User fees are funds collected by government agencies for the services or goods they provide to the public or other agencies. In compliance with the laws or regulations that set them, these fees either are retained by the agency to fund continuing operations or are turned over directly to the treasury or fiscal agency of the government. Licenses of all kinds are considered to be user fees, although many are used to raise revenues well beyond the actual cost of services or goods provided.

Nonappropriated Funds

The revenues and resources that come from other than tax appropriations—including earnings, gifts, grants, and other lawful conversions to cash of agency services and products—fall within the category of nonappropriated funds. Among the many sources of such funds are employee association dues and club fees, agency fund-raisers, fees for and profits from vending machines installed in agency buildings, profits from sales of logo items, donated frequent flyer credits, interest on agency deposits from other sources, and any other income not derived from tax revenues or other legislated sources such as user fees, fines, and forfeiture. The rules governing expenditures of such funds may differ from those associated with appropriations, and often an agency manager will have far greater latitude in spending these funds. They are commonly used for social events and gifts within the workforce or to purchase items that cannot be acquired with appropriated funds. However, when legislation or rules require that nonappropriated funds be returned to the treasury or reported in the budget and managed in the same fashion as appropriated funds, then these will be treated as if they were appropriated funds.

Other Budget Terms

A variety of additional terms are used in relation to budgeting in government service. A contemporary criminal justice manager is quite likely to encounter most of the terms that follow.

Capital Budget

The line items in an agency budget that pay for long-lasting agency assets, such as its buildings and durable goods—that is, those items of equipment that will last for many years—often are treated separately from other categories of funds. These are referred to as the **capital budget.**

Operational Budget

In contrast to the capital budget, the expenditures that will be consumed in the ordinary operations of the agency are classified as parts of its **operational budget.** Usually salaries; consumables such as gasoline, electricity, water, and other utilities; short-lived equipment; office supplies; postage; and other expendable items fall within this category.

Personnel Budget

Agency expenditures that have to do with staffing often are identified and separated into a **personnel budget** or staffing budget category. Such items as salaries, training costs, medical insurance, withholding taxes, Federal Insurance Contributions Act (FICA) tax, and agency contributions to retirement plans are all typical personnel items in a budget.

Expendables

Items that are consumed ("expended") or rendered to be of no further value by their use are classified as **expendables.** In policing, bullets and paper clips are typical expendables. In any office, copier paper, envelopes, pens, and pencils are typical expendables. In standard accounting practice, the issue of the item to an "end user" will terminate its audit record. As soon as it is placed in the hands of an appropriate user, it is considered expended, even if it has yet to be consumed.

Accountables

Items of agency property that have greater value and that can endure after initial use are classified as **accountables.** Uniforms, weapons, and some kinds of equipment (such as office machines, computers, scanners, telephones, office furniture, and recording equipment) eventually will wear out or become obsolete, but for some time they will be inventoried and their users will be held accountable for them. The audit train of an accountable item ends only when it is turned in and sold as scrap or is properly disposed of. For example, when old weapons no longer are considered safely serviceable, they will be destroyed and a witnessed destruction certificate will be put on file to document their disposal.

Supplemental Appropriations

Legislatures and local legislative bodies can authorize additional funds to an agency in the middle of a budgetary term to meet unplanned needs or urgent requirements. These are called **supplemental appropriations.**

Encumbered Funds

Encumbered funds are funds against which obligations already have been made, although not yet paid.

Sequestering

Withholding or canceling a previously approved (appropriated) government expenditure or obligation occasionally becomes necessary. **Sequestering** may be ordered by either the executive or the legislative branch of government, and it can be conditional or absolute.

Proration

In difficult economic times, government or agency budgets may be cut "across the board" by legislative or executive action. In some states such uniform cuts are referred to as **prorations,** the proportional reduction of an entire budget or select budget lines.

Diversions

Under legislation, regulation, or executive orders, funds can be redirected from one agency or budget category to another. For example, because of a drop in fuel prices, a surplus that develops in the Vollmer City Police Department "fuels" line item can be diverted to cover the increased expenditures in the local courts caused by an unexpected postal rate increase. A **diversion** often takes the form of a supplemental appropriation for the beneficiary.

"Bill-Payers" and "Beneficiaries"

The **bill-payers** are the agencies that give up funds under diversions. The **beneficiaries** are the agencies or programs that gain funds under diversions. As another example, the Vollmer City Police Department becomes the bill-payer when it is instructed to reallocate $1.5 million in operating funds to the Vollmer City Fire and Rescue Department (the beneficiary) to cover its operational shortfall due to a massive chemical spill.

Return on Investment (ROI)

In economics, the **return on investment (ROI)** is the realized gain of an investment minus the cost of that investment divided by the cost of the investment:

$$ROI = [gain - cost]/cost$$

In a criminal justice application, the Vanderbilt County Courts have been paying $1.8 million in overtime salaries to clear a backlog of paperwork. The chief clerk secures an appropriation of $800,000 to purchase new computers and software and to hire a contractor to help install the new system and train the existing clerical staff. In the first year of the program, overtime salaries are cut in half to $900,000, and most of the backlog is caught up. ROI = [$1,800,000 – $900,000]–$800,000/$800,000 = 12.5%. In this illustration, the new equipment, software, and training produce a savings of $100,000 in the first year and reduce overtime demands on the staff. Most ROIs are not this profitable as quickly, but new cost-cutting technologies and methods do repay their initial costs over time.

Value-Added Contributions (VACs)

An expenditure for new equipment or training can add to the productivity of the organization or the work output of the newly trained staff. These expenditures are referred to as **value-added contributions (VACs).** In some cases this can be measured by making before-and-after comparisons, but more often this is not possible. If a new technology or new training strategy makes the agency more efficient, often work output will increase, but new tasks that had not been considered before also will be undertaken. Some VACs are either hypothetical or defy actual calculation, such as improved skills and confidence, better worker relations, or personal workplace fulfillment. Some VACs are simply estimated. Some can be identified via surveys of those involved (i.e., managers, workers, and clients). Often it is difficult to assign a definite dollar amount to a savings on such a theoretical abstraction, but some do try (Whetten, 1989). Even if they defy accurate measurement, these value-added contributions are real consequences of some agency expenditures.

Subscriptions

Subscriptions are rarely used now, but once governments actively served as collection agencies for "subscriptions" for public services or projects. For example, when several civic groups in Vollmer City wished to build a monument to commemorate the city's hero and namesake, August Vollmer, the city council voted to appropriate no public funds for the purpose. Instead, it instructed the city treasurer to collect donations and hold them until sufficient funds were donated to build the monument. Many employees of the police department took part in the fund-raising efforts when off duty, and the money was "subscribed" in just 8 months. In many states, there are items on tax return forms that permit and encourage the taxpayer to donate to various state-approved endeavors. These are contemporary subscriptions to which you can contribute when you file your state tax return. By doing so, you give up some part of your tax refund, which then is held by the state for use by this state-sponsored fund.

Check-Offs

Check-offs are provisions of the tax-collection process that allow small sums of tax dollars to go to specific purposes. These are modified subscriptions. Two contemporary check-offs with which you might be familiar are the federal and state election campaign withholdings, both collected when a taxpayer voluntarily elects to designate a small part of their tax payment to these funds. Some states make extensive use of both tax check-offs and subscriptions, wherein you transfer a small part of your state tax return to some state-endorsed public fund or activity.

Pass-Throughs

When an agency serves to transfer funds from one source to another, with little or no direct benefit to itself, it is understood to be passing such funds through as a convenience to both the spending and receiving parties. Police and sheriff's departments and other criminal justice agencies occasionally allow their officers to take private employment for which the agency functions as an employment agency. Officers are hired out to private parties who pay the agency and then see that the officers are paid overtime rates for their services. These sources of income and expenditure are classic **pass-through** items.

Sunk Costs

Sunk costs are the historical expenditures of an organization that cannot be effectively recovered by cessation of their use and that cannot be liquidated for their original value because the actual and book value has declined or depreciated substantially. **Book values** are market-based or depreciation-based assessments of the value of property or equipment belonging to the organization. The "book" referred to is the ledger of the organization wherein the property is listed as an asset.

Depreciation

Depreciation is the process whereby an asset declines in value over its useful life. It can be calculated as either "straight-line" or by some "accelerated" formula. Some assets will depreciate to zero value, while others will retain a salvage value (a term described below).

Surplus Properties

Surplus properties are assets of the organization that no longer are needed for current and anticipated organizational operations. When laws and regulations permit, these surplus properties may be sold off and the funds received will be returned to the treasury or added to the selling agency's budget. Police departments routinely sell off high-mileage police cars, and all criminal justice agencies have old computers and other outdated technologies that can be sold, often only as scrap. Occasionally, real estate becomes surplus and unused land and buildings will be offered up for sale.

Salvage Value

Salvage value, also known as scrap value, is the price that can be anticipated when an organizational asset is disposed of at the end of its useful life. Rarely is aged surplus property of much value, and the return is a very small fraction of the original expense.

However, there are other advantages to disposing of surplus property for its salvage value, one of the most obvious being freeing up storage space and reducing the labor of maintaining inventories of obsolete and broken equipment.

Budgeting Approaches

Budgeting is an important aspect of fiscal management in criminal justice. It is a specific subarea of organizational planning (Fox 1983). There are four commonly used approaches to budgeting:

1. traditional, line-item, and incremental budgets
2. program planning and budgeting system (PPBS) and performance budgets
3. pay-as-you-go (PayGo) budgets
4. zero-based budgeting (ZBB)

Line-item budgeting (or **incremental budgeting**) is the traditional approach to preparing a budget. Usually this method uses expenditure from past budget periods to project expenses for the coming period, usually done by "line item":

- salaries
- copiers
- vehicles
- stationery
- uniforms
- gasoline

It is the easiest form of budgeting to do, the most reliable in a static organizational environment, and the easiest to modify if there are cost increases in any particular areas. If postage rates rise, the amount of the increase will be added to the prior year's postage expenses. If gasoline costs drop, a savings will be reflected in the new budget. If new people are hired, their salaries will be added to the existing personnel line. In this way, the budget is modified up or down with "incremental" adjustments from the prior budget term (Tucker 1982).

The **program planning and budgeting system (PPBS)** and the closely related **performance budgeting** are related to management by objectives (MBO). Just like in other MBO applications, the manager preparing or revising the budget first considers the agency mission and then its needs, goals, and objectives; he or she then conducts a search for alternative ways to accomplish the objectives. When a good alternative is found, a program is designed or modified and its budget prepared.

A large organization often will prepare separate subunit budgets, using either the same PPBS approach or by requiring subunits to use traditional line-item budgets for their components. For example, a large correctional institution may use PPBS overall, but its central kitchen may be given a line-item budget for its budget planning.

Another aspect of PPBS performance budgeting is that the actual work done is recognized in the budget allocation for operations. A jailer will be given a fixed amount for each inmate for each day that inmate is held. If the number of inmates in custody rises, the funds available will automatically rise in direct proportion. If the number in custody declines, the total amount available will decline. The amount per person remains constant, but the available funds will increase or decrease to match the jail population. PPBS commonly is used in preparing a budget for a new program or activity. It is heavily used in grant development. It is performance- and program-oriented (Schick, 1966). When new activities are being planned, PPBS methods can be adapted as activity-based budgeting (Shane, 2005).

The **PayGo (pay-as-you-go) budgeting** process involves matching expenditures to revenues. Some criminal justice agencies and activities actually raise revenues. In a PayGo budgeting plan, the more revenues collected, the more will be available for agency operations, equipment, or facilities. The approach approximates the approaches of private, for-profit businesses. Top-end expenditure levels may be set by the legislation or regulations governing the process, but actual expenditures or obligation of funds cannot occur above the level of funds actually taken in by the agency or the government setting the PayGo terms. Revenue sharing between police agencies and the courts will occur by the allocation of fines and court costs. Parking ticket collections can be set aside for supporting the ordinance enforcement costs. Profits from correctional industries can be used to initiate new correctional activities. The PayGo process often is used when severe financial restrictions are being encountered, especially in governments having strict balanced-budget rules.

Zero-based budgeting (ZBB) is related to MBO, using a "from-the-ground-up" approach to building a budget. An agency's activities are subdivided into its components, and programs are then prioritized. Then each program is divided into its component activities, and these are prioritized, using a task-oriented approach. Within each program, a PPBS or line budget is prepared. If full funding cannot be provided, the lowest-priority activities and programs are cut. Funds are allocated to the most effective aspects of the organizational activities. In this way, every activity and program is reassessed for its importance in each budgetary term. ZBB often is used when agencies are facing severe financial and program reductions.

Summary

A contemporary criminal justice manager is responsible for the allocation of money, time, equipment, and facilities within the organization in support of the organizational mission. This function is supported by complex time-management and budgetary systems. There may be a time when you, as a future junior manager, will be responsible for allocation functions within your unit. Knowing that such resources exist and knowing how to recognize them will help you acquire the knowledge you will need to schedule and budget, allocate scarce resources, and best use facilities that have been entrusted to you.

LEARNING OBJECTIVES

Upon finishing this chapter, you should be able to do the following:

1. Identify the four major assets of a criminal justice organization that its manager is responsible for allocating.
2. Recognize and explain the data elements graphically represented on a Gantt chart and a PERT network analysis chart.
3. Compare the differences in the four major types of agency budgeting systems.
4. Distinguish between appropriated and nonappropriated funds, and discuss the possible sources of both in a criminal justice agency.
5. Identify key facilities and equipment of a criminal justice agency that its manager can allocate as rewards.

IMPORTANT TERMS AND NAMES

- *accountable*
- *activity*
- *activity arrows*
- *allocation function*
- *appropriation*
- *beneficiaries*
- *bill-payers*
- *book values*
- *capital budget*
- *check-offs*
- *court costs*
- *critical path*
- *Critical Path Method (CPM)*
- *depreciation*
- *diversion*
- *encumbered funds*
- *event*
- *expendables*
- *fines and forfeitures*
- *fixed shifts*
- *float time*
- *follower events*
- *free float*
- *Gantt chart*
- *harmonogram*
- *incremental budgeting*
- *interfering float*

- *leader events*
- *line-item budgeting*
- *network analysis*
- *operational budget*
- *pass-through*
- *pathways*
- *PayGo/pay-as-you-go budgeting*
- *performance budgeting*
- *perk*
- *personnel budget*
- *physical plant*
- *plum assignment*
- *Program Evaluation Review Technique (PERT)*
- *proration*
- *PERT Chart*
- *program planning and budgeting system (PPBS)*
- *return on investment (ROI)*
- *rotating shifts*
- *rotation plan*
- *salvage value*
- *sequestering*
- *subscriptions*
- *sunk costs*
- *supplemental appropriation*
- *surplus properties*
- *user fees*
- *value-added contributions (VACs)*
- *zero-based budgeting (ZBB)*

References and Supplemental Sources

Caldeira, G. A., & Cowart, A. T. (1980). Budgets, institutions and change: Criminal justice policy in America. *American Journal of Political Science, 24*(3), 413–438.

Clayton, R. (1980). Techniques of network analysis for managers. In: White, M. J., Clayton, R., Myrtle, R., Siegel, G., & Rose, A. (Eds.), *Managing public systems: Analytic techniques for public administration.* North Scituate, MA: Duxbury.

Fox, V. (1983). *Fiscal management: Correctional institutions.* Englewood Cliffs, NJ: Prentice Hall. (pp. 264–280)

Gantt, H. L. (1903). A graphical daily balance in manufacture. *Transactions of the American Society of Mechanical Engineers, 24,* 1322–1336.

Gantt, H. L. (1916/1973). *Work, wages, and profits* (2nd ed.). New York: Engineering Magazine. (Reprinted 1973, Easton, MD: Hive)

Gantt, H. L. (1919/1973). *Organizing for work.* New York: Harcourt, Brace, and Howe. (Reprinted 1973, Easton, MD: Hive)

Marion, N. E., & Oliver, W. M. (2009, June). Congress, crime, and budgetary responsiveness: A study in symbolic politics. *Criminal Justice Policy Review, 20-2,* 115–135.

Marsh, Edward R. (1975). The harmonogram of Karol Adamiecki. *The Academy of Management Journal, 18*(2), 358–364.

Massie, J. L. (1987). *Essentials of management* (4th ed.). Englewood Cliffs, NJ: Prentice Hall.

Schick, A. (1966, December). The road to PPBS, the stages of budget reform. *Public Administration Review, 26,* 243–258.

Shane, J. M. (2005). Activity-based budgeting: Creating a nexus between workload and costs. *FBI Law Enforcement Bulletin, 74*(6), 11–23.

Shiftwork Solutions (2003). Fixed shift schedules or rotating shift schedules. *Shiftwork Solutions LLC.* Retrieved from <http://www.shift-work.com/law.htm/>.

Shiftwork Solutions (2005). Fixed shift schedules or rotating shift schedules? *Shiftwork Solutions LLC.* Retrieved from <http://www.shift-work.com/shiftwork-search.htm/>.

Sylvia, R. D., Sylvia, K. M., & Gunn, E. M. (1997). *Program planning and evaluation for the public manager* (2nd ed.). Prospect Heights, IL: Waveland Press.

Tucker, H. J. (1982). Incremental budgeting: Myth or model? *Western Political Quarterly, 35*(3), 327–338.

Whetten, D. A. (1989). What constitutes a theoretical contribution? *Academy of Management Review, 14*(4), 490–495.

Yates, D., Jr. (1985). *The politics of management.* San Francisco: Jossey-Bass.

Yates, D., Jr. (1989). Identifying and using political resources. In: Ott, J. S. (Ed.), *Classic readings in organizational behavior* (pp. 500–509). Pacific Grove, CA: Brooks/Cole.

11

Reporting for Criminal Justice: Information Management and Organizational Communications

In both POSDCORB and LODESTAR the "R" represents the "reporting" functions of the criminal justice manager. In Luther Gulick's time, most reporting was done orally or in writing on paper. The earliest applications of electronically assisted communications were in use then. The telephone had been in use since the 1880s, the two-way radio was in use in police operations, and intercom systems existed within some correctional units. However, other than the telephone, these criminal justice applications were quite limited in their impact on managerial communications. In contemporary times, that reporting function has been expanded via the use of additional communications media such as television (including cable channels), fax machines, voice mail, e-mail, and other computer-based communications, such as blogs, podcasting, instant messaging, and the use of Internet **social-networking** sites like Facebook (Abram & Pearlman, 2008; Sahlin & Botello, 2007), YouTube (Fahs, 2007; Miller, 2007), Twitter, Flickr, LinkedIn, and so many more (Wikipedia, 2011). If anything, the modern criminal justice manager is facing a severe communication overload—too much information coming from too many sources of information.

Trained in psychology and in the principles of scientific management, Mary Parker Follett nevertheless clearly foreshadowed the human relations school. In 1926, in her frequently reprinted article (1989), "The Giving of Orders," she advocated coordination as the key to successful management. Arguing against authoritarian commands, she observed that, "One might say that the strength of favorable response to an order is in inverse ratio to the distance the order travels. Production efficiency is always in danger of being affected whenever the long distance order is substituted for the face-to-face suggestion" (1926/1989, p. 256). "It is not the face-to-face suggestion that we want so much as the joint study of the problem" (1926/1989, p. 260). As mentioned earlier in this text, she wisely observed that "orders will not take the place of training" (1926/1989, p. 256). "One person should not give orders to another person, but both should agree to take their orders from the situation" (1926/1989, p. 259).

Follett advocated a three-part process to giving instructions: (1) they should not be orders, but the law of the situation; (2) one should recognize that situations are always evolving, so rigid orders are quite out of place most of the time; and (3) orders should be circular (reciprocal) in character, not linear (unidirectional) behavior (1926/1989, p. 263).

Reporting Obligations

The contemporary criminal justice manager has reporting obligations to superiors, to the public, to the press, to peers, and to subordinates. Precisely what those reporting requirements are varies according to the information possessed by the manager, laws, confidentiality regulations, security classification rules, and policies of the agency. As a general principle, more information is better than less information, but there are clear exceptions. Modern criminal justice managers have numerous means of communicating the information they possess, including direct communication in spoken and written messages, broadcast methods such as e-mails and organizational memos, and formal reports. Managers also are called on to address the mass communications media, including newspapers, radio, and television, especially in crisis situations and when dealing with major criminal cases.

Communication Styles

Communication styles vary with the individual manager. Some criminal justice managers are excellent communicators and enjoy the opportunity to convey their ideas by various means. Others are reluctant communicators and uncomfortable expressing themselves. Some prefer to write messages rather than speak in public, or vice versa. The type of manager will predict the preferred method of communication. Type A managers who use Theory X strategies generally prefer direct orders and explicit directions. Type B managers generally prefer dialog and discussion.

How does a criminal justice manager best convey ideas? Recall that Mary Parker Follett advocated, "not the face-to-face suggestion ... so much as the joint study of the problem." Follett favored circular or reciprocal communications. She advised against giving orders. Even the Type A, Theory X manager (the authoritarian order giver) cannot be sure his or her orders will be followed. The Type B, Theory Y manager faces an even more difficult problem because this style lacks the clarity of direct orders.

Communicative Behavior

Four basic patterns of managerial communication have been described: (1) *controlling:* the manager dominates discussions, gives direction, and does not listen much to subordinates or peers; (2) *relinquishing:* the manager gives up most of his or her influence and allows others to dominate exchanges; (3) *defending:* the manager withdraws from exchanges passively, or withdraws altogether, is not involved in the discussions, and avoids the issues that are raised; (4) *developing:* the manager encourages and participates in reciprocal exchanges of ideas, acknowledges and uses other's ideas, shares thoughts, and remains involved in the process throughout.

Communications Audiences

A criminal justice manager has obligations to report to superiors, to the public, to the press, to peers, and to subordinates. The reporting obligations differ according to the audience. Within the organization, formal communications should follow the chain of command (Klofas, Stojkovic, & Kalinich, 1990, pp. 56–57) and often must conform to rigid rules and procedures regarding issues such as the number of copies and their distribution, who must be informed, in what sequence, and so on.

The communications process involves organizing a thought, referred to as "encoding." The message then is "transmitted" through some communications medium, known as the "channel." Those receiving that message then "decode" that message into their own thoughts (Klofas, Stojkovic, & Kalinich, 1990, p. 54). Both the encoding and decoding processes involve the science of semantics, the study of meaning in communication. Both the coder and decoder of the message apply their interpretations to the words used. Ronald Lynch (1986) was the first to note that there are two elements to communication in criminal justice contexts: (1) what is said or written in a given exchange, and (2) the history of interactions among the principles sharing the communication (Lynch & Lynch 2005).

Moreover, there are many forms of communication. How do we communicate?

- spoken words
- written words
- tonal qualities merged with spoken words
- body language
- symbolic and other nonverbal means

Some managers want to see everything; others are experts at triage: dealing with crisis issues at once, dumping hopeless cases in the trash, putting less critical items into a delayed suspense file or system, and so on. As the "communications load" (Klofas, Stojkovic, & Kalinich, 1990, p. 60) rises, the importance of informal channels rises.

Communications networks are constructed within organizations to facilitate formal communications. But rarely do these function well. Hence, supplemental, informal networks spring up, and these are sometimes referred to as "back channels." A phone rings, you pick up the receiver, and a friendly voice from another unit in the organization says, "The warden will be sending your division head a memo on the widget works project later today. Your division will get the lead assignment but will have only 3 days to carry it out. I thought you might like to know." In virtually all large organizations, informal communications supplement formal ones.

Reporting and Communications Problems

A number of communications problems have been identified by various authors on management topics. Gossip and rumors are troublesome, and serve to supplement back-channel communications. Communications problems are common to most organizations. Joseph Massie cites several types of communication problems (1987, p. 113):

1. Technical transmission problems
   * noise
   * redundancy
2. Semantic problems (proper meanings)
   * past communication experiences
   * communications environment (context)
   * facts-versus-opinions problems
   * abstractness of symbols
   * complexity
3. "The effectiveness problem"—the balance of effects and results
   * levels through which information must be transmitted
   * the size of organization
   * acceptance of message (psychological dimensions)

Line loss is the condition of informational loss as a message passes from one person or hierarchical level to another. Anyone who has played the parlor game of whispering a message to one person, then that one whispers it to another, and so on, until all have heard it, knows how much the message will have changed. Stewart and Dixon (1983, p. 107), citing a report by William Conboy (1976), noted one managerial study that revealed the scope of the problem. At a meeting of a board of directors, 100 percent of them received the message correctly. However, as it was passed to their vice presidents, just 67 percent of those vice presidents acquired the correct information, as did only 56 percent of the general supervisors, 40 percent of the plant managers, and 30 percent of the foremen. As a result, only 20 percent of the workers received the message correctly.

Andrew J. DuBrin (1978) identified eight common communications barriers (Klofas, Stojkovic, & Kalinich 1990, p. 54): (1) preconceived ideas; (2) denial of contrary information; (3) use of personalized meaning; (4) lack of motivation or interest (MEGO: "my eyes glaze over"); (5) noncredibility of the source; (6) lack of communications skills; (7) poor organizational climate; and (8) use of complex channels.

Massie named three communications barriers (1987, p. 117): (1) distortion, (2) filtering, and (3) overload. **Distortion** is similar to line loss, but it reflects interpretational biases of the listener. The listener received the message but interprets it to fit his or her preconceptions. This approximates DuBrin's preconceived ideas and use of personalized meaning.

Filtering also is similar to line loss. The listener retains the part of the message that fits his or her own interests without retaining the parts that do not. It is similar to DuBrin's denial of contrary information.

Overload is one of the most common communication problems facing the contemporary manager. Load is a measure of the rate and complexity of the communications being processed. Overloads easily occur in an organization. Too much paper passes through the channels, and important items are smothered among the routine items.

Load crises are related to: (1) organizational instability (rigid, traditional, hierarchical bureaucracies are considered stable in this context); (2) the individual capacity to manage message inputs and output; (3) reading speed, and the ability to communicate in print or orally, memory, etc.; and (4) the individual and systemic desire for information.

Jargon

Some communication problems arise from **jargon,** which is an overuse of technical and professional language and obscure vocabulary. In public service agencies, there also is a vast overuse of abbreviations, slang, and almost incomprehensible terminology. Within the closed work group, such usages may not be a problem, but people from outside the organization listening to such terms may not comprehend.

Optimum Legibility Formula

Learning how to avoid the difficulties and problems of poor communications requires effort and practice. B. R. S. Silverman gave guidance on how to communicate more clearly in an article, "The Optimum Legibility Formula" (1980, July). According to the **optimum legibility formula,** one should:

1. Write the complete message down as quickly as possible.
2. Determine the purpose of the message by listing a few potential sentence subjects it implies or states.

BOX 11.1 JARGON: "MARY HAD A LITTLE LAMB"—THE POLICE REPORT

The subject, a female Caucasian, hereinafter known as Mary, surname unknown, has been frequently observed in the close company of an immature member of the Bovidae family ... whose remarkable flocculent albino surface resembles frozen precipitation in the form of hexagonal snow crystals. It appears that regardless of Mary's migratory habits, the woolly juvenile maintained pursuance. Such pursuit of the subject led the unfledged species of the genus, Ovis, to the subject's institute of learning—in absolute violation of Section 63.55 of the Municipal Code. The subject's academic peers subsequently engaged in exultation, jubilation, frolic, and general rejoicing at the incongruous apparition of a callow member of the Hollow Horn Ruminant family at a place of academia (*The Legal Guide to Mother Goose*, "translated" by Don Sandburg, 1978).

   "Mary Had a Little Lamb"
   Mary had a little lamb
   With fleece as white as snow,
   And everywhere that Mary went
   The lamb was sure to go.
   It followed her to school one day.
   That was quite against the rule.
   It made the children laugh and play
   To see a lamb at school.

---

3. Attempt to answer the six basic journalistic questions: who, what, when, where, why, and how.
4. Rearrange the sentences in priority order.
5. Place verbs immediately after their subjects.
6. Eliminate all linking verbs.
7. Use one verb per sentence.

Nonverbal Communication

David Givens (1984a,b) is a linguistic anthropologist who publicized his studies of non-verbal communications in the 1980s. His research included a critique of judges in their courtrooms (Klahn, 1981). "In the courtroom, judges don't have to say a word to make their feelings perfectly clear—and perhaps unfairly influence juror's decisions." He added, "Unlike Justice, the blindfolded lady weighing the evidence on her scale, courtroom participants consider more than what they hear. What they see, especially in the judge, makes an impression on jurors and others in courtrooms", says anthropologist David Givens. Givens was quoted further as saying, "If a judge's opinion is clear, people will try to follow his lead. … [I]f his opinion is clear non-verbally, the same things happen."

Givens's point is that we communicate in unspoken and unwritten ways, some of which we may not even realize. Our faces, our postures, our gestures, our movements, how we occupy space, touching and avoiding touching, and symbolic emblems we display all add to our communication messages.

Facial Expressions and Eye Contact

Faces can reveal pleasure, tension, hostility, or fear. There is eye contact when people want to exchange ideas, and eye contact is broken when there is disinterest. To stare is to express exaggerated interest. A smile can be genuine or false, and there are ways to tell which is which. A real smile is revealed in the muscles that orbit the eyes (Tavris, 2003, pp. 87–88). Paul Ekman's *Emotions Revealed* (2003) discusses such clues.

Basic Body Language

Basic body language includes kinesics, gestures, and posture (Birdwhistell 1970). **Kinesics** is the interpretation of such things as facial expressions and gestures or nonverbal behavior related to movement, either of any part of the body or of the body as a whole. Posture will reveal whether a person is tense or relaxed. Other gestures and indicators of body language can be decoded as well. Some, like **illustrators,** are quite obvious. These include pointing, waving someone forward, nodding one's head to indicate yes or no, and raising one's hand to answer a question or to get a speaker's attention. **Affect displays** are facial expressions that send a message rather than just reveal a state of mind. Common examples are a frown, a smile, blushing, and sticking out one's tongue. **Regulators** are gestures such as nodding in agreement as someone else speaks, making encouraging or discouraging facial signals as someone is speaking, answering a question, and looking upward or out a window when bored with the topic. **Adapters** are mannerisms that are not meant as communication but can be translated by a perceptive observer (Ekman & Friesen, 1969).

Space and Territory

The manipulation of space and territory, known as **spatial distribution**, can communicate feelings as well. Commonly used expressions such as "you're crowding me," "he's in my face," "she's stand-offish," "he's distant," and "I need my space" all reflect a subtle awareness of this fact. Deference can be revealed in a person's posture and use of space. For instance, because of military training, most veterans shift to a "position of attention" in the presence of those feared or respected but remain relaxed while among equals and inferiors and those who are not found to be threatening.

Environment

Messages can be found in the arrangement of furniture. Do you have to talk to a manager "across a desk," or does your supervisor have a pair of overstuffed chairs in which both parties sit during a conversation? If the director's office is buffered by a secretary's desk or an anteroom to filter access, this communicates a wish to be left alone. An easily accessible ground-floor office and an open door suggest a willingness to communicate.

Touch (Tactile Communication)

Messages are sent through the rules of touching (**tactile communication**)—whom one may and will touch, the kinds of touching, and even the duration of physical contact. Friends shake hands, but usually rivals do not. Putting an arm over a friend's shoulder or patting a buddy on the back is acceptable behavior with close associates, but not with strangers or those with whom one does not have a close personal relationship. Stricter rules govern contact between males and females (Henley, 1977), and a mistake can lead to a complaint of sexual harassment. The rules of etiquette vary by culture and subculture. For example, East European friends kiss in situations in which few Americans would. When a person puts an arm around your shoulder, is it a friendly gesture or a control posture? Who can do this to whom?

Emblems

Emblems include various graphic symbols and hand or body gestures. The 1960s peace sign, the "A-OK" popularized by pilots and astronauts, the Vulcan salute copied from *Star Trek,* and the "New York salute" (or "flipping the bird") each communicates a message.

Nonverbal Speech Cues (Paralanguage)

When people speak, it is not just the word but also the other nonverbal vocal cues that help them convey what they are thinking. All of it is communication. The methods used, consciously or unconsciously, by one person to convey an idea to another are not limited to the vocabulary used. An astute criminal justice manager learns to use these added features of communication to convey additional meaning to his or her words.

Tonal Cues

Tonal cues are factors such as vocal pitch and whine, which augment and alter the meaning of the words a person speaks. The words "I could kill you" can be spoken jokingly, neutrally and unemotionally, or threateningly. It is the tone of voice that conveys whether the speaker is being humorous, factual, or threatening.

Pace of Speech

People speak more rapidly when tense and more slowly when relaxed.

Volume

People may shout at someone whom they feel is inferior or stupid. Raising one's voice is generally an indicator of anger.

Silence and Pauses

The so-called pregnant pause, when all conversation ceases after some remark, also is communication. The delay while a person considers a question, the time lag in returning a call, or the failure to reply at all ("If he really wants to speak to me, he can call back.") reveals disinterest. Placing a subordinate's memo or report aside as it is turned in means "This is not as important to me as it is to you."

Using False Signals

All of the above cues can be used to send **false messages**. Imagine a police officer who is quiet, passive, and a model of courtesy until he needs to make an arrest. Then he turns livid, speaks with a violent rasp to his voice, and stands with fists clenched. His posture is very threatening, but it could be an act to intimidate the person he is planning to arrest.

The Language Itself: The Choice of Words

Samuel Hayakawa (1906–1992) was a distinguished university professor of English, president of San Francisco State University, and former U.S. Senator from California from 1977 to 1983. He was a major language theorist and a leading expert on semantics. His major contribution to English is his book, *Language in Thought and Action,* published in five editions since 1949 (a revision of his 1941 *Language in Action*). He was greatly influenced by Alfred H. S. Korzybski (1879–1950), a Polish-American philosopher who developed the theory of general semantics. Korzybski thought that knowledge is limited

> **BOX 11.2 HAYAKAWA'S CLASSIFICATION OF STATEMENTS**
>
> **Reports** are statements that can be independently verified or disproved.
>
> **Inferences** are statements of the unknown made on the basis of what is known, the essence of all theory.
>
> **Judgments** are expressions of approval or disapproval, usually opinions about something that tell more about the speaker than about the subject under discussion.

by the structure of the human nervous systems and the structure of language. Humans experience life through linguistic "abstractions," yet our linguistic understandings can deceive us. Hayakawa expanded on Korzybski's concepts on the study of semantics, which he defined as "the study of human interaction through communication" (1972, p. ix). Hayakawa founded the organization, U.S. English, which sought to make English the official language of the United States, even though he was of Japanese ancestry.

Hayakawa taught that words are symbols. As he would say, "The word is not the thing. The symbol is not the thing symbolized. ... The map is not the territory." Hayakawa (1972, pp. 34–42) divides communications into three categories of statements: reports, inferences, and judgments (see Box 11.2).

We must forever be aware of the ease of confusing facts and inferences. What one actually knows and what one may sincerely believe are quite different. A **fact** is first-hand, empirical observation, while an **inference** is an assumption or a probability statement.

An even greater risk is assuming that judgments actually convey any information about the topic under consideration. On the contrary, they are statements that tell only the speaker's personal opinion or prejudices about the topic under discussion. Thus, they tell the listener very little about the topic but much about the speaker.

Semantic Problems with the Spoken Word

Hayakawa coined the phrases *snarl words* and *purr words*. **Snarl words** are unfavorable adjectives and nouns used in conjunction with persons or things that we dislike (e.g., "incompetent," "flip-flopper," "terrorist"). **Purr words** are favorable adjectives and nouns about things we like (e.g., "bright," "beautiful," "witty," "sweet"). Police occasionally are spoken of as "Nazis," "Gestapo," and "Fascists" when used to express displeasure with their actions. Words like "hero," "leader," "champion," and "star" are used to characterize those whom we like (Hayakawa, 1972, pp. 40–41).

The "one-word, one-meaning fallacy" (Hayakawa, 1972, p. 54) is the mistake of taking a word to mean one thing when it can mean another. In your mind, think of a "cat," and jot down the following information about "your cat," the one you were thinking about: the sex, long or short hair, color or fur pattern, age group (a kitten, young adult, old adult), frisky versus taciturn. Or did you describe a piece of construction equipment, also a "CAT." Or maybe you still remember the abbreviation for "cable access television" (CAT) broadcasting. The same words have multiple meanings according to their context and the "history" of the user and listener.

"Words with built-in judgments" (1972, pp. 68–71) are terms that convey information but also subtly reveal one's prejudice for or against the person or thing identified. Less obvious than snarl and purr words, their use still will identify people or concepts that are disliked: a man who has been convicted of a minor criminal offense is "a criminal"; a disliked woman who has been involved in a casual sexual affair is a "tramp" or a "slut"; a businessman who is doing too well for our taste is "a shark" or "a white-collar criminal." On the other hand, someone who is liked or sympathized with might be "a man who made a mistake," a "liberated woman," or a "successful entrepreneur." Racial and ethnic appellations obviously convey prejudice. The so-called N-word has become an infamous term in our public vocabularies—too value-loaded to be used even in a neutral academic context such as this passage. Such a word offends, and each such word suggests prejudice in the person using it, even if that is not the case.

"The language of social control" (1972, pp. 88–91) permits language to be used to give directions without the obvious force of orders. When we speak of the future as fact we can see how language directs us to act: for example, "There will be a test in the next class." Sometimes the direction is more subtle. A manager may express a vague hope that something will be done in anticipation that it will be taken as an order without having the officiousness of making it one: for example, "Will someone find me the case report?" may sound like a question, but it is a direction to a junior subordinate to find and bring back the case report.

Written Communications

Most governmental communication involves a great deal of paperwork. The quantity of paperwork in most criminal justice administrative jobs can be frightening. The "action occupation" of police work is overwhelmed by the reports required for each request for assistance, investigation, search, arrest, booking, and release from custody.

A routine investigation leading to an arrest, booking, and custody will involve: (1) a case or incident report, (2) one or more follow-up reports, (3) an arrest report or record, usually with one or more sets of fingerprint cards, each requiring basic information on the suspect and the charge, (4) an arrest warrant issued by a magistrate, but containing service-execution information supplied by the police, (5) an inventory of personal effects taken from the suspect in custody, (6) a mittimus to record the transfer of the prisoner out of police custody, and (7) a request for paid overtime to get all of the paperwork done. In addition, each police officer is advised to keep a police notebook of his or her activities, summarizing all of the above.

As modern bureaucracies, all criminal justice agencies must keep and rely on files. Documentation is required within every agency in the criminal justice system in order to produce records on every legal action and procedure. The courts must keep records of all judicial proceedings. Prosecutors must keep extensive case files. Correctional units must keep files on all inmates and all correctional operations. Probation and parole offices must keep extensive records on client caseloads. Felony criminal cases require transcripts that have to be available if there are appeals. Appeals are filed with extensive "briefs" of the case law and legal arguments behind the appeal. Criminal justice managers have to ensure that the extensive files in their possession are stored in an orderly manner, are classified and categorized, and can be retrieved when needed.

Document Classification and Protecting Sensitive Information

In an open society it is often too easy to ignore the fact that some knowledge and information is not public but is instead **proprietary information** (i.e., privately owned information). Governments freely give away great quantities of knowledge and information (or try to), but in some cases their goal is to shelter critical, sensitive knowledge from the general public.

In this computer age, access to information has expanded greatly. Everyone with access to a computer has at his or her fingertips more information than exists at any major library. Even so, there are those who want more: they want to see the proprietary information of corporations, the defense secrets of the nation, or the financial information of private individuals. Using a computer it is possible to "hack" into computer systems to steal these data.

Protecting information is the purpose of **information security (INFOSEC)**. Part of the security effort of a criminal justice manager is defining what information needs protection and why. Often referred to as **document security**, many managers use systems that are the same as or similar to those used by the Department of Defense to protect their documents and data banks. These systems rely on **document classification**, the terminology of which usually matches the security clearances and access controls of the Department of Defense.

"For Official Use Only" (FOUO) is used to identify information that is sensitive and could violate basic privacy rights of persons named in the documents, or could result in interference in an investigation or a case. Records and documents containing a name, birth date, and social security number together are typical FOUO materials, as are medical records. Releasing the addresses and telephone numbers of witnesses and crime victims can result in persons being harassed by offenders or the media. Access requires employment or affiliation with the organization possessing the information, and typically that involves a simple background check.

"Confidential" is used to identify information that would be prejudicial to the interests of the agency or its clients. What is meant by "prejudicial" is deliberately vague. The practical definition is based on the harm that may be done if the information falls into the hands of an unauthorized user. In law enforcement, it might include leaks of evidence that could help a suspect better evade detection or prepare a better alibi. Access again usually requires employment or affiliation with the organization possessing the information as well as a simple background check.

"Secret" is used when unauthorized disclosure could bring about real and substantial damage to the state, the United States, its allies, or the organization. Real damage can be measured in major dollar losses, injuries, and deaths. The planning of a police raid to capture dangerous criminals would be classified as secret. Authorized access requires a more thorough background investigation and a clear need to know about the information, operation, or activity that has been classified as secret.

"Top Secret" is used when grave damage would be expected to result from the unauthorized disclosure of such information. "Grave damage" is not specifically defined, but it is assessed by the worst-case scenario that can be projected from such information being released to an enemy. Imagine a domestic Al Qaeda terrorist cell gaining access to names, addresses, and identifying information of all of the FBI and state and city anti-terrorist agents and investigators working in your state. Access to top secret information requires a comprehensive, thorough background investigation and a clearly defined need to know.

"Top Secret with Special Access" implies caveats and compartments, which define access and will require additional authorization based on need-to-know criteria. A **caveat** is a broad categorization of who may or may not see the data. "NOFORN" (no foreign nationals may see the information) and various "EYES ONLY" notations naming which groups may see the information are examples. Assigning **compartments** involves identifying the units within a government agency that may be allowed to see the raw data or the finished product. Prior to September 11, 2001, "9-11," the CIA often "overcompartmentalized data" so that the FBI did not know what the CIA knew, and the FBI frequently denied access to state and local police and even the Defense Intelligence Agency (DIA) about criminals and ongoing investigations.

In the federal government the National Security Agency is tasked with interagency **operational security (OPSEC)** training. An Interagency OPSEC Support Staff (IOSS) exists to train and coordinate OPSEC efforts of the National Security Agency (NSA), FBI, CIA, General Service Administration (GSA), and Department of Defense (DOD), among others. A state or local OPSEC plan or standard operating procedure (SOP) should be developed for criminal justice agencies of the states or localities where sensitive information is generated, kept, or used. Initially, it may seem that localities and states do not need to be concerned with such matters and will not be dealing with secret and top-secret matters. But in the aftermath of 9-11 and with the continuing threat of terrorist threats to the United States, this thinking is naive. A terrorist cell or violent criminal gang could be active anywhere in the country, and every county and city in the country has targets at risk. Most terrorist cases will be handled by federal authorities, but many gang-related cases remain under local jurisdiction. Court administrators and correctional managers will find themselves dealing with such individuals in their facilities.

The criminal justice manager who finds his or her agency involved with such cases or handling sensitive information about dangerous groups or individuals must develop its own INFOSEC plan. According to G. F. Jelen (1994), the plan needs to accomplish five aims (quoted in Ortmeier, 2005, p. 180):

1. Identifying and assessing the value of the information the agency routinely handles, the criminal justice manager must determine what data in the agency needs to be protected.
2. Identifying the potential threat, the criminal justice manager needs to know who this information should be kept from and why.
3. Identifying organizational vulnerabilities is another criminal justice managerial responsibility. The agency needs to be aware of how protected data can get out.
4. Assessing the impact of the threat versus the costs of the protection systems used is another managerial priority. The criminal justice manager needs to calculate the cost to the agency if its data were leaked and also compute the costs of each additional level or layer of information security. The manager needs to assess the return on investment (ROI) and value-added contribution (VAC) of the new security procedures.
5. Designing countermeasures is the final step in developing an agency information security plan. A countermeasure is a response to a known or suspected disclosure of sensitive information. Countermeasures can include changing access codes, passwords, or encryptions immediately if they have been compromised; changing the timing or the details of the plans that have been revealed; or changing features of protective procedures that have been exposed.

State and local government agencies engaging in coordinated security operations working in cooperation with the U.S. government typically use the hierarchical security classification system of the Department of Defense. However, they may use their own systems for internal security.

Criminal justice agencies are obligated to release some information to the press and the public under the Freedom of Information Act and state "**sunshine laws**" (federal and state laws requiring regulatory authorities' meetings, decisions, and records to be made available to the public), so the criminal justice manager needs to conform agency INFOSEC practices to meet the requirements of the law. Often these managers are authorized or obligated to protect unclassified information as well, such as private personnel information kept in their files. The INFOSEC plan needs to address these legal requirements. Criminal justice employees can be obliged to sign security, confidentiality, or secrecy agreements that bar them from disclosing any protected information they acquire during their employment. Any failure to comply can result in lawsuits and payment of damages.

Computer and Communications Security (COMSEC)

A contemporary criminal justice manager must be aware of the communications security measures that can be used and also should know what the most common threats to communications and computers are. The following topics should be considered.

Encryption and **ciphers** (algorithms for performing encryption and decryption) are used to protect classified information and limit access. Passwords, access codes, key-card systems, and secure safes and vaults for confidential storage of information all can use encryptions. *Cryptography (cryptology)* is the science of both encryption and code-breaking.

Cryptographic security is a managerial responsibility that includes protecting encryption codes and machines as well as other security devices. It includes *line security,* the security equipment, procedures, and practices needed to protect the organization's own internal communications systems. Increasingly more criminal justice agencies are relying on various forms of *space-radio communications,* such as cellular and wireless phones, fixed and mobile radio systems, satellite radio systems, microwave transmissions, and many other communications systems using the open airwaves to send communications. *Transmissions security* must be considered when using such equipment. Any such transmission can be heard by unintended listeners who are willing to acquire the equipment and apply the effort to listen in. Related to this is *emanations security,* which tries to protect or disguise the electromagnetic signature of the communications equipment in use.

Computer and Internet Security

The threat to computer data cannot be underestimated. **Firewalls** and antivirus protections, usually achieved through commercial software, should be installed to help protect computers. Even with these protections, weaknesses common to most computer systems include unintentionally sending out passwords on wireless networks and other methods of losing passwords. When protecting sensitive communications or stored documents, access codes must be limited to as few users as possible and should be changed frequently to avoid compromise. Computer crimes can target criminal justice agencies just as easily as commercial businesses and private individuals (Britz, 2004; Schmalleger & Pittaro, 2008; Taylor et al., 2006). These include online computer fraud, identity theft, hacking into data and resultant data theft, data alteration, computer attacks such as contriving to overload Web sites, and the insertion of **malware** (malicious software), such as virus and worm programs.

Information Sharing and Communication Networks

It is possible to overly restrict access to criminal justice information. Limiting access and overcompartmentalization can keep data from members of other component agencies of the criminal justice system who will need it. Often it is learned that one police agency has released a suspect sought by another or that a correctional unit is holding a person who is suspected in an earlier case and cannot be found; or police may have in custody a person who is under probation or parole supervision but neither the police nor the community corrections officers are aware of their common interest in the person. To help overcome such common, self-imposed limitations on information sharing, a criminal justice manager must determine in advance what kinds of information should be shared with other criminal justice agencies and what information it will want from them in exchange. The result will be the establishment of interagency communications networks. Larger agencies also should establish coherent information-sharing plans for internal use.

Numerous writers on management topics refer to the several variations in communications networks. Pioneering work on internal communications and social networking in organizations was done by Alex Bavelas and Dermont Barrett (1951). Massie (1987, pp. 115–116) describes direct, star, circular, radial, and serial patterns. Klofas, Stojkovic, and Kalinich (1990, pp. 62–65) illustrate similar wheel-and-spoke, chain, circle, and all-channel (star) networks. Souryal (1985, p. 58) describes networks as vertical, horizontal, diagonal, and circular. Stewart and Garson (1983, p. 110) apply similar models taken from an article by Alex Bavelas and Dermat Barrell (1951, March, pp. 370–371). Most organizations have both formal and informal communications networks (Klofas, Stojkovic, & Kalinich, 1990, pp. 67–69). In the informal network, there is a **linking pin** (also called a "lynch pin" or "linchpin"), that is, a person who is the central cohesive element and key to keeping communications open and flowing. When the linking pin functions informally, the information often is considered office gossip, and such networks are known collectively as the "**grapevine**" (Massie, 1987, p. 115). The reliability of the grapevine is difficult to ascertain, and a wise manager will independently verify information before acting on it.

Face-to-Face Communicating: Giving a Formal Briefing

The formal staff meeting briefing often is used as the means of achieving face-to-face communications, but it can fail when certain rules are not followed. There are some practical communication rules that a manager should use to make best use of a formal briefing opportunity (see Box 11.3). A common form of briefing will be an agency's routine staff briefing.

BOX 11.3 FEATURES OF A WELL-PREPARED STAFF MEETING

1. There should be an agenda announced in advance, but it need not be followed slavishly.
2. No staff member should brief the whole group on any topic that does not require knowledge by the chief manager and at least two others. An item, even if very important, that involves only the boss or only one staff member—or just other staff, not to include the boss—ought be discussed directly between affected parties.
3. Petty informational items ought to be kept to a minimum, but items that may seem petty but will affect internal functions and routines should be addressed. Any change of routines affecting most staff should be included. Examples would be conveying that the copier is down; important visitors will be visiting in the afternoon; three secretaries are out with flu, producing a typing backlog; the cafeteria will be closed tomorrow for a special function; or the new phone system goes online next Tuesday.
4. Decision items should be previewed in an advance memo. If this is not done, then decisions should be deferred until all parties involved can have the time to research and consider the impact of the decisions being sought.

Speaking to a group often results in confusion as to whom an assignment or responsibility has been given. The chair or staff person tasked should restate new decisions and missions: for example, "So I'll send X to support Y for today and tomorrow." or "It's agreed then, that Bill and Tom will assist Frank on the XYZ Project." Other methods involve sending the participants in the meeting a "memorandum for record" to summarize the decisions made and tasks allocated. The taking and circulating of meeting "minutes" serves a similar function. In each of these examples, any receiver of the communication has a duty to respond with corrections or clarifications.

Information Storage and Retrieval Systems

A massive amount of criminal justice information is generated by the various components of the criminal justice system. With the addition of various kinds of electronic media to the great quantity of written and printed material, a criminal justice manager must have a system in place to store and retrieve information.

The police generate incident and investigative reports, arrest records, inventories of property seized and evidence collected, and much more. Police managers are responsible for the collection and storage of this information, much of which is sensitive and not available to the public. Other police data are made public regularly, in the format of the Uniform Crime Reports, prepared by local police agencies around the nation and compiled for the public by the Federal Bureau of Investigation. Police managers have a duty to inform the public via the news media about major criminal cases under investigation, but it is part of their managerial responsibility to be cautious and selective about what information to reveal (Sewell, 2007).

Prosecutors also have access to great quantities of criminal case information that is highly sensitive. Information given to grand juries is held under a seal of secrecy and may be disclosed only in the furtherance of criminal due process. A prosecutor can reveal indictments, presentments, and "no bills" of a grand jury to the public. Prosecutors also compile summary statistics on cases reviewed, dismissed, *nolle prosequed*, plea-bargained, brought to trial, or producing convictions or acquittals. By their rules of ethics they are obligated to avoid generating prejudicial pretrial publicity. In court, their cases are fully public and available to the news media, except in some cases involving juvenile defendants and witnesses.

The courts compile and publish their performance records, transcripts of the trial proceedings in major cases, sentence data, appeal records, and similar public reports.

Correctional agencies and community correctional units are limited in what information they can reveal about those in custody or under supervision, but keep extensive files on the people under their control. They do publish and share data on the numbers of people they manage and people under sentence of death, parole data, recidivism statistics, and similar information about the offenders in their care.

Agencies have some of their data stored in print form in traditional files; on microfilm; on microfiche; on electromagnetic data cards; on reel-to-reel magnetic tapes; on 8-inch,

---

BOX 11.4 COMPONENTS OF INFORMATION MANAGEMENT SYSTEMS

1. Reporting systems = input systems
2. Record-keeping systems = storage systems
3. Data-retrieval systems = output systems
4. Data analysis =
    process systems
    management summaries
    consolidated reports
5. Transmission systems

5.25-inch, and 2.5-inch computer disks; on beta-cassettes; on 8-mm and 16-mm film; on VHS cassettes; on audio cassettes; on servers; on hard drives; on zip drives; on CDs; on DVDs; and other storage devices. Some of these storage media no longer are supported by equipment maintained in the agency. If data can no longer be retrieved, they no longer can be used. In this age, when "cold cases" can be solved using technologies that did not exist when the crime occurred, when courts allow appeals of convictions rendered decades earlier, and when researchers want long-term recidivism data to evaluate correctional programs, this loss of access to stored data can be critical. Therefore, it becomes necessary that criminal justice agencies have means of accessing old data. Options include transferring data to new storage formats, making print copies for archives, and keeping older data-retrieval technologies available and serviceable for decades to come.

Making Use of Criminal Justice Data: Reporting Revisited

Having good data is almost meaningless if the criminal justice manager is not using the data that are available to support other managerial functions. Formal analysis of routine information is a key managerial responsibility. Knowing how to use the data the agency already has in storage can enhance agency performance and identify better ways to manage the organization. Numerous aids can be used to make data analysis easier for the criminal justice manager:

- spatial distribution graphics
- temporal distribution reports
- individual performance summaries
- unit performance summaries
- client-characteristic summaries
- case-characteristic summaries
- caseflow reports (offense or offender-based reports)
- financial summaries

Agency data also can be used to undertake special research projects. Such data will be needed for an internal research or auditing unit. Outside evaluation teams, accreditation committees, and commissions also will need to have access to appropriate information. If management consultants are to be employed for some purpose, they too need key data.

Summary

Ultimately, the information generated by a criminal justice agency will be needed by its political superiors to help them plan and make policy. Moreover, criminal justice information needs to be provided selectively to the general public. Each criminal justice agency head and every senior manager must be held accountable to the public, and proper reporting of police, prosecutorial, judicial, and correctional data in accurately analyzed formats will help the criminal justice manager meet that mandate.

LEARNING OBJECTIVES

Upon finishing this chapter, you should be able to do the following:

1. Discuss the three types of communication statements defined and described by S. I. Hayakawa.
2. Name several advantages and disadvantages to using "informal communications" within an organization.
3. Explain vertical, horizontal, diagonal, and circular communications patterns and the merits of each.
4. Explain the communications security measures that a criminal justice agency should use.

IMPORTANT TERMS AND NAMES

- *adapters*
- *affect displays*
- *back channels*
- *caveat*
- *ciphers*
- *communication overload*
- *compartments*
- *distortion*
- *document classification*
- *document security*
- *emblems*
- *encoding*
- *encryption*
- *fact*

- *false messages*
- *filtering*
- *firewalls*
- *Mary Parker Follett*
- *for official use only (FOUO)*
- *grapevine*
- *Samuel I. Hayakawa*
- *illustrators*
- *inference*
- *information security (INFOSEC)*
- *jargon*
- *judgments*
- *kinesics*
- *line loss*
- *linking pin*
- *malware*
- *operational security (OPSEC)*
- *optimum legibility formula*
- *overload*
- *pace of speech*
- *proprietary information*
- *purr words*
- *regulators*
- *semantics*
- *snarl words*
- *social networking*
- *spatial distribution*
- *sunshine laws*
- *tactile communication*
- *tonal cues*

References and Supplemental Sources

Abram, C., & Pearlman, L. (2008). *Facebook for dummies*. New York: For Dummies, Wiley.

Bavelas, A., & Barrell, D. (1951, March). An experimental approach to organization communication. *Personnel*, 370–371.

Birdwhistell, R. L. (1970). *Kinesics and context: Essays on body motion communication*. Philadelphia: University of Pennsylvania Press.

Britz, M. (2004). *Computer forensics and cyber crime: An introduction*. Upper Saddle River, NJ: Pearson/ Prentice Hall.

Conboy, W. A. (1976). *Working together: Communications in a healthy organization*. Columbus, OH: Merrill.

DuBrin, A. J. (1978). *Fundamentals of organizational behavior*. New York: Pergamon.

Ekman, P. (2003). *Emotions revealed*. New York: Time Books.

Ekman, P., & Friesen, W. (1969). The repertoire of non-verbal behavior: Categories, origins, usage, and coding. *Semiotica, 1*, 49–98.

Fahs, C. (2007). *How to do everything with YouTube*. New York: McGraw-Hill.

Follett, M. P. (1926). The giving of orders. In: Metcalf, H. C. (Ed.), *The scientific foundations of business administration*. Baltimore, MD: Williams & Wilkins.

Follett, M. P. (1926/1989). The giving of orders. In: Ott, J. S. (Ed.), *Classic readings in organizational behavior*. Pacific Grove, CA: Brooks/Cole.

Givens, D. B. (1984a). What is nonverbal communication? *Nonverbal Q & A*, American Anthropological Association. Retrieved from <http://www.geocities.com/marvin_hecht/givens.html/>.

Givens, D. B. (1984b).What body language can tell you that words cannot. *Nonverbal Q & A*, American Anthropological Association. Retrieved from <http://www.geocities.com/marvin_hecht/givens.html/>.

Hayakawa, S. I. (1972). *Language in thought and action* (3rd ed.). New York: Harcourt Brace Jovanovich.

Henley, N. M. (1977). *Body politics: Power, sex, and nonverbal communication*. New York: Simon & Schuster.

Jelen, G. F. (1994). OPSEC for the private sector. *Security Management, 38*(10), 67–68.

Klahn, J. (1981, June 7). Body talk. *The Charlotte Observer*, p. D-1.

Klofas, J., Stojkovic, S., & Kalinich, D. (1990). *Criminal justice organizations: Administration and management*. Pacific Grove, CA: Brooks/Cole.

Lynch, R. G. (1986). *The police manager: Professional leadership skills* (3rd ed.). New York: Random House.

Lynch, R. G., & Lynch, S. (2005). *The police manager*. Newark, NJ: LexisNexis Matthew Bender.

Massie, J. L. (1987). *Essentials of management* (4th ed.). Englewood Cliffs, NJ: Prentice Hall.

Miller, M. (2007). *YouTube 4 you*. New York: Macmillan Computer.

Ortmeier, P. J. (2005). *Security management* (2nd ed.). Upper Saddle River, NJ: Pearson/Prentice Hall.

Sahlin, D., & Botello, C. (2007). *YouTube for dummies*. Indianapolis: Wiley.

Sandburg, D. (1978). *The legal guide to Mother Goose*. Los Angeles: Price/Stern/Sloan.

Schmalleger, F., & Pittaro, M. (Eds.). (2008). *Crimes of the Internet*. Upper Saddle River, NJ: Pearson/Prentice Hall.

Sewell, J. D. (2007). Working with the media in times of crisis. *Crime and Justice International, 23*(98), 32–35.

Silverman, B. R. S. (1980, July). The optimum legibility formula: A written communications system. *Personnel Journal, 56*, 581–583.

Souryal, S. S. (1985). *Police organization and administration*. Cincinnati: Pilgrimage/Anderson.

Stewart, D., & Garson, G. D. (1983). *Organizational behavior and public management*. New York: Dekker.

Tavris, C. (2003). A polite smile or the real McCoy?. *Scientific American, 288*(6), 87–88.

Taylor, R. W., Caeti, T. J., Liper, D. K., Fritsch, E. J., & Liederbach, J. (2006). *Digital crime and digital terrorism*. Upper Saddle River, NJ: Pearson/Prentice Hall.

Wikipedia. (2011). List of social networking websites, *Wikipedia, The Free Encyclopedia*. Retrieved from <http://en.wikipedia.org/wiki/List_of_social_networking_websites/>.

12 ■■■
Future Issues in Criminal Justice Management

What does the future hold for criminal justice managers? While we cannot be certain, forecasts can prepare us for what we may experience in years to come. Forecasting is one of the planning tools mentioned in Chapter 6. Forecasts typically look to the past and consider contemporary developments to make predictions about the future. A criminal justice manager in the 21st century can expect to face many of the same issues that challenged managers in the past.

An entire new discipline appeared in the 1960s called **futuristics**, the prediction of the future based on the scholarly study of existing conditions. Futurologists (also called "futurists") in criminal justice have offered numerous insights into what may be in store for your career as a criminal justice manager in the decades to come.

Two organizations have been leaders in the study of the future: the World Futures Studies Federation (WFSF), founded in 1967 in Oslo, Norway, and the World Future Society (WFS), founded in the United States in 1966. The WFS publishes two journals, *Futures Research Quarterly* and *The Futurist.* The *Journal of Futures Studies,* published by the Graduate Institute of Futures Studies of Tamkang University in Taipei, Taiwan, is another scholarly outlet for such studies. Many futurists have looked ahead to the risks that we will face from crime and terror. None, though, is more distinguished than Wendell Bell (2000), one of the founders of futurology, and the author of one of its major works, *Foundations of Futures Studies* (1996, 1997).

The Society of Police Futurists International is a nongovernmental organization dedicated to applying futuristics to policing. In 1991, **William Tafoya**, then with the FBI, cofounded the Society of Police Futurists International. He has lectured and consulted on various futuristic challenges and threats, the changing nature of policing (1990), and on **cybercrime** when it was in its infancy (1998).

Another leading futurist in criminal justice, studying for more than a quarter century, is **Gene Stephens**. In 2005, he summarized some of the predictions that he and others have for American law enforcement, including such things as the expanded use of non-lethal force, customization of police and criminal justice services to meet specific public needs, greater demands on first responders, cybercrime, and terrorist incidents including the threat of bioterrorism.

FIGURE 12.1 William Tafoya Tafoya is a retired special agent of the FBI and widely renowned futurist. He was a cofounder of the Society of Police Futurists International and predicted the problems of cybercrime when that concept was still in its infancy. *Photo provided by William Tafoya.*

FIGURE 12.2 Gene Stephens Stephens is a former journalist who later taught criminal justice at the University of South Carolina. He was a cofounder and past president of the Southern Criminal Justice Association. He is a pioneering futurist, focusing on projected developments in policing. He also was studying the phenomenon of terrorism years before the Oklahoma and 9-11 attacks, warning of the threat the United States would be facing. *Photo by Richard R. E. Kania.*

One of the leading futurists looking at the court system is Sohail Inayatullah (1990, 1992). Having worked on a judiciary improvement project with the Hawaiian courts, Inayatullah writes of futures for judicial bureaucracies (Inayatullah & Monma, 1989). Some results of that project were the initiation of a problem-oriented planning process and consideration of options for the future, including some low-probability issues such as the rights of robots, sentencing offenders using natural brain drugs, and even the secession of Hawaii from the United States.

Many others also are looking ahead. Georgette Bennett sought to predict future crime trends in her 1987 book, *Crimewarps* (revised in 1989). Her predictions relied heavily on demographic trends and foresaw the problems of cybercrime.

Another future-looking expert on demographic trends and crime is **Alfred Blumstein**, whose work (1995; Blumstein & Rosenfeld, 1998; Blumstein & Wallman, 2000, 2006) was recognized with the 2007 Stockholm Prize in Criminology; his predictive work on human rights, age-based crime trends, and studies of incarceration rates in American correctional institutions among other subjects were so honored. His advanced statistical analyses have produced complex predictions on the productivity of deterrence, the growth of prison populations, and the problems and future of drug-enforcement policies. He developed the statistical concept of "**lambda**" as a reliable predictive measurement of an individual's offending frequency within a possible lifelong criminal career. He has examined declining trends in violent crime to identify suitable predictors that policy-makers can apply (Blumstein, Rivara, & Rosenfeld, 2000).

Roslyn Muraskin and Albert Roberts have compiled a collection of essays, *Visions for Change* (2009), that addresses future issues for the 21st century. The authors look at recent developments and future directions in technological applications, forensic sciences, globalization, victimology, drug policy, cybercrimes, juvenile justice issues, media matters, gender issues, and all of the components of the justice system.

These leading futurists and others have looked ahead to the future of criminal justice. Others have undertaken efforts to direct that change toward improved futures. These kinds of managers are change agents in the pattern of great criminal justice reformers of the past such as Cesare Beccaria, Jeremy Bentham, Zebulon Brockway, Dorothea Dix, August Vollmer, Orlando W. Wilson, Bruce Smith, Arthur Vanderbilt, Katharine Bement Davis, Mary Belle Harris, and George Beto. Each of these leaders was a **change agent** for the improvement of the criminal justice system. Future criminal justice managers have a potential role as change agents and need to recognize three distinctive patterns of change: (1) straight-line change, (2) rise–plateau–crash change, and (3) cyclic change.

FIGURE 12.3 Alfred Blumstein Former dean of the Heinz School of Carnegie-Mellon University, Alfred Blumstein was the recipient of the 2007 Stockholm Prize in Criminology for his statistically based predictive work on human rights, age-based crime trends, and studies of incarceration rates. He continues to serve as the director of the National Consortium on Violence Research (NCOVR), a major think tank doing futuristic studies on crime (Heinz College, 2010). *Photo provided by the American Society of Criminology.*

Natural Patterns in Change

Straight-Line Change

Change often will follow a trend in a consistent fashion, either steady-state, rising, or falling. In criminal justice, **straight-line change** patterns have involved training requirements, entry educational requirements, and in-service educational achievements, all rising gradually over the decades.

Rise–Plateau–Crash Change

In criminal justice, specific technologies have appeared, become popular (the rise), then become commonplace (the plateau), only to be replaced by new technologies and thus vanish (the crash). This **rise–plateau–crash change** has been evident especially in the applications of communications technologies (the call box, one-way radio, two-way radio, and in-car computer) and in suspect and offender identification (the Bertillon system, inked fingerprints, scanner prints, and DNA identification). Correctional innovations also have followed this pattern (the Pennsylvania silent penitentiary movement, the Auburn congregate system, the rehabilitation movement, correctional boot camps, and, more recently, three-strikes legislation and career-offender long-term incarceration programs). Media attention to spectacular criminal cases also follows this pattern (Marsh, 1991).

Cyclic Change

The most predictable events undergo **cyclic change** or follow an **oscillating change pattern,** in which frequencies of some feature will rise, then fall, only to rise again. This cyclic change is obvious in the long-term history of criminal justice; consider issues such as brutality complaints, corruption scandals, and the bias against minorities.

Issues Criminal Justice Managers Will Face in the Future

Brutality and Excessive Force Issues

Police and correctional officers are obliged to use force in the performance of their duties. Several hundred people are killed each year by police and correctional officers, far more than are lawfully executed. This use of force, whether *deadly force* or *nonlethal force,* can be used wrongfully. When serious abuse of force occurs, there will be news media attention (Hirschfield & Simon, 2010), protests, lawsuits, and changes made in criminal justice training standards to prevent future abuses. Criminal justice managers also are looking to new nonlethal force devices to reduce the number of police-caused homicides and to reduce cases of **excessive force**. The *crisis-planner* manager will react to such cases; the manager who is a *purposeful planner* will anticipate such problems and prepare for them before they occur.

In 1985, a change in case law (*Tennessee v. Garner*) altered the standards by which police could use deadly force. Even before the U.S. Supreme Court made its ruling, though, the International Association of Chiefs of Police (1981) was anticipating what the future would bring to deadly force practices by police. Police managers were preparing to apply more restrictive shooting standards. When the court rendered its decision, these managers' agencies were prepared to accept the new standards. These progressive police managers used a process like that described by Kurt Lewin (1890–1947), who wrote that the process of effecting change involves a three-step procedure (Lewin, 1989, pp. 546–547; Souryal, 1995, pp. 128–129):

> *Unfreezing: to "break open the shell of complacency and self-righteousness, it is sometimes necessary to bring about deliberately an emotional stir-up."*
>
> *Moving or Changing: make the change-oriented decisions and begin the process of implementation.*
>
> *Refreezing: allow the new ways to become established as the replacement habits.*

By the time the court decision was made, most progressive police departments already were training their officers in the procedures recommended by the IACP that were to be expressed in the court ruling. Old procedures, especially the outdated "fleeing felon" rule, already had been discredited (unfreezing). When the new standard was promulgated, police all over the country were anticipating it (changing), and most were ready to apply it (refreeze).

General Ethical Failures and Shortcomings

Periodically new scandals arise because criminal justice officials have engaged in corrupt or immoral activities. There are seven recurring ethical problems facing all those who take on responsibilities in the name of justice: (1) wrongful pursuit of personal gain, (2) favoritism and bias, (3) abuses of power, (4) a flawed personal life, (5) deceitfulness, (6) denial of due process to those involved with criminal justice, and (7) neglect of duties (Kania & Dial, 2008, p. 169).

Personal Gain

The criminal justice manager must avoid unlawful personal gain from the position, and similarly must be aware that such misconduct is prevented, detected, investigated, and punished when it occurs within the organization. The criminal justice manager must

---

BOX 12.1 SEVEN RECURRING ETHICAL PROBLEMS IN CRIMINAL JUSTICE

1. Wrongful pursuit of personal gain
2. Favoritism and bias
3. Abuses of power
4. Flawed personal life
5. Deceitfulness
6. Denial of due process
7. Neglect of duties

238 of MANAGING CRIMINAL JUSTICE ORGANIZATIONS

enforce the prohibitions, both in law and in ethical guidelines, against using public service for personal enrichment, profit, pleasure, or benefits not specifically authorized by law, the work contract, or the rules. Included in this category are the rules against:

- taking bribes and extorting payoffs
- accepting gratuities and unauthorized benefits
- receiving excessive compensation and benefits
- using the office to promote personal aims
- harboring and advancing excessive ambition (Kania & Dial, 2008, p. 170)

Favoritism and Bias

Because it is unethical to use one's office to aid those whom we like or to interfere with those whom we dislike, a criminal justice manager must be attentive to this perpetual threat to the agency's integrity. These biases often arise from divided and mixed loyalties, holding one's obligation to the public interest below that of oneself (egoism), family (paternalism, nepotism), friends, personal associates, co-workers and peers (peer bias), one's political party and programs (patronage, ideological bias), or church and spiritual faith (theological bias). Included in this category are rules against:

- political and ideological patronage
- racial, ethnic, and religious bias (favorable and unfavorable)
- nepotism and other family favoritism
- overt and covert discrimination (racial, ethnic, sexual, political, etc.) (Kania & Dial, 2008, p. 170)

Abuses of Power

The prohibitions against public officials using their offices to place their values, desires, needs, or preferences above those of the public they serve, and over the rules and laws they must uphold, are sometimes broken, leading to abuses of power. Criminal justice managers must be alert to such abuses. These violations need not involve personal material gain and include such activities as:

- authoritarianism, coercion, and harassment
- arranging or condoning unjustified arrests
- seeking to deny opportunities for reasonable bail
- denial of liberty by lengthy detention prior to trial (Kania & Dial, 2008, p. 170)

Flawed Personal Life

Criminal justice managers must maintain socially respectable private lives and also must enforce among their employees and subordinates the prohibitions against personal activities outside the workplace that bring discredit on the public servant and the servant's agency or profession. These include private violations of the criminal law and moral violations that are not necessarily illegal but are generally frowned upon by the public, such as:

- criminal wrongdoing by criminal justice officials
- financial improprieties and tax evasion by criminal justice officials
- sexual misconduct, deviance, or unconventionality by criminal justice officials
- civil illegality (tax, regulatory, and civil law violations)
- questionable associations and membership in controversial organizations
- private prejudicial expressions and actions (Kania & Dial, 2008, p. 171)

Deceitfulness

Deceitfulness includes violations that run counter to the expectation that public officials will be honest and forthright with the public on matters involving their work. Criminal justice managers must set an example for honesty and truthfulness for the employees of their agencies to emulate. When they do not, managers must take action to root out dishonesty and restore truthfulness within their agencies. The rules against deceitfulness include:

- overt lying, duplicity, loopholing, and evasions
- covering up misdeeds
- unwarranted secrecy in the conduct of the public business
- fraud, trickery, and hypocrisy (Kania & Dial, 2008, p. 171)

Denial of Due Process

Due process comprises the rules for procedural correctness in dealing with all administrative matters, both within the justice system and in all public service bureaucratic activities. Criminal justice agents are required to follow the policies set out for them, and should not invent their own solutions to the situations they encounter. Criminal justice managers have the responsibility to train staff, monitor their conduct, and take disciplinary action when due process is not followed properly. Citizens have the right to expect that their cases will be dealt with fairly, in accordance with the rules for such cases. Failures include:

- ignoring civil rights and constitutional guarantees
- not following the rules and procedures
- failing to comply with internal bureaucratic rules
- ignoring regulatory and statutory guarantees (Kania & Dial, 2008, p. 171)

Neglect of Duties

All criminal justice occupations and positions have associated duties and obligations that must be fulfilled. A criminal justice official who does not fulfill these duties is violating that mandate, and sometimes even will be violating laws against:

- malfeasance
- nonfeasance
- misfeasance
- disobeying lawful orders
- abuse of discretion
- failing to comply with regulations and standing orders (Kania & Dial, 2008, p. 172)

BOX 12.2 NEGLECT OF ONE'S DUTIES

Both the law and ethical standards obligate those who hold public office to be faithful to their lawful duties. Three common failures are:

nonfeasance—the failure to perform one's duty by oversight or omission, usually inadvertent (willful nonfeasance typically will be considered malfeasance)
misfeasance—the wrongful performance of one's duties, usually in the form of making mistakes, not following procedures correctly, or other unintentional blunders
malfeasance—the intentional performance of an official act or use of one's official powers to achieve an end that is circumstantially illegal, harmful, and/or unjustified

---

Actual ethical failures in practice have often overlapped two or more of these categories. A criminal justice manager must anticipate that each and every one of these failures will occur. They may be reduced, minimized, or mitigated, but the wise criminal justice manager must be aware and prepared for these failings to recur.

Ethnic, Race, and Community Relations

Implicit in the discussion of the failures above, under the categories of bias, abuses of power, and due process especially, are the seeds of public dissatisfaction with the performance of criminal justice agencies. These result in poor criminal justice–community relations. In the 1950s, progressive leaders in criminal justice began the effort to reeducate criminal justice agencies, especially the police, about better community relations. Many programs were developed and experiments attempted. Efforts to improve the image of the police and the justice system have included programs such as community-oriented policing, yet problems in race and ethnic relations continue to occur.

Sometimes the criminal justice agency is not the source of the problem. Some members of racial and ethnic groups engage in behaviors that clash with the customs and laws of the United States and the criminal justice system must maintain a balance between enforcing the law and respecting the customs and behaviors of such groups. To add to the problems managers will face, leaders of these groups occasionally confront U.S. laws and hope to create an us-versus-them conflict. A good criminal justice manager will stay ahead of the conflict, anticipating the reasonable and lawful demands of minority groups, striving to meet those by training agency employees, hiring people able to communicate effectively with minority groups, and creating programs to achieve cooperation and harmony. Police managers in many cities are intent on closing the gap between officers and citizens.

Since the 1990s, a more cooperative approach between police and citizens, often called **community-oriented policing (COP),** has helped criminal justice managers and community leaders work together to solve issues (Peak & Glensor, 2007). A new generation of police managers came up through the ranks while the community-oriented policing model was being implemented. In this model, officers are trained to become a part of the community and to engage in partnerships.

In Chapter 9, we discussed that police culture has, in the past, bred resentment toward the community. This is a problem that managers try to deal with in both academy training and continuing education. Shifts in policy indicate the movement toward a more community-centered model has been implemented in many departments. One trend that exemplifies this is the **civilianization** of certain positions, particularly those that deal directly with the public. Crime-prevention practitioners are often civilians and are responsible for teaching crime-prevention techniques throughout the community. Another example is making officers more approachable, particularly to young people. School resource officers in many districts switched to "soft" uniforms (knit shirts with embroidered police badges) to make officers seem more approachable to young people.

When bias, prejudice, or injustice occurs, the criminal justice manager has an obligation to address it promptly and judiciously. To suppose that good relations existing today will last indefinitely is naive. Communities are forever in flux. Good relationships with adults of the minority communities will not guarantee good relationships with their offspring, and new groups will enter the community or the client population. The future-oriented criminal justice manager must prepare for new challenges.

Applying New Technologies to Criminal Justice

What will be the new technologies of 2025? Of 2050? Certainly we can do no more than guess, but judging by the past and present, we can be sure that new technologies that apply to criminal justice will emerge.

Existing technologies certainly will be improved upon. Communications, computers, video, transportation, criminalistics, nonlethal weapons, and emergency medical technologies have been improving so dramatically in the past 35 years that the practice of criminal justice is far different from what it was when the Law Enforcement Alliance of America (LEAA) was helping agencies acquire their first computer systems, upgrade their telecommunications, and add nonlethal controls to supplement the use of firearms. In the 1990s, **CompStat** and **Geographic Information Systems (GIS)** provided law enforcement managers with new managerial and crime-fighting tools (Canter, 2000; McDonald, 2002; Shane, 2004). As computer programs and digital applications improve, new generations of technological innovations will be integrated into the service of criminal justice management.

Criminal justice managers with foresight will stay informed about new technologies and think of ways that they can be applied to criminal justice roles. More than one hundred years ago, August Vollmer and his peers applied the new inventions of their age to police applications, including the patrol car, the police radio, fingerprint identification, and ballistics. In the 1960s, progressive criminal justice managers were exploring ways to use computers to enhance criminal justice operations. Using the unique features of DNA for identification was a new idea just two decades ago. The criminal justice managers who conceived of using it to solve crimes were highly original thinkers (Wambaugh, 1989). What new technology might you apply to criminal justice if you come to hold a managerial position? You might be the change agent who brings about a major improvement in criminal justice practices in the future.

Union Conflicts

Dealing with union demands is a recurring, cyclical pattern that future criminal justice managers are sure to face again. In 2011, the conflict over collective bargaining by public service unions between Governor Scott Walker of Wisconsin, a Republican, and Democrats in the state legislature revived the issue on the American scene.

Police unions in the United States arose in the 1880s. Dissatisfaction with low wages and poor working conditions led police to turn to unions for **collective bargaining** with the localities and the states. In 1919, when the Boston Police Department went on strike, the strikers were fired and subsequently blacklisted by the Commonwealth of Massachusetts. The governor, Calvin Coolidge, wrote to Samuel Gompers, a key union leader, "There is no right to strike against the public safety by anyone, anywhere, any time." Governor Coolidge's strong anti-union stance made him a national celebrity and popular figure and was a factor in his selection as the Republican vice-presidential nominee in 1920.

The anti-union sentiment in this country led to numerous states either outlawing public service unions or prohibiting collective bargaining with them. The First Amendment right to peaceful assembly and to petition the government meant the bans on union membership were constitutionally questionable, but nothing in the First Amendment requires a city or state to bargain with a union. In the 1930s, the political hostility toward public service unions was replaced with a more sympathetic outlook, especially within the Democrat Party, which drew much of its strength from union support. Led by Wisconsin, states legalized collective bargaining rights and recognized public service employee unions as the agents of various public employee groups. Anti-union states supported "**right-to-work**" laws, while pro-union state legislatures approved "closed-shop" rules and compulsory union dues subscriptions for union members and nonmembers alike. The 1981 strike of the air traffic controllers early in the first term of President Ronald Reagan led to the mass firing and blacklisting of fired controllers, denying them any future federal employment (Schalch, 2006).

After Reagan's Coolidge-like response to the air traffic controllers, unions were again in public disfavor. But through the 1990s, public service unions again gained strength and public acceptance. In 1993, President Clinton lifted the ban on rehiring the air traffic controllers Reagan dismissed in 1981. Public service unions continued to support the Democratic Party and in turn received political support from Democrats in public office. So the events of 2011 in Wisconsin predictably developed along partisan political lines.

The issue of collective bargaining for public employees has taken on new relevance with the budget battles in Ohio, Wisconsin, New Jersey, and several other states. The midterm elections of 2010 brought in a wave of politicians who believed they had a mandate to make significant cuts in state budgets without raising taxes. Media attention focused specifically on the battle between Governor Scott Walker of Wisconsin and the unions that represented public employees in that state. Wisconsin had been the first state to grant collective bargaining to public workers, and it has a strong union tradition. The budget battle in Madison was symbolic for the national media and also national labor leaders. If collective bargaining rights could be lost in this state, then it could happen anywhere. Conservative magazines such as the *National Review* strongly supported Walker and wrote strong editorials about the need for cutting benefits to workers in hard economic times (Costa, 2011). Protestors representing unions from across the nation as well as leaders from most of the major labor organizations showed up for around-the-clock marches and protests. Ultimately, Walker was successful in his bid to end collective bargaining in Wisconsin.

However, the issue will not end there. The predictable end result is a reenergizing of employee unions that include many workers in the criminal justice field. The pro-labor publication *The Nation* has laid out political strategies for public employees who are intent on not losing further ground in the state budget battles (Nichols, 2011). After years with little controversy, public-employee unions are once again very relevant to the criminal justice manager.

Media Attention

A criminal justice manager cannot necessarily predict when a major case within his or her jurisdiction will grab the attention of the mass communications media (Mannion, 1993). Crimes that are clearly serious will justify major media attention, as will crimes with socially important victims or suspects (Chermak, 1998; Chermak & Chapman, 2007). When "the big one" hits, the prudent criminal justice manager will have a plan in place to handle the media onslaught (Mannion, 1993). Otherwise, there is a great risk of conflict between the media and the agency (Mozee, 1987). There are 12 lessons that a criminal justice manager can learn from the past to anticipate the future:

1. A major disaster or crisis can happen anywhere, anytime. Even the smallest criminal justice agency in the smallest of communities must be prepared to face this reality (Mannion, 1993).
2. The criminal justice manager must prepare for two aspects of the crisis: the major crime or disaster case itself and the media onslaught that will follow it (Mannion, 1993).
3. The media will be invasive and lack respect for the people involved. For them, the story always takes precedence (Skolnick & McCoy, 1985, p. 114; Wilson & Fuqua, 1975, p. 124). The criminal justice manager must be prepared to thwart the media's desires to invade the crime scene and exploit morbid curiosity, while still giving the media opportunities to get key visuals to support their stories (Mozee, 1987, p. 143).
4. Such a case invariably will have a long-term impact on relationships among and within the criminal justice agency, the community, and the news media (Mannion, 1993).
5. The media are a criminal justice agency's most direct link with the public, and they can be helpful to the police, the prosecutor, the courts, or corrections if the right

lessons are learned and the proper steps are taken to prepare for such a catastrophic event (Garner, 1987, pp. 15–16; Graber, 1980; Skolnick & McCoy, 1985, p. 132).

6. The media will cooperate with criminal justice agencies when they are given useful information, sensible direction, and assistance (Jones, 1987; Mannion, 1993; Skolnick & McCoy, 1985, p. 132).

7. The media will not go away, but if ignored by official sources, they will seek out less well-informed and less reliable ones to get a story (Jones, 1987, p. 164).

8. Criminal justice agencies need to know the variety and informational requirements of the news and entertainment media organizations and freelancers that now exist (Mannion, 1993).

9. The criminal justice manager must have advanced knowledge about how various media organizations operate and their technology and facility requirements (Garner, 1987, pp. 110–113), organization, and ethics.

10. The criminal justice manager must be aware of the capabilities, possible consequences, and hazards of instantaneous live broadcasting (Jones, 1987, p. 160).

11. Criminal justice agencies need knowledge of the objectives, rivalries, ideologies, and hidden agendas of media organizations (Mozee, 1987, pp. 144–145; Sherizen, 1978).

12. The "media" are not limited to the traditional local and national news-gathering organizations. Criminal justice agencies should expect movie producers, book writers, tabloid newspapers, and television and radio talk shows to join the "feeding frenzy" at the crime scene, and all will likely claim full First Amendment rights and freedoms (Mannion, 1993).

Educational and Training Standards

When criminal justice managers were recruiting staff a century or more ago, a high school diploma was considered to be the symbol of an advanced education. By the beginning of this century, this has become a minimal standard for most criminal justice occupations. A law degree was not even required to practice law when Abraham Lincoln hung out his shingle as an attorney. Today, no one in the United States can practice law without having been educated in the law and having passed

FIGURE 12.4 Marea Mannion Mannion is a former news anchor and reporter who teaches for the Pennsylvania State University and frequently lectures on media issues for the FBI National Academy in Quantico, Virginia. *Photo by Richard R. E. Kania.*

the bar examination. A century ago, most police departments and correctional agencies provided no training to their employees. Now in-service training is an essential part of personnel practices in most agencies.

What will the future bring in criminal justice education in the next several decades? What initial training will be required? How much more in-service training will be provided? Straight-line change predicts that all of these will increase gradually over time.

Criminal justice managers will have to revise their recruiting requirements and budget for more training to prepare for the future. Higher educational standards for entry and specific educational curricula may need to be specified. In-service training will have to prepare agencies to deal with each of the future challenges anticipated above. Flexibility and intellectual agility will be needed to deal with these and any other challenges not anticipated in the preceding pages.

Summary

The criminal justice system needs to be future-oriented. The past is behind us and cannot be redone. We may try to correct past errors and injustices, but they never will go away completely; some old wounds will last forever. However, the future holds out hope for our society, the justice system, and criminal justice agencies. We can make progress—old mistakes need not be repeated. We can add new technologies and improve upon ineffectual methods. Our objectives can be better met. Moreover, we can preserve the best of the past. The values of our society are worthy of respect. A future criminal justice manager will be responsible for upholding and preserving our constitutional protections and the political values that are associated with them.

We began this book by stating that the job of the criminal justice manager may be summed up by the mnemonic LODESTAR. In fact, though, this is not enough. The criminal justice manager has other important tasks and responsibilities. Maintaining high standards of ethics is an important aspect of criminal justice for managers, for individual criminal justice employees, and for each criminal justice organization. Maintaining good community relations also is important. Acting to reduce the level of ethnic, racial, class, and social strife will benefit the entire society as well as the criminal justice agencies serving it. Achieving community harmony and public consensus is a goal that can be attained through effective criminal justice performance and a sensitivity to public needs and concerns. Good media relations are important as well. It is through these media that the public learns of the activities of our criminal justice agencies, decides how well they are doing their jobs, and either supports or turns against them. An ethical, educated, community-oriented, well-trained, and wisely supervised workforce can be a very powerful tool in the kit of an effective criminal justice manager. It is, therefore, the additional task of the criminal justice manager to create such a workforce, to build for a better future.

LEARNING OBJECTIVES

Upon finishing this chapter, you should be able to do the following:

1. Name and describe three patterns for change.
2. Identify the seven most common patterns of ethical failures occurring across the criminal justice system.
3. Discuss the 12 principles for dealing with the mass communications media that a criminal justice manager should consider.
4. Discuss what future challenges you predict for criminal justice.

IMPORTANT TERMS AND NAMES

- *Georgette Bennett*
- *Alfred Blumstein*
- *change agents*
- *civilianization*
- *closed shop*
- *collective bargaining*
- *community-oriented policing (COP)*
- *CompStat*
- *cyclic change*
- *excessive force*
- *futurists*
- *futuristics*
- *futurologists*
- *Geographic Information Systems (GIS)*
- *lambda statistic*
- *open shop*
- *oscillating change pattern*
- *right-to-work laws*
- *rise-plateau-crash change*
- *Gene Stephens*
- *straight-line change*
- *William Tafoya*

References and Supplemental Sources

Bell, W. (1996, 1997). *Foundations of futures studies* (2nd vol.). Edison, NJ: Transaction.

Bell, W. (2000). Futures studies and the problem of evil. *Future Studies*, 5(2).

Bennett, G. (1989). *Crimewarps: The future of crime in America* (Revised ed.). New York: Anchor Books.

Blumstein, A. (1995). *Youth violence, guns, and the illicit-drug industry.* Retrieved from <http://www.drugtext.org/library/articles/blumstein.htm/>

Blumstein, A., Rivara, F. P., & Rosenfeld, R. (2000). The rise and decline of homicide – and why. *Annual Review of Public Health, 21*, 505–541.

Blumstein, A., & Rosenfeld, R. (1998). Exploring recent trends in U.S. homicide rates. *Journal of Criminal Law and Criminology, 88*(4), 1175–1216.

Blumstein, A., & Wallman, J. (Eds.). (2000). *The crime drop in America.* New York: Cambridge University Press.

Blumstein, A., & Wallman, J. (Eds.). (2006). *The crime drop in America* (2nd ed.). New York: Cambridge University Press.

Canter, P. (2000). Using a geographic information system for tactical crime analysis. In: Goldsmith, V., McGuire, P. G., & Mollenkopf, J. H. (Eds.), *Analyzing crime patterns: Frontiers of practice* (pp. 3–10). Thousand Oaks, CA: Sage.

Chermak, S. M. (1998). Predicting crime story salience: The effects of crime, victim, and defendant characteristics. *Journal of Criminal Justice, 26*(1), 61–70.

Chermak, S. M., & Chapman, N. M. (2007). Predicting crime story salience: A replication. *Journal of Criminal Justice, 35*(4), 351–363.

Costa, R. (2011, March 21). The badgered state: Wisconsin Governor Scott Walker is the left's public enemy no. 1. *National Review.*

Garner, G. (1987). *Chief, the reporters are here.* Springfield, IL: Thomas.

Graber, D. A. (1980). *Crime news and the public.* New York: Praeger.

Heinz College (2010). Alfred Blumstein: J. Erik Jonsson University Professor of Urban Systems and Operations Research; Former Dean of the Heinz School. The Heinz College, Carnegie-Mellon University. Retrieved from <http://www.heinz.cmu.edu/faculty-and-research/faculty-profiles/faculty-details/index.aspx?faculty_id = 9/>

Hirschfield, P. J., & Simon, D. (2010). Legitimizing police violence: Newspaper narratives of deadly force. *Theoretical Criminology, 14*(2), 155–182.

Inayatullah, S. (1990, March). Deconstructing and reconstructing the future: Predictive, cultural and critical methodologies. *Futures.*

Inayatullah, S. (1992). Linking the future with the present in judicial bureaucracies: Learning from the Hawaii judiciary case. In: Mannermaa, M. (Ed.), *Proceedings of the eleventh world futures studies federation conference.* Turku, Finland: World Futures Studies Federation and Hungarian Academy of Sciences.

Inayatullah, S., & Monma, J. (1989, Spring). A decade of forecasting: Some perspectives on futures research in the Hawaii judiciary. *Futures Research Quarterly, 5*(I), 520.

International Association of Chiefs of Police (IACP) (1981). A balance of forces: A study of justifiable homicide by the police: *IACP Newsletter.* Gaithersburg, MD: IACP.

Jones, R. B. (1987). The press at the emergency scene: Issues and answers. In: Kelly, P. A. (Ed.), *Police and the media: Bridging troubled waters* (pp. 159–167). Springfield, IL: Thomas.

Kania, R. R. E., & Dial, A. (2012). Prosecutor misconduct. In: Braswell, M. C., McCarthy, B. R., & McCarthy, B. J. (Eds.), *Justice, crime and ethics* (pp. 147–163) (7th ed.). Boston: Anderson.

Lewin, K. (1989). Group decision and social change. In: Ott, J. S. (Ed.), *Classic readings in organizational behavior* (pp. 543–548). Pacific Grove, CA: Brooks/Cole.

Mannion, M. (1993). Handling the fallout when the "big one" arrives. *The Justice Professional, 8*(1), 123–145.

Marsh, H. L. (1991). A comparative analysis of crime coverage in newspapers in the United States and other countries from 1960–1989: A review of the literature. *Journal of Criminal Justice, 19*(1), 67–79.

McDonald, P. (2002). *Managing police operations: Implementing the New York crime control model—CompStat*. Belmont, CA: Wadsworth.

Mozee, D. M. (1987). Police/media conflict. In: Kelly, P. A. (Ed.), *Police and the media: Bridging troubled waters*. Springfield, IL: Thomas.

Muraskin, R., & Roberts, A. (Eds.). (2009). (5th ed.). Upper Saddle River, NJ: Pearson/Prentice Hall.

Nichols, J. (2011, May 20). AFL-CIO's Rich Trumka on the post Wisconsin GAME Plan. *The Nation*. Retrieved from <http://www.thenation.com/blog/160828/afl-cios-rich-trumka-post-wisconsin-game-plan/>

Peak, K., & Glensor, R. (2007). *Community policing and problem solving* (5th ed.). Upper Saddle River, NJ: Pearson/Prentice Hall.

Schalch, K. (2006, August 3). *1981 strike leaves legacy for American workers*. NPR (National Public Radio). Retrieved from <http://www.npr.org/templates/story/story.php?storyId = 5604656/>

Shane, J. M. (2004). CompStat design. *FBI Law Enforcement Bulletin, 73*(5), 12–19.

Sherizen, S. (1978). Social creation of crime news: All the news fitted to print. In: Winick, C. (Ed.), *Deviance and mass media* (pp. 203–222). Beverly Hills, CA: Sage.

Skolnick, J. H., & McCoy, C. (1985). Police accountability and the media. In: Geller, W. A. (Ed.), *Police leadership in America* (pp. 102–135). New York: Praeger.

Souryal, S. S. (1995). *Police organization and administration* (2nd ed.). Cincinnati: Anderson.

Stephens, G. (2005, March–April). Policing the future: Law enforcement's new challenges. *The Futurist*.

Tafoya, W. (1990, February). The changing nature of the police: Approaching the 21st century. *Vital Speeches of the Day, 56*, 244–246.

Tafoya, W. (1998, August 7). How cybercops fight terrorism. Online Chat with William Tafoya, for *The Washington Post*. Retrieved from <http://www.washingtonpost.com/wp-srv/zforum/national/tafoya080798.htm/>

Tennessee v. Garner, 471 U.S. 1 (1985).

Wambaugh, J. (1989). *The blooding*. New York: William Morrow.

Wilson, J. V., & Fuqua, P. Q. (1975). *The police and the media*. Boston: Little, Brown.

Appendix ∷∷
Key Case Law for
Criminal Justice Managers

Randal L. Wood, J.D.

The work of the criminal justice manager differs from that of the line officer in criminal justice. Most criminal justice employees learn key criminal law cases and principles in their academy training and college preparation, but few are exposed to the key cases in civil law that govern the practices and procedures of criminal justice managers in much the same way that *Miranda v. Arizona* governs police arrest procedures.

Elsewhere in this book the authors mention some of the important federal laws governing criminal justice personnel matters and practices. In this appendix, five important cases are covered, with the objective of helping future criminal justice managers be prepared for the important jobs they have to do. The cases are presented in reverse chronological order, with the most recent first.

Connick v. Thompson
131 S.Ct. 1350 (2011)

In this case, the U.S. Supreme Court was called upon to determine whether a district attorney has demonstrated "deliberate indifference" to the constitutional rights of persons prosecuted by his office by failing to specifically train prosecutors working under him (A.D.A.s) in regard to their legal duty to turn over exculpatory evidence (*Brady* material) to those being prosecuted, such "deliberate indifference" being in violation of 42 U.S.C. 1983.

In 1985, Thompson was charged with murder by the Orleans Parish District Attorney's Office (Louisiana). Due to publicity related to that murder charge, victims of an unrelated armed robbery came forward and identified Thompson as the perpetrator of the robbery. The robbery case was tried first and Thompson was convicted. During the subsequent murder trial, Thompson chose not to testify due to his previous conviction for robbery. Thompson was convicted of murder and sentenced to death.

In 1999, just weeks before Thompson's scheduled execution, a private investigator looking into Thompson's murder conviction discovered that the New Orleans Police Crime Laboratory had analyzed a swatch of clothing from one of the victims of the armed robbery that was stained with blood from the actual perpetrator of the robbery. The blood on the swatch of clothing was type B. This information had not been made available to Thompson's counsel. Thompson's blood had not been analyzed for comparison. When analyzed, it was determined that Thompson's blood was type O. The D.A.'s office moved to vacate the robbery conviction. The Louisiana Court of Appeals subsequently reversed Thompson's murder conviction. Thompson was retried on the murder charge and acquitted.

Thompson then brought suit against the D.A.'s office, the D.A. himself (Connick), and the A.D.A.s who prosecuted the case, alleging that their failure to provide him with the exculpatory blood evidence as required by *Brady v. Maryland*, 373 U.S. 83 (1963), led to his wrongful convictions, his multi-year incarceration, and his near-execution. Thompson also alleged that Connick had demonstrated "deliberate indifference" to his constitutional rights by failing to specifically train his A.D.A.s in relation to their duties under *Brady*. Thompson was awarded $14 million in damages as well as $1 million in attorney's fees and costs. Connick appealed, stating that there was no "obvious need" to train his subordinates in regard to *Brady* standards due to there being no evidence of a pattern of *Brady* violations within his office, therefore, there was no "deliberate indifference" on his part to support the judgment against him. The U.S. Court of Appeals for the Fifth Circuit ultimately rejected Connick's arguments and affirmed the judgment of the trial court. Connick appealed to the U.S. Supreme Court.

Among other things, the Supreme Court noted that "[i]n limited circumstances, a local government's decision not to train certain employees about their legal duty to avoid violating citizen's rights may rise to the level of an official government policy for purposes of Section 1983." However, the Court distinguished between the need to specifically train police officers in relation to giving or acquiring medical care for citizens with whom they come into contact (as set out in *Canton v. Harris*, 489 U.S. 378 (1989)) and the need to specifically train prosecutors in relation to legal principles.

The Court pointed out that police officers come into the job with little, or no, knowledge of their responsibilities and therefore need extensive training therein. In contrast, prosecutors come into their jobs after graduating from law school, passing the bar exam, and being required to maintain continuing legal education. There is no obvious need to train them in specific areas of the legal principles related to their job responsibilities until a specific problem arises in relation thereto. "A pattern of similar constitutional violations by untrained employees is ordinarily necessary to demonstrate deliberate indifference for purposes of failure to train. ... A district attorney is entitled to rely on prosecutors' professional training and ethical obligations in the absence of specific reason, such as a pattern of violations, to believe that those tools are insufficient to prevent future constitutional violations in the usual and recurring situations with which [the prosecutors] must deal."

Ultimately, the Supreme Court ruled that because Thompson did not prove "a pattern of similar violations" that would have demonstrated that specific training in relation to *Brady* material was needed for the A.D.A.s, Connick had not shown a "deliberate indifference" to Thompson's constitutional rights and ruled in Connick's favor, reversing the judgment of the Court of Appeals.

Canton v. Harris
489 U.S. 378 (1989)

In this case, the U.S. Supreme Court was called upon to determine the standard under which a municipality can be held liable under 42 U.S.C. 1983 for "failure to train" an employee whose actions lead to damages suffered by an individual.

In 1978, Harris was arrested by Canton police officers. Upon arriving at the station, Harris was discovered sitting on the floor of the patrol wagon in which she was transported. Upon being asked if she needed medical attention, Harris responded incoherently. While being processed inside the station, Harris slumped to the floor twice. After the second time, she was left lying on the floor to prevent her from falling again. Harris was released from custody shortly after being processed and was taken to the hospital by an ambulance hired by her family. She was hospitalized for one week and received outpatient treatment for one year for several emotional ailments.

Under Canton Police Department policy, the shift commanders were responsible for determining when to provide immediate medical care for people in custody, but were given no special training to aid them in determining when such care was necessary. Harris sued the city, making several claims, including a 1983 action for violation of her constitutional right to receive medical care while in custody due to a "failure to train" the shift commanders. At trial in the U.S. District Court, the jury found for Harris. The Court of Appeals reversed and remanded the case for a new trial. The City of Canton appealed, based on the Court of Appeals' interpretation of municipal liability under 1983.

The U.S. Supreme Court determined that in 1983 actions a municipality is liable for failure to train its police personnel "only where the failure to train in a relevant respect amounts to deliberate indifference to the constitutional rights of persons with whom the police come into contact." Citing its decision in *Monell v. New York City Dept. of Social Sciences*, 436 U.S. 658 (1978), the Court said "a city is not liable under 1983 unless a municipal 'policy' or 'custom' is the moving force behind the constitutional violation. Only where a failure to train reflects a 'deliberate' or 'conscious' choice by the municipality can the failure be properly thought of as an actionable city 'policy'." In setting this "deliberate indifference" standard for "failure to train" actions, the court stated that neither *respondeat superior* nor *vicarious liability* principles would attach under 1983. The ruling by the Court of Appeals was vacated and the case remanded for further proceedings in accordance with this decision.

In 1983 actions a municipality is liable for failure to train its police personnel "only where the failure to train in a relevant respect amounts to deliberate indifference to the constitutional rights of persons with whom the police come into contact."

Firefighters v. Cleveland
478 U.S. 501 (1986)

The issue in this case was whether Section 706(g) of Title VII of the Civil Rights Act of 1964, which "precludes a district court from entering an order requiring the hiring or promotion of an individual who was refused employment or promotion for any reason other than discrimination" (which would require actual proof of discrimination against a particular individual), applied to a consent decree entered into by the direct parties to a class action alleging discrimination based on race and national origin.

In October 1980, the Vanguards of Cleveland, an organization of black and Hispanic firefighters in the city of Cleveland, filed a complaint against the city and various city officials charging discrimination in the "hiring, assignment and promotion of firefighters" within the city's fire department on the basis of race and national origin. The local chapter of the International Association of Firefighters (the "Firefighters" in the title of the case) was permitted to intervene in the case. The city, having had eight years of litigating "these types of cases" unsuccessfully, decided to settle with the Vanguards. After several months of negotiations, the city and the Vanguards presented the court with a proposed consent decree regarding the distribution of upcoming promotions among minority and non-minority firefighters.

Because of the consent decree, no proof of actual discrimination by the city's fire department had been made. The Firefighters objected to the consent decree (as well as "any form of affirmative action"), alleging that the court would be violating Section 706(g) by entering "an order" that would benefit individuals who had not proven that they had been "refused employment or promotion" due to discrimination. The District Court eventually approved an amended consent decree over the objections of the Firefighters. The Firefighters appealed. The Court of Appeals affirmed the District Court's decision.

The U.S. Supreme Court affirmed the lower courts' decisions, stating that a consent decree does not fall within the meaning of "an order" as set forth in Section 706(g). The court stressed the voluntary nature of a consent decree as opposed to "an order" by a court mandating certain actions by the parties to the case. Citing its decision in *Steelworkers v. Weber*, 443 U.S. 193 (1979), the court stated that "voluntary action available to employers and unions seeking to eradicate race discrimination may include reasonable race-conscious relief that benefits individuals who were not actual victims of discrimination" and, applying that to the present case, said that such a plan is not "rendered impermissible by Title VII simply because it is incorporated into a consent decree."

Section 706(g) of Title VII of the Civil Rights Act of 1964 does not prohibit parties from entering into consent decrees leading to affirmative action programs benefiting employees who have not been proven to be victims of discrimination.

Davis v. City of Dallas
777 F.2d 205 (1985)

In this case, the U.S. Court of Appeals for the 5th Circuit was called upon to determine whether certain job eligibility criteria, that, through no discriminatory intent, had an adverse disparate impact on black applicants, were in violation of the Civil Rights Act of 1964, Title VII, or were sufficiently job-related to not be in violation of said Act.

The Dallas Police Department required the following criteria, among others, for applicants for positions as police officers: (1) completion of 45 semester hours of credit from an accredited college or university with at least a "C" average; (2) no history of "recent or excessive marijuana usage"; and (3) no conviction of more than three "hazardous traffic violations" in the 12 months, nor more than six convictions of such violations in the 24 months, preceding the date of application. A class action was filed against the City of Dallas in the U.S. District Court for the Northern District of Texas claiming racial discrimination in that the criteria had an adverse impact on black applicants. That court held that the criteria were sufficiently job-related to not be in violation of Title VII. The plaintiffs appealed.

In relation to criteria #1, the Court of Appeals reviewed several cases from the U.S. Supreme Court (including *Griggs v. Duke Power Co.,* 401 U.S. 424 (1971)) as well as its sister Courts of Appeals, finding a "business necessity" in the education requirement in that "the position of officer on (a) police force combines aspects of both professionalism and significant public risk and responsibility…[that it] bears a manifest relationship to the position of police officer." The requirement involved the "issue of bona fide occupational qualifications" in that police officers are "entrusted with the lives and well-being of citizens." The appellate court restated the trial court's position that "few professionals are so peculiarly charged with individual responsibility as police officers. Officers are compelled to make instantaneous decisions, often without clearcut guidance from the Legislature or departmental policy, and mistakes of judgment could cause irreparable harm to citizens or even the community." The court further stated that "(t)he extraordinary risk posed by an officer who is not adequate for the job is such that the City is justified in requiring applicants for positions on the police force to possess the professional maturity gained through education."

In addressing the "marijuana usage" issue, the court reviewed the testimony of experts who considered "three perspectives: (1) the propensity for an officer to use marijuana in the future if he has used it in the past; (2) his willingness to enforce the law concerning marijuana if he used it in the past; and (3) the credibility of the officer in the eyes of the public once the information (regarding his previous usage) becomes known." The experts testified that someone who has previously used marijuana is likely to use it again in the future and that a police officer who has used marijuana is less likely to enforce the laws related to marijuana.

Turning to the "hazardous traffic violations," the court again referred to the testimony of experts whose testimony was based on numerous studies, their own as well as others. As with the marijuana issue, the experts stated that past behavior is a good predictor of future behavior and that police officers who have engaged in previous hazardous driving practices are likely to do so in the future. Considering the amount of time that police officers spend behind the wheel of patrol cars, the court stated that there was a clear "job relatedness factor" to this criterion for employment.

The court ultimately determined that all three criteria were sufficiently job-related so as to not be in violation of the Civil Rights Act of 1964 despite having an "adverse disparate impact on black applicants."

The U.S. Supreme Court denied *certiorari*.

Griggs v. Duke Power Co.
401 U.S. 424 (1971)

In this case, the U.S. Supreme Court was called upon to determine "whether an employer is prohibited by the Civil Rights Act of 1964, Title VII, from requiring a high school education or passing of a standardized general intelligence test as a condition of employment in or transfer to jobs when (a) neither standard is shown to be significantly related to successful job performance, (b) both requirements operate to disqualify Negroes at a substantially higher rate than white applicants, and (c) the jobs in question formerly had been filled only by white employees as part of a longstanding practice of giving preference to whites."

Duke Power Co. had five departments — Labor, Coal Handling, Operations, Maintenance, and Laboratory. In 1955, the company began requiring completion of high school for employment within any of the departments except Labor. Prior to 1965, Negroes had been restricted to employment within Labor. In 1965, the company added the requirement of successful completion of two "professionally prepared" aptitude tests for the hiring of new employees. This did not apply to employment within the Labor department. "Incumbent" employees could be transferred to one of the more desirable departments if they had completed high school. Later that year, a policy was instituted allowing incumbents without high school educations to transfer to an "inside" department (Operations, Maintenance, and Laboratory) by passing the two tests. "Neither (test) was directed or intended to measure the ability to learn to perform a particular job or category of jobs."

The Court stated that the objective of Congress in enacting Title VII "was to achieve equality of employment opportunities and remove barriers that have operated in the past to favor an identifiable group of white employees over other employees. Under the Act, practices, procedures, or tests neutral on their face, and even neutral in terms of intent, cannot be maintained if they operate to 'freeze' the status quo of prior discriminatory employment practices." The Court went on to say that the "Act proscribes not only overt discrimination but also practices that are fair in form, but discriminatory in operation." Noting that "whites register far better on (Duke Power Co.'s) alternative requirements than Negroes," the Court cited the "inferior education" in segregated schools received by the petitioners as a barrier to employment in, or transfer to, any of the company's departments other than Labor.

"Congress has not commanded that the less qualified be preferred over the better qualified simply because of minority origins... What Congress has commanded is that any tests used must measure the person for the job and not the person in the abstract."

Summary

Numerous other cases could be presented, but these five were chosen on two bases, their overall great importance, or their currency. A criminal justice manager need not be a lawyer to function in today's workplace, but one does to stay abreast of the law and occasionally will need to rely upon the services of a person trained in the law.

Glossary

AA affirmative action programs intended to increase the participation of certain sub-groups within the community in public service or publicly provided opportunities. As most commonly experienced in criminal justice, it involves programs to increase the hiring and promotion of minority members and women in criminal justice agencies; but is not limited to only this.

AA associate of arts, two-year college degree, usually awarded for a curriculum strong in the liberal arts.

AAS associate of administrative sciences, two-year college degree, usually awarded for a curriculum strong in technical and administrative subjects.

abuse of force the use of excessive force, far in excess of that necessary and sufficient to make an arrest, to deal with a difficult citizen or a troublesome inmate already in custody; a common ethical failing in criminal justice, which criminal justice managers must combat.

abuse of powers because criminal justice officials are given extensive powers of investigation, interrogation, and arrest, it is possible for them to misuse these powers for personal reasons or to discriminate against select individuals or groups. Such abuses of otherwise lawful powers for illegitimate purposes must be controlled by criminal justice managers.

accelerated depreciation in accounting practice, assessing the declining value of an item spread out over a period of time, normally the expected lifetime of a facility or a major piece of equipment but weighted more to the earlier years. It is calculated by taking the purchase price of an asset, subtracting by the likely salvage value, and distributing the estimated decline in value over the years the asset reasonably can be expected to remain in service. For example, a $1,000 computer may be assumed to be useful for about five years, and be worth only $100 at the end of that time. In the first year of use its value may be assumed to decline by 40%, 20% in the second year, and 10% a year in the third, fourth and fifth years of use.

Ackerman's question in subtle opposition to civil service laws, Amos T. Ackerman, President Grant's Attorney General, raised the constitutional question of how much influence the Legislative Branch should have in influencing the "**contracting process**" whereby the Executive Branch selects its workforce.

accountables the non-perishable property of an organization for which an official accounting or inventory should be made periodically; for example, laptop computers allocated to organization members, which they may take home, but which remain property of the agency until such time as they are disposed of as salvage.

activity in general usage, an action or task regularly undertaken by an agency or its employees. For example, writing speeding tickets is a routine activity for a police department and officers assigned to traffic duty. As used in a PERT chart, this is the linkage between two successive events in a plan. See "activity arrow."

activity arrow as used in a PERT chart, this is the graphic representation of the linkage between two successive events in a plan; the arrow's point indicates the direction of the action, leading from one event to the next.

administration [1] this is the group of people in the organization charged with seeing that the duties of the organization are carried out, not necessarily by doing those duties themselves, but by directing the efforts of others or providing the technical support and managerial oversight to insure that they are done; and [2] the art, science and practices of successfully ministering to an organization, as in the "principles of administration."

administrator a person whose primary function within an organization is administrative, logistical or technical support to the organization, rather than the actual performance of the mission, assigned tasks and labor for which the organization was created.

affect display in communications theory this is the additional expression of emotions or supplemental feelings within a communication, revealed by tone of voice, gestures, concurrent laughter or tears, facial expressions, or other body language accompanying the basic communications message.

agency another term for an organization or department within the larger governmental structure having a specific function to serve.

agent in law an agent is an individual or group which is empowered to act on behalf of another, as distinct from "the principle," the individual or group whom the agent represents. In federal investigative agencies, the term agent is used for officials who have been entrusted with the investigative and arrest powers of that agency, as in an FBI or DEA agent.

allocation function one of the major managerial duties, the distribution of the scarce resources of the organization among the sub-units and individuals of the organization in the most productive fashion.

apex in the organizational system of Henry Mintzberg, there are five basic parts of the modern organization, and the apex is one of these; the top management team responsible for leading the organization achieve the central mission of the agency.

appeal in personnel actions, a basic right to respond to and offer counter-arguments to an unfavorable personnel action, such as punishment, an unsatisfactory performance assessment, a denial of a promotion or assignment to an unfavorable work assignment. It is a responsibility of a manager to have in place a process for hearing and resolving appeals to personnel actions taken within the organization.

applied ethics the application and use of abstract ethical principles and guidelines for pragmatic moral guidance and direction in both organizational management functions and discretionary decision-making and behaviors.

applied technology any technological innovation which can be used to enhance the efficiency, security, reliability and effectiveness of the criminal justice system.

appointment the hiring or an individual, usually based upon merit criteria, for employment in the agency.

appraisal the process of making an assessment or evaluation of an individual or work unit; or the document or record of that assessment or evaluation.

appropriation an allocation of funds by a legislative entity (federal, state or local) to an agency intended to sustain its operations. Usually appropriations are enacted as laws outlining in very general terms how much an agency may spend on very general categories of expenditures (personnel, facilities, equipment, etc.).

arbitrariness the exercise of excessive, unjust or non-rational discretion by a manager or administrator, seemingly randomly, either without regard to organizational rules or in the absence of existing guidelines.

assessment the process of making an appraisal or evaluation of an individual or work unit; or the document or record of that appraisal or evaluation.

attached borrowed from military jargon, this is the temporary assignment of an agency member from one unit to another to perform a specific task serving the needs of both. A common form of attachment might be the assignment of a veteran police investigator to the office of the district attorney for the duration of a major trial; the police investigator remains an employee of the police department but for the duration of the attachment takes all work assignments and direction from the DA.

authoritative/authoritarian leader similar to an autocratic leader, an authoritarian freely uses the authority and power of one's office to make decisions and take actions with little or no input from others in the organization.

autocratic/autocratic leader a leadership style and leader who rules absolutely, employing an extremely domineering, assertive style of leadership; using the power of the office with little or no internal, organizational limitations.

BA the bachelor of arts, the four-year college degree.

BFOQ Bona Fide Occupational Qualification, a set of specific exemptions to the more general rules prohibiting all forms of discrimination in hiring of work assignments. For example, denying employment to a person on the basis of one's political affiliation normally is unlawful, but an elected official has the right to require his or her chief deputy to hold the same political affiliation – in this case political affiliation is a BFOQ. In another example, denying employment on the basis of one's sex or age normally is unlawful, but in hiring only mature women to be residential counselors for a home for delinquent teenage girls would be an acceptable BFOQ.

BS the bachelor of science, four-year college degree, often required as an entry credential to certain criminal justice occupations; especially in the federal investigative agencies.

back channel in organizational communications, a network of information sharing that does not follow the official chain of command; an informal communications network.

beneficiary in accounting practice, the individual or unit within a larger organization to which resources are allocated or reallocated.

best qualified in personnel practice, a civil service standard that uses objective criteria to rank order applicants for new positions or promotions and then offers the position or promotion to the individual whose objective score is the highest. See also "rule of three."

bill payer in accounting practice, informal jargon for the individual or unit within a larger organization whose resources or funds are reduced or reallocated to another individual or unit, usually during a period of agency expenditure reductions or emergency reallocations.

book value in accounting practice, the estimated value of the facilities or accountables owned by the agency, based upon objective criteria such as current market prices for comparable facilities or equipment.

bounded rationality originating with the criticisms of Herbert Simon of the rational choice model, this concept proposes that most decisions are only rational some of the time, with decision-makers limited by the data available, their past experiences, personal preferences, and other empirically non-rational [though not necessarily irrational] factors. In some cases there is too much relevant information to be digested successfully in the time available for making a decision, so a decision-maker will develop non-rational devices to help limit the options and inputs.

bureau originating with the French word for a multi-compartmented office desk, subsequently morphed into meaning a governmental office, the bureau is a functional unit of government, and a key component of the bureaucracy.

bureaucracy the collective term of the civil service, organized along bureaucratic principles, such as those employed by Cardinal Richelieu in the 17th century in France, and later defined by Max Weber, including a system of fixed jurisdictions, enumerated tasks and duties, explicit rules and procedures, a hierarchical system, delegation of authority with supervised span of control, and career officials (the bureaucrats).

bureaucrat an official of a bureaucracy, a civil servant hired and employed under the criteria for a bureaucracy.

CALEA the Commission on Accreditation for Law Enforcement Agencies, Inc., was established in 1979 as the primary organization credentialing (accrediting) law enforcement agencies; website at http://www.calea.org/.

CPM the critical path method, a planning approach similar to PERT, which depicts time graphically, as an aid to planning and project management in which both time and effort are depicted graphically, and in which the sequence of events which will determine the total time required for a complex project is indicated.

capital budget in accounting practice, that part of an organizational budget used for major facilities, buildings, infrastructure, and similar expenditures.

caps in accounting practice, upper limits placed on certain categories of spending.

captain a military rank borrowed by police and corrections agencies to identify a managerial position with major supervisory authority. A mid-level manager in a larger police or correctional hierarchy.

career a long-term line of employment, a chosen profession, or a path from an entry-level position rising upward into the higher ranks of one's occupation.

caveat a pre-stated condition in an agreement; an exception, qualification, or advanced clarification of a proposed relationship; or a warning or limitation on whom may have access to information, resources, or other agency assets.

chain of command in a hierarchal system, the formal channel for giving orders and supervising, also along which formal communications move both up and down. A series of hierarchal positions or ranks, one reporting to the next one higher, in sequence so that every individual is connected somewhere between the apex of the agency and its base via one single, unitary path.

change agent a person who brings about significant change within the organization; often one of the duties of a manager.

check-off in accounting practice, as a noun, an item on a tax or other form which is to be marked so that a deduction or transfer of is authorized. See also subscription.

chief a term commonly used for the chief executive officer or top manager of a law enforcement agency; the person in the organization with the highest rank or position of authority.

cipher a code, usually using some form of letter or number substitution; in a more general meaning, the practice of encrypting sensitive organizational information, now most often via some form of computer encryption software.

civil servant a public employee, functionary, or official whose duties involve serving the interests of the public; usually chosen via civil service rules involving examination, merit selection, probationary appointment, etc.

civil service law administrative legislation setting out the procedures for recruiting, hiring, assigning, promoting, and even dismissing an appointed public official; most often modeled on the Pendleton Act of 1883.

civilianization the use of non-sworn, civilian employees within police, emergency services, and correctional organizations to do tasks that do not require full police or correctional officer powers and authority.

clerk of court a functionary of the court system, either elected or appointed, to administer the court records, schedule cases for trial, collect fines and do the other administrative work of the courts.

closed shop a workplace, where a union has successfully bargained for it or state law requires it, that requires union membership as a condition of employment.

coercive change compulsory, involuntary change; compelled upon subordinates by their managers or higher officials.

cold case in police and prosecutorial jargon, a criminal investigation that has not been solved or prepared for trial in a timely manner, usually for lack of critical evidence, and which ceases to be investigated further.

collective bargaining a process in which a collective bargaining agent, often from a union or professional association, represents the employees *en masse* in negotiations with their employers in reaching agreements on wages, working conditions, or other conditions of employment.

collegiate academy in police and correctional training, a training approach that follows the methods of colleges, with a formal curriculum, classes, lectures, tests, etc., usually at a non-residential training center that functions like a college campus. Often these are conducted at actual community colleges and typically are commuter academies.

comb in the design of an organizational chart, a comb is a graphic representation of numerous subordinate units connected to a single supervisory unit, graphically resembling a comb.

communication adapter a mannerism that is not meant as communication by the sender, but can be translated by a perceptive observer into additional meaning; for example, an experienced investigator can detect deceit or concealment of information in a suspect or witness by various signs of nervousness and tension unintentionally revealed.

communication audience the intended recipients for any form of communication.

communication illustrator body language or gestures that are attached to other forms of communication intentionally, such as pointing, waving someone forward, nodding one's head to indicate yes or no, or raising one's hand to answer a question or to get a speaker's attention.

communication overload the problem of having far too much information input for an average manager or employee to review, digest, and act upon.

communication regulator a gesture such as nodding in agreement as someone else speaks, making encouraging or discouraging facial signals as someone is speaking, answering a question, looking upward or out a window when bored with the topic, and so on.

community corrections: various measures employed to bring about the reform and rehabilitation of an identified offender within the community, rather than via incarceration and imprisonment, including probation and parole.

community-oriented policing (COP) an approach to police-community relations that attempts to solve community problems with both input from and participation by the public in concert and cooperation with their police.

commuter academy in police and correctional training, a training location that lacks residences for the academy cadets. Such a non-residential training center often functions like a college campus, and often these are conducted at community colleges.

comparable worth derivative from the legal concept of "equal pay for equal work," the argument is that occupations requiring similar amounts of education and training, even if the actual work is not the same, ought to receive similar salaries. The argument does not accept the validity of market forces in determining wages.

compartmentalization in security and intelligence work, the selective denial of information or access to those lacking a "need to know," useful in reducing the number of individuals who have access to sensitive information, and thus limiting the likelihood of leaks and loss of information.

compensation the total package of wages and benefits a worker lawfully receives from his or her employment.

CompStat an abbreviation for computer statistics or comparative statistics (both are correct, based on the context), best known from the widely emulated New York City Police Department accountability process, which uses real-time information and current statistical data to enhance both managerial decision-making and evaluation.

conflict theorist in the social sciences, a person holding the perspective that our social institutions and laws are inherently coercive, the imposition of the will of the few with power against the wishes and best interests of those with little or no power.

consideration deliberate thought and reflection; in law also, something offered in exchange for something desired in return.

contingency theory an approach to leadership and decision-making that advocates decisions and decision-making procedures that are highly flexible and adaptive to changing situations. See situational leadership.

continuing education study undertaken after one has secured professional employment, usually as a condition for continued employment. For example, to retain membership in the state bar association, lawyers must take additional courses in new legislation, procedures, and court rulings after admission.

contracting process the managerial duty, following legal or regulatory procedures, of acquiring equipment, facilities or resources for the agency.

co-optation (co-opting) to take an idea from another, often an opponent, for one's own use; to use the criticism of others by employing it in revised programs; to win over opposition via assimilation into the dominant group.

cost-benefit analysis an analysis of the effectiveness of different decision alternatives to determine in which the benefits best outweigh the costs; this pattern of analysis separates the whole of a project into its constituent parts in order to calculate the costs and advantages of each of these parts.

court the building, chamber, or meeting room in which such cases in law are heard and determined; as a metaphor in the plural, the courts, that part of the criminal justice system dedicated to adjudication.

court costs fees attached to judicial decisions to help collection the costs of holding trials from one or both of the principles to the case; typically in a criminal proceeding the one found guilty is assessed court costs; in a civil proceeding the judge assesses court costs as part of the decision of the case.

court recorder: an administrative employee of the courts whose duty is to transcribe what is said during a court hearing or trial; see also **stenography/stenographer**.

court reporter: a term having two commonly encountered meanings, one synonymous with **court recorder** or **stenographer**, and the second referring to a journalist assigned to report on the courts.

credentialism in bureaucracy and in social life, an emphasis on earned diplomas or degrees in qualifying for employment or conferring social status.

critical path on a PERT chart, the sequence of events that will determine the time required for a complex project. See also CPM.

cyclic change pattern of change in which there is an oscillation, a regular, recurring rising and falling, as in a sine curve in mathematics, with a consistent periodicity.

deadly force in police and correctional work officers are entitled by law to take human lives without prior judicial review of their decisions. This exercise of discretion will be reviewed after the fact, but having taken a life, it cannot be reversed.

decentralization the delegation of powers and authority from a central source to subordinate or independent units or individuals.

decision process models also known as decision trees, these provide a formal structure for making decisions, often with either/or or multiple-choice options at key decision points, which are linked in sequence from left to right. Decisions, events, and end results are connected by branching lines. The result is a branching structure with the starting point or root to the left and various optional choices split off to the right, so that it resembles a horizontal tree branch.

decision trees see **decision process models** above.

decoding in communication theory the activity of the recipient of the message in attempting to interpret the meaning of the transmission.

defense counsel in criminal procedure the official, either an attorney in private practice or an employee of a public defender's office, who represents a suspect or an accused as a criminal case develops, especially in court, but also while a suspect is in pre-trial custody or being interrogated.

delegation as a process, the act of assigning one's powers or authority to a subordinate (delegating), and the status of power or authority being delegated.

Delphi Method decision-making process in which a team of experts are engaged to offer experienced opinions or recommendations to a decision-maker via a process of questioning, comparing answers, and ranking options. The Delphi Method was developed by the RAND Corporation for the U.S. Department of Defense.

democratic/democratic leader a leadership style and leader who actively seeks the input of subordinates, co-workers, and colleagues in making decisions or in taking actions, with decisions influenced by their preferences.

department distinct, specialized division of a larger organization, an administrative division of any large governmental agency; also one of the executive divisions of the federal government of the United States, headed by a cabinet officer.

depreciation in accounting practice, the decrease in value, because of age, normal wear, or evolving market conditions; an allowance or factor in an agency's fiscal records made for a loss in value of organizational property.

deputy a person appointed or empowered to act for another; an assistant having the full authority of a superior in the absence of that; also a deputy to the sheriff, clerk of court, or other criminal justice official who is hired to act on behalf of that elected official.

detailed borrowed from military jargon, this is the temporary reassignment of a unit, team, or key individual from its normal hierarchy to another command hierarchy for some specialized purpose.

deterrence any action that serves to deter or discourage criminal actions. A principle aim of sentencing, punishment, and corrections of offenders to keep them from further offending (specific deterrence);

also serves as a warning to discourage those who might be considering criminal offending (general deterrence).

detective a police official or private investigator whose specialty is the investigation of a crime or other suspicious event in order to determine the facts of such a case. See investigator.

director a top manager or chief executive officer of an organization; in the federal government of the United States, the appointed leader of an executive agency below the cabinet level, as in the Director of Central Intelligence, or the Director of the FBI.

discretion the delegated power to decide responsibly on behalf of one's agency; the authority and freedom to act or exercise judgment on one's own and to act as one sees fit.

distortion in communications theory, the changes in meaning or comprehension that occur in a message between the transmission form the source to the interpretation by the recipient.

diversion in accounting practice, the shifting of funds from the budget of one agency or program to another by a supervising authority.

diversion in criminal justice practice, the policy and practice of resolving criminal and juvenile delinquency cases outside the formal procedures of arrest, trial, conviction, and sentencing. A case may be diverted by the police, a prosecutor, or a judge when alternative remedies are employed, such as restitution or treatment.

diversity heterogeneity in the composition of the workforce, having employees selected from a wide range of ethnical, racial, social, class, and community interests.

division a unit within a larger organization, an administrative element of a department or agency.

division of labor the specialization of cooperative labor in coordinated, specific, allocated tasks, and roles, intended to increase the overall productivity of labor.functional – those divisions of labor based on the functions performed. *Temporal* – those divisions of labor based on the time that the functions are performed. *Spatial* – those divisions of labored based on the location or space where those functions are performed.

document security the procedures established for the protection of the content of files or other documentation generated or possessed by an agency from unauthorized access or disclosure.

documentation the records and files of a bureaucracy; recording the official activities of the agency.

EEO Equal Employment Opportunity.

EEOC Equal Employment Opportunity Commission.

economies of scale there is efficiency to be gained by doing things on a larger scale, so this refers to the decreased cost per unit as output increases. The initial investment of capital or any resource is spread over an increased number of units, and therefore, cost per unit is reduced. For example, combining 9-1-1 dispatching services in a city for police, fire, and rescue is far more economical than providing separate dispatch services for each.

egalitarianism a philosophical ideal that advocates one form or another of full equality, be it of opportunity, distribution, or result, for all participants in a political, economic, or social system.

election a method for making a group decision by allocating each participant (voter) equal say in process and going with the plurality or majority; also a selection that each individual can make for himself or herself. For example, the chief says that police officers may "elect" to carry either pepper spray or a Taser.

emblem in symbolic communication via a sign, badge, logo, or similar item, or hand sign, gesture, or salute that is a distinctive attribute of the agency, organization, or profession, and has clear meaning within that group.

employee a person hired by and in the employ of an agency or organization.

employee classification a scientific approach to the description of positions in an organization, defining which are managerial, which are labor, which require specialized skills and licenses, etc., and which defines which are "exempt" and which are covered by the protections of various personnel laws and policies.

emulative change demonstrating change by example; for example, showing co-workers new ways of performing their duties by demonstration of new methods and techniques.

encoding in communication theory, the activity of the person composing a message so that the recipient of the message is able to interpret the meaning of the transmission successfully. Encoding involves the selection of the medium of communication as well as the words chosen for it.

encryption in document security, the use of codes or computer algorithms to disguise the actual meaning of a transmitted message from all but the intended receivers.

encumbering in accounting practice, the commitment of funds for an anticipated expense, such as an order placed for new equipment which must be paid for upon delivery.

endorser in personnel evaluation, usually the next manager in the chain-of-command is designated as the "endorser," and his or her responsibility is to see that the personnel evaluation is timely, reasonable, and appropriate.

equality of opportunity an approach based on the idea of equal treatment and respect for all, applied in personnel matters, intended to provide employment and advancement opportunities, via practices and measures taken by organizations to ensure fairness.

equality of result measuring success in affirmative action or other programs by measuring the end results in preference to procedures or equality of opportunity

ethnic bias prejudice, either favorable or unfavorable, based on ethnic identity; giving preference to or placing disadvantages in the way of persons from specific ethnic groups on that basis.

evaluator in personnel evaluation, the person who prepares an evaluation of an employee, usually that employee's immediate supervisor.

event in CPM or PERT, the concluding point of an activity, usually understood as the completion of that activity.

exempt employee in personnel classification, an employee who is not protected under the provisions of the Fair Labor Standards Act (FLSA), usually on contract and paid a fixed salary, and those classified as managerial employees.

excessive force that physical force or constraint used by police or corrections officers which exceeds the reasonable minimum most likely needed to achieve a lawful enforcement or custodial purpose. While it need not match the level of resistance, it should be greatly out of proportion to that resistance.

executive the top managerial position in an organization, or the members of the organizational apex.

expendables in accounting practice, those items that may be considered used up once they are issued, and therefore are not accountable after their allocation. Pens, paper, light bulbs, staples, and the like often are classified in this way.

FOUO in document security, this identifies information that is intended "for official use only."

FTO field training officer, a veteran officer with the additional duties for mentoring a new officer, used in both law enforcement and corrections organizations. See OJT.

failure to train liability in civil law, a category of litigation based on the legal theory that a public agency such as a police department or correctional agency, has an affirmative duty to train its employees properly, and its failure to do so creates its liability for lawsuits.

false signal in communications theory, a message intended to be deceptive or to conceal one's actual meaning, emotion, or intention. Maintaining a calm demeanor in a crisis when actually upset is an example of a positive application of a false signal. Lying is a negative one, and maintaining a "poker face" is a neutral one.

felicific calculus a term used by Jeremy Bentham to describe the rational process whereby an individual decides on a course of action; an integral part of utilitarian reasoning, it is quite similar to cost-benefit analysis done at an individual level. See also hedonistic calculus.

filtering in communications theory, the process, intentional or inadvertent, whereby one selectively hears or comprehends only part of a larger or more complex message; one of the major problems in organizational communications.

fines and forfeitures collections from those convicted of criminal or regulatory offenses taken as part of the sentence; a fine is in the form of money assessed as a penalty and a forfeiture is a confiscation of property or assets.

firewall in computer applications and security, a system utilized to enforce access control between network entities. The firewall consists of a pair of mechanisms: the first exists only to block traffic and the second one exists to permit traffic. This allows users inside the organization, protected by the firewall, to access information on the outside while preventing people on the outside from getting into the user's system.

fitness of character a personnel doctrine dating to the times of Thomas Jefferson which expects that a prospective public servant will possess a high standard of personal morality, ethics and previous achievement, including good education, patriotism, loyalty to the nation, and a good family background.

fixed shifts defined periods of work, usually between eight and twelve hours in duration, which are the same from week-to-week and month-to-month, not changing or rotating. See also rotating shifts.

float time in PERT and CPM, this is the amount of time available for the performance of an activity that will not delay the completion of the overall project, although it might delay follower events not on the critical path. See also free float and interfering float.

following [or follower] event in CPM or PERT, the next event in a sequence; one that must come after the completion of the one preceding it.

forecasting predicting likely future events based on the knowledge of past trends and an understanding of patterns of change.

free float in PERT and CPM, this is the amount of time available for the performance of an activity that will not delay the completion of other activities or the overall project.

fully qualified in civil service practice, a category of prospective candidates for an office who meet all of the necessary criteria for the position for which the candidate is being considered.

functionary a person who carries out specific functions and roles in an organization, a person acting in an official capacity, such as for a government; an official or other person invested with a government office.

futurist a futurologist, one who undertakes the scientific study of the future, making informed predictions and forecasts based on change patterns and past trends.

futuristics the techniques of prediction of the future, based on patterns of change and the study of previous trends.

futurologist a futurist, one who undertakes the scientific study of the future, making informed predictions and forecasts based on change patterns and past trends.

futurology the scientific study of the future based on analysis of past trends, using the techniques of futuristics.

GED the general education development certificate is the equivalent of the high school diploma for public employment purposes.

Gantt Chart developed by Henry L. Gantt (1861-1919), it is a form of bar chart in which each task is given a horizontal line scaled to reflect how long that task should require, as an aid to planning and project management. Time and effort thus are depicted graphically.

grapevine slang for informal communications networks within an organization that spread gossip, rumors, news, and advanced information among the workforce.

grievance a complaint, usually in the context of personnel actions, that an employee has a lawful right to make, following organizational procedures. A grievance can be filed in cases of unfavorable personnel actions, such as non-selection for promotions or better assignments, transfer to undesirable assignments, and in cases of unfavorable evaluations.

harassment a form of discrimination in violation of the Civil Rights Act of 1964; can include unwelcome verbal or physical conduct based on race, color, religion, national origin, age, disability, sex, or sexual orientation, even when the offending behavior is not of a sexual nature, and including same-gender harassment and gender identity harassment, or retaliation. The conduct need only create a hostile work environment or result in a tangible, disadvantageous change in an employee's employment status, assignments, or benefits.

harmonogram/harmonograf a graphic representation of time and effort, developed by the Polish engineer Karol Adamiecki (1866-1933), as a precursor to the Gantt Chart, as an aid to planning and project management.

Hawthorne Studies a series of empirical studies conducted in the 1930s that originally sought to evaluate workplace innovations, but discovered the existence of informal but powerful workplace norms that could offset and even cancel out technological and managerial innovations. The study of these norms led to the development of the Human Relations School of management.

hedonistic calculus a term used by Jeremy Bentham to describe the rational process whereby an individual decides on a course of action; an integral part of utilitarian reasoning, it is quite similar to cost-benefit analysis done at an individual level. See also **felicific calculus**.

Human Relations School an approach to the study of management drawing on the findings of the Hawthorne Studies, leading to an emphasis on worker motivation, correction of employment mental hygiene problems, and greater involvement of the worker in organizational decision-making, and policy formation.

hierarchy a feature of modern bureaucracies; an arrangement of people, offices, grades, or classes, in a ranked order, connected to one another via a system of supervisors and subordinates.

hierarchy of human needs a management model and theory proposed by Abraham Maslow, which sought to understand employee motivation by recognizing employees' unmet human needs and finding creative and innovative ways of satisfying them while advancing the interests of the organization at the same time. Maslow saw those needs falling into five broad categories, with physiological needs being the most basic, followed by safety, affiliational, achievement, and self-actualization needs.

hygiene factors in the "Motivator-Hygiene" system of Frederick Herzberg (1923–2000), dissatisfaction is primarily the result of hygiene factors, those features of the work such as pay and benefits, company policy, relationships with co-workers and supervisors, the physical environment, status, and job security. Their presence has little effect on long-term satisfaction, but their absence or insufficiency is the cause of employee dissatisfaction.

ideal type a concept derived from the ideas of Max Weber that attempts to describe a complex social phenomenon in terms of its most likely and most distinctive attributes, components, and features. While actual cases of the phenomenon may not possess all of these attributes, and certainly will contain other features as well, if they are to fit into the category of the ideal type, they will possess most of the defined diagnostic attributes.

incremental budget a traditional approach to preparing a budget in which the prior budget and expenditure records are examined and become the basis of the next budget. Minor increases or decreases reflect the prior patterns and known or anticipated changes, such as increased postal rates or rising fuel costs.

indoctrination instruction in a doctrine, principle, or value set in the workplace intended to convey a specific point of view and identification with the work group.

inertia in organizations, retaining a steady-state condition, with regard to effort and action, inactivity showing little initiative, and offering passive resistance to change.

inference in the semantic system proposed by S. I. Hayakawa, an inference is a statement about the unknown that is based upon that which is known; a conclusion. It stands in contrast to a report and a judgment.

influence associated with power, the ability to produce an effect without apparent exertion of force or direct exercise of command.

information security (INFOSEC) practices intended to protect information and information systems from unauthorized access and disclosure, misuse, disruption, modification, damage or destruction. Related to both document and computer security practices, its aim is the protection of proprietary, sensitive and classified information.

initiating structures in the discussion of leadership traits, those factors defining and structuring the leadership role; identifies such things as active or passive approaches to planning, directing, and scheduling work activities.

inspector a police and civil service rank or title reflecting the role of its holder, the inspection of parts of the organization for compliance with proper practices and procedures. In some organizations inspectors are middle-level supervisors and managers. In other cases, they are organizational specialists within internal affairs, internal investigations, inspections, or ombudsmen units.

interactional change such change arises from the normal interaction of people in social relationships, includes mutual goal setting, equal power distribution, but no conscious deliberation. See influence.

interfering float in PERT and CPM this is the amount of time available for the performance of an activity within the overall project, but such that any delay in completing that activity will delay the completion of other activities or the overall project.

investigator a police official or private detective whose specialty is the investigation of a crime or other suspicious event in order to determine the facts of such a case. See detective.

Jacksonian egalitarianism referring to President Andrew Jackson, a viewpoint that carried the political value of equality under the law a step further, by assuming equal potential to perform well in public service, given equal education and employment opportunity.

jail a short-term confinement facility, used primarily for pre-trial detentions, but also used for short sentences to incarceration, usually managed by a county or city, often under the supervision of a sheriff. Spelled "gaol" in British English.

jargon in linguistics and communications, the technical terminology or workplace idioms of a work group, often characterized by obscure, pretentious language or specialized meanings for otherwise conventional words and the excessive use of abbreviations that only insiders would understand in lieu of the more comprehensible full words.

Jefferson ideal referring to President Thomas Jefferson, a viewpoint that incorporated the concepts of *noblisse oblige* and fitness of character into the criteria for a civil servant, who was indeed a public servant, and not an overseer of the citizenry.

job description in personnel practices, the objective, scientifically developed statement of the essential principle and regular duties of the incumbent in an office.

judge an official or functionary of the courts, having the responsibility for rendering legal opinions and judgments in an adjudicary hearing or trial.

judgment in the semantic system proposed by S. I. Hayakawa, a statement that conveys only an opinion and thus says little about the matter being discussed, but instead informs us of the values of the speaker or writer. It is contrasted with a report and an inference.

jurisdiction in the law, the power, right, or authority to interpret and apply the authority of a sovereign power to govern or legislate, the power or right to exercise authority under the law, or the control one may exercise within the geographical limits or territory wherein which such authority may be exercised. Agencies in the criminal justice system have both jurisdiction "under"—that is under the authority given in the laws of some governing entity, and "over," a geographical entity (city, county, state, or nation) or a particular activity or enterprise (drugs, guns, taxable income, etc.).

justice as a philosophical concept, it may be defined in terms of equality, that all should be treated alike, or in terms of equity, that people should receive benefits in proportion to what they contributed. Others focus on the due process of justice as fairness; if all procedures are followed correctly, then the process is fair and just. It also is the adjective that helps identify all those components of the political system associated with law enforcement, adjudication, treatment, and punishment of offenders, as in "the justice system."

justice of the peace a lower court judicial official; see also **magistrate**.

juvenile justice system that part of the criminal justice system having special criteria when dealing with juvenile suspects, offenders, or victims; usually involving custodial, treatment, adjudication, and supervisory arrangement, similar to but separate from those intended for adult.

kinesics in communications theory, the use of gestures of the body or various motions to convey additional messages or information.

laissez-faire/laissez-faire **leader** from the French for "to allow to act," a leader and leadership style that gives subordinates, co-workers, and colleagues great freedom to make decisions and pursue their responsibilities with little obvious direction and supervision.

LEAA the Law Enforcement Assistance Administration, an agency once existing within the U.S. Department of Justice, created under the authority of Omnibus Crime Control and Safe Streets Act of 1968, to oversee innovative federal crime control programs, administer grants to states and localities, conduct research, and collect useful crime data; functioning until 1982, with many of its functions shifted to the National Institute of Justice (NIJ), starting in 1979.

leadership continuum the range of leadership styles available (from autocratic, to authoritarian, to democratic to *laissez-faire*); as an aspect of situational leadership, the manager selects a leadership style from this range of options according to the situation and the manager's best judgment.

LEEP the Law Enforcement Education Program of the LEAA, which provided seed grants to create criminal justice education programs in colleges and universities, and to fund the college tuition of serving criminal justice practitioners in the 1970s.

Leader Behavior Descriptive Questionnaire (LBQD) this survey provides a work group the opportunity to describe the behavior of the leader of any organization, as long as the subordinates routinely have observed their leader in action. It was developed by the Ohio State Leadership Studies Office, then directed by Dr. Carroll L. Shartle.

leading [or leader] event in CPM or PERT the preceding event in a sequence; one that must be completed before the one following it.

lieutenant a military rank that also is widely used in police and correctional organizations for a middle-level manager, usually immediately above a first-line supervisor. It's usual insigne is a single brass or silver bar worn on the shirt collar or shoulder epaulets.

line item in budgeting, a category into which funds are assigned, such as postage, salaries, utilities, etc.

line loss in communications, the problem of information being lost or distorted, occurring as a message is passed from its point of origin along a lengthy communications chain, as is found is a multi-tiered hierarchal organization.

linking pin in communications, that person or unit in the organization that provides the communications connection among participant in a communications network; also called a linchpin.

LODESTAR a mnemonic device employed in this book to identify the key responsibilities of a contemporary manager: leading, organizing, deciding, evaluating, staffing, training, allocating, and reporting.

MBO Management by Objectives. A managerial process first popularized by Peter Drucker that sets objectives for the employee or the work team, which must be SMART (specific, measurable, achievable, relevant, and time-specific), and which keep work effort focused on the mission and goals of the organization.

MPA Masters of Public Administration.

MSW Masters of Social Work.

magistrate a judicial official, also referred to as a justice of the peace in some jurisdictions, who may set bonds, issue warrants, and hear simple cases, usually involving only infractions and misdemeanors.

Malek Manual an unofficial set of instructions that appeared during the presidency of Richard Nixon, attributed to Frederic V. Malek, a guide to the political appointees under Nixon, which emphasized achieving managerial control by establishing political control and offering techniques designed to pressure or eliminate uncooperative civil servants in a quasi-legal manner. The techniques proposed all were legal, but were not originally designed with the intention of stripping away civil service protections from federal workers.

malware computer software designed to damage or interfere in the operations of a computer; can included a computer virus or other programs that take over computer operations in the service of an unauthorized user.

management workshop a team-building exercise, similar to a management retreat; a brief period of time when a work team can come together to discuss agency needs, strategies, goals, objective, future projects, or plans.

manager a person in an organization whose principle duties are the control, supervision, and direction of the unit managed. In this book a manager is a person whose primary duties are found within the LODESTAR functions, rather than the actual performance of the mission, assigned tasks, and labor of the organization.

marshal a traditional law enforcement office, originally having both civil and military functions, but which now is used to describe both local and federal law enforcement officers.

media in mass communications jargon, these are the various forms of communications available to disseminate news, information, and entertainment, including, but not limited to, the print press, radio, television, cinema, the Internet, and social networking; important as management communications tools.

merit selection under civil service procedures, the rules that govern hiring, promotion, and assignment are supposed to be based on objective, work-related criteria based on the competitive merit of candidates for positions in a public service organization. Often merit is determined by competitive examination or the acquisition of essential licenses and credentials.

middle-level manager supervisory personnel under the apex or executive level of the organizational hierarchy, usually those above the first-line supervisors, who support the central mission of the agency but do not participate in the actual labor or output of the agency.

middle line in the organizational system of Henry Mintzberg, there are five basic parts of the modern organization, and the middle line is one of these; the middle-level managers responsible for supervision within the organization in support of the central mission of the agency.

Missouri Plan a procedure of the selection of judges, whereby a bipartisan commission recommends judicial nominees to the governor or other appointing authority, and if that recommendation is accepted, the judge is appointed to the office until the time of the next elections, at which time the voters opt to retain or remove the judge in a special retention election. There are no opponents challenging the sitting judges in theses retention election.

motivation factors in the "Motivator-Hygiene" system of Frederick Herzberg (1923–2000), workplace satisfaction is primarily the result of motivational factors, those features of the work such as challenging work, recognition, and responsibility, which can give employment a positive nature, and thus be used to encourage more productivity and employee morale – hence motivation.

National Crime Victimization Survey (NCVS) a recurring, federal government–sponsored, nationwide telephonic survey that asks those contacted about their recent experiences as possible victims of crime.

NIJ the National Institute of Justice, created by the Justice System Improvement Act of 1979, replacing and continuing many of the research functions of the LEAA.

NGO a non-governmental organization.

network analysis the application of systems approach to planning complex activities, associated with PERT and CPM, indicated by graphic illustrations of interconnected tasks and activities.

noblisse oblige French term literally meaning the obligations of the nobility, referring to the greater responsibilities of those more fortunate socially, politically, and economically.

nominal group technique a form of group decision-making in which a team of experienced employees are engaged to offer experienced opinions or recommendations to a decision-maker via a process of questioning, comparing answers, and ranking options.

non- exempt employee in personnel classification, an employee who is protected under the provisions of the Fair Labor Standards Act (FLSA), usually paid an hourly wage, and typically not part of the management of the organization.

non-lethal weapons in law enforcement and corrections, tools that can be used to control and subdue persons under arrest or in custody who are resisting their custodians or seeking to escape without high risk of death or serious permanent injury.

non-merit selection the hiring of public service employees by criteria other than those of strict competitive merit, such as political patronage, nepotism, or other criteria not part of a civil service system.

OFCCP Office of Federal Contract Compliance Programs

occupational socialization the process of learning the attitudes and practices associated with one's employment, including those skills acquired via formal training and informal peer-group workplace relationships.

office a position of trust and responsibility in a government agency, whose holder, an officer, is invested with the authority to act on behalf of the agency.

officer a person who occupies a position of trust and responsibility as an employee of a government agency, invested with the authority to act on behalf of the agency. See also official and functionary.

official a person holding an office in an organization, with specific responsibilities, authorities and powers bestowed by that organization.

on-the-job (OJT) training a method of training new employees by pairing them with veteran members of the organization, who teach them work skills by example and by mentoring. See FTO.

operating core in the organizational system of Henry Mintzberg, there are five basic parts of the modern organization, and the operating core usually is the largest of these; usually the "labor" element of the agency, comprising those employees who carry out the duties that are the central mission of the agency.

operational budget that part of an agency budget used to sustain operations, and not used for salaries or capital expenditures. See also capital budget.

operational control borrowed from military jargon, this is the delegation of authority for specific major activities (the operations) from one supervisory entity to another for the duration of such activities. For example, a multi-jurisdictional police task force may contain police investigators from several police agencies, all placed under the command and control of one of those participating agencies for the duration of the mission.

operational security (OPSEC) procedures of an agency intended to identify critical and sensitive information, facilities, or assets essential to the successful conduct of "operations," the major activities of an agency; for example, a police department planning a major "sting" will want to protect its plans, its officers, its chosen locations, and the identities of its "targets" until the sting is successfully concluded.

optimum legibility formula in written or spoken speech, a series of rules for maximizing the understandability of the message.

organizational development (OD) in planning and achieving planned change, the complex process of improving an organization's capacity to perform its missions and sustain itself in doing so. As developed by Warren Bennis and others, it is a managerial strategy for changing attitudes, basic beliefs, values, and structures to achieve greater productivity and efficiency.

oscillating change pattern one of the three major patterns to change, in which the frequency of some phenomenon will rise and fall cyclically, usually with a uniform amplitude and periodicity; as in a sine curve in mathematics.

over-compartmentalization in security matters, a common problem whereby too few people are given access to controlled or classified information, so that they do not have the intelligence upon which to make correct decisions.

PERF Police Executive Research Forum, a non-governmental organization (NGO) formed in 1976 by the leaders of several larger police agencies, dedicated to working with public officials, scholars, and researchers to innovate and improve policing; website at http://www.policeforum.org/.

pace of speech in linguistic analysis of spoken speech, the rate of word production, usually assuming that rapid speaking suggests tension while slower pace of speech reflects a more relaxed demeanor, and very slow and deliberate enunciation suggests anger, disrespect, or status inequality (as when speaking slowly to children).

paramilitary academy in police and correctional training, a training approach that follows the methods of the armed services ("boot camps" and military-style basic training) with uniforms worn, marching and drill common, strict discipline, and a heavy emphasis on skills mastery, usually at a residential training center.

parole in corrections, the conditional early release of an adjudicated offender from prison under some form of community supervision and with certain conditions that the offender obligated to obey while in this status.

parole officer the official, usually employed by the state correctional organization, who supervises those adjudicated offenders given conditional early release from prison.

pass-thru in accounting practice a pass-thru is the transfer of funds from one entity to another via an intermediate agency; for example, a jewelry store wanting more police protection will pay the police department a fee to assign to them an off-duty officer as a security guard – the money paid to the police department is passed thru the police department's budget and accounting office, and added to the officer's salary as supplemental overtime income.

path or pathway in PERT charts, the continuous linkage among successive events in the plan, leading from the inception to the conclusion. There can be multiple pathways, but the one that determines the amount of time the overall project will require is the "critical path" of the project.

patronage the system of awarding government positions, contracts, or other benefits under the control of a high public official to that official's friends and political allies, rather than by a strict merit system of allocation.

PayGo/pay-as-you-go budgeting in the federal system, as enacted under the 1990 Budget Enforcement Act, an agency is not allowed to spend funds beyond those they take in for certain functions; so that an increase in expenditures in one area would, therefore, require a "bill-payer" in another category to give up funds or some external rise in income to be developed. PAYGO sources can include the sales of government services or products; for example, the sales of FBI print versions of annual *Uniform Crime Reports* may generate revenue for the printing of additional copies of FBI documents for public distribution.

performance appraisal another term for an evaluation or assessment on an individual or work team.

performance budget in accounting practice, an approach to budgeting that provides for flexibility in an organizational budget related to the activities undertaken; for example, a prison may be allocated an amount per prisoner-day served, so that the budgeted amount available from the state will rise when the prison population rises, and decline when the prison population falls.

perk a benefit of one's employment beyond the basic salary, either authorized, such as a take-home automobile, or unauthorized and proscribed, such as free coffee and donuts given to a police officer.

PERT chart the graphic representation of the program evaluation review technique, similar to the critical path method, as an illustrative device used as an aid to planning and project management in which both time and effort are depicted graphically, identifying the "critical path" that indicates which sequence of events will determine the time required for a complex project.

personnel budget that part of the agency budget reserved for employee salaries, matching tax payments (FICA), health benefits, pension plans, etc.

physical plant the buildings and structures and their major components [i.e.: heating and cooling systems, installed telephone and computer wiring, security systems] used by the agency in its operations, which may be wholly owned or leased by the agency.

plum assignment a duty that has additional rewards or perks, either because of its location or other advantages to the official assigned to it, that most other assignments do not offer.

policy a plan of action or guide to decision-making procedures, set in place in anticipation of certain events or circumstances, in order to shape those events or circumstances toward favorable outcomes.

POSDCORB: a mnemonic device created by Luther Gulick in 1937 to identify key functions of a traditional scientific manager: planning, organizing, staffing, directing, coordinating, reporting, and budgeting.

practice a routine manner in which some activity is undertaken, similar to a procedure or rule for action.

premise an assumption, inference, or other basis upon which decisions will be made, assumed to be true or correct in its application in the case at hand.

primary/first order policy making those policies made by senior level managers, executives, and legislative bodies that create or dramatically alter goals and objectives for public agencies. For example, when a state legislature decided to do away with parole as a correctional option and implement "truth in sentencing" laws, this becomes the policy that state correctional managers and workers must implement.

prison a long-term punitive or correctional residence for adjudicated offenders, usually under state management, but occasionally contracted out to private vendors providing the same custodial services.

prison classification a practice of categorizing adjudicated offenders within the prison system by offense and offense severity, past criminal history, age, education, health issues, or other non-discriminatory organizing principles to provide better correctional supervision and rehabilitative services to them.

private police law enforcement and security personnel employed by non-governmental entities and organizations to provide them more protection than routinely available from public law enforcement agencies.

probation in correctional practice, the supervision of an adjudicated offender in the community, thus supplanting incarceration as a punitive or correctional option. One on probation (a probationer) usually is under the supervision of a probation officer, and is obligated to conform to certain rules of conduct and behavior while in this status.

probation officer the official, usually employed by the courts or the state correctional system, who supervises adjudicated offenders given supervised probation in the community.

problem analysis the process of thoroughly studying an issue or problem, so that one may determine how it originated, what factors are associated with it, which of these are causal versus coincidental or derivative, and what, therefore, can be done to correct, reduce, or eliminate it.

procedure a set of actions or steps that need to be followed to properly and legally to achieve a desired outcome or decision.

profession an occupation requiring extensive specialized education and skills, usually meeting credential requirements for licensing or certification.

professionalism a career orientation or vocational perspective which relies upon a philosophy, a body of technical knowledge, guidelines for practice, admission criteria and educational requirements, based upon that body of technical knowledge that all members of the profession are expected to acquire.

program evaluation review technique (PERT) A planning and evaluation methods employing a PERT Chart, a visual representation of the inter-related elements of complex major projects involving many inter-dependent components and tasks.

program planning budgeting system (PPBS) this approach to agency planning and budgeting divides the larger organization into the discrete units responsible for performing specific functions or operations; for example, preparing the budgets for a prison work-release program, in-prison industries, drug-counseling programs, etc. separate from each other and from other prison programs so that the planners and decision-makers can determine operational costs for each.

programmed decision decision-making formulae, usually using step-by-step procedures, or if-then decision-trees, to lead one to the correct decision.

proprietary information privately owned or classified (confidential, secret, and top secret) public data, formulae, and information on technologies and procedures, protected as if material property; this may include private financial information, operational plans, investigative information, trade secrets, commercial marketing information, or other forms of data that are of great value to the organization or individual generating them.

proration in budgeting, a uniform, across-the board percentage reduction in budget line items as a cost-reduction measure.

prosecutor the criminal justice official who brings criminal charges to court, prepares the cases against accused persons, and conducts the state's case during the trial. Trained as a lawyer, and known also as the city, county, circuit, or district attorney (DA), public solicitor, state's attorney, commonwealth's attorney, and other such titles, this official may be elected or appointed, according to state laws, to present the state's side in criminal actions.

public servant any person employed by a government operating under the Jeffersonian ideal, whose duties are to serve the interests of the public at large.

rater the supervisor whose duties include evaluating or assessing the performance of subordinates.

ratings in personnel practice, comparative scores given to individuals or work teams, usually on an interval or ordinal scale, to record their evaluations or assessments.

rational choice a model for decision-making, also known as rational choice theory and rational action theory; this is a utilitarian approach to decision-making that assumes the actor is rational and aware of the likely costs and consequences of decisions made and actions taken. In this view, the actor will seek to minimize cost or labor in favor of maximizing the returns, benefits, or rewards from the action.

rehabilitative ideal in corrections, the belief that the primary purpose of the corrective experience of an incarcerated offender is to change one's character and behavior for the better; often attributed to John Howard and Alexander Maconochie in British penology and later to Zebulon Brockway at Elmira State Reformatory in New York.

residential academy in some police and correctional training programs, the training is scheduled at a residential campus, where the trainees are removed from their homes and families briefly while enrolled in their studies; a form of total immersion in the sub-culture of the new occupation.

retreat a brief period away from the workplace in which a work team can come together to discuss agency needs, strategies, goals, objective, future projects, or plans, free from the interruptions of the job.

return on investment (ROI) also know as the rate of return, this is the ratio of income or value gained, usually per year, on an investment. In public service, where profit is not a primary motivation in implementing new ideas or installing new equipment, the cost-earnings ratio is not the key factor, as it is in business, but savings returned or major increases in productivity can be factored to assess the rate of return on any investment on new and improved technologies or practices.

right-to-work law legislation that restricts or prohibits union shop (closed shop) rules, thus permitting workers to be employed without having to join the union or pay union dues.

rise-plateau-crash change one of the three major patterns for change in which there is a rapid rise in the frequency of a phenomenon, followed by a leveling off (plateau), followed by a rapid decline when a new approach to that phenomenon becomes accepted; a common pattern in the rapid rise, continuation, and quick termination of technologies when newer and better technologies come along to replace them.

rotating shifts a cycle or template of changing hours or days for work assignments in agencies maintaining work days longer that that of the normal 8-hour work-day and/or requiring week-end staffing.

rotation plan in personnel assignments, a schedule that outlines in advance any shift changes for workers in organizations needing to maintain 24-7 coverage (police, jails, and prisons, for example), and does so with rotating shifts.

rule of three under the original civil service rules in the 1880s, it was the practice to identify the three individuals with the highest score on a civil service test (the three best qualified) and have the person or committee making the hiring decision select one of those three as the new hire. Some state and local government civil service systems still employ the rule of three.

running the numbers in accounting practice and some decision-making, the practice of determining the costs and benefits, or otherwise using quantification to determine the value of assets or resources or the cost-efficiency of certain decisions.

salvage value in accounting practice, the residual value of equipment or facilities no longer of use to an organization, and hence declared surplus and available for disposal sale outside the agency.

satisficing a term created by Herbert Simon, from "satisfying" and "sufficing", to capture the nature of decisions made in a pseudo-rational process in which a decision-maker settles on an immediate solution or makes a decision, not always the best rationally and objectively, which will be sufficient and will satisfy immediate needs.

scientific management an approach to managing organizations that is associated with the theories of Henri Fayol and Frederick Taylor, placing emphasis on careful empirical examination of labor, the development of job descriptions and task analysis studies for employees, formal training, and managerial supervision of the workers.

secondary/second order policy-making those policies made by agencies and managers to implement broader decisions and policies from higher authorities or the law.

secrecy agreement because of the confidential nature of the work, many people in the criminal justice system do, an employer can require that such employees sign a contractually binding agreement to make no disclosures of those kinds of information outside of the criminal justice system.

semantics in linguistics, the science of linguistics meanings; study of relationships between words, signs, and symbols and what they represent; interpreting the actual meaning of statements, words, sentences, texts, or other forms of language.

sequestering in accounting practice under which previously allocated funds or other resources are "frozen," so that the agency no longer is authorized to spend them. Sequesterization may be temporary, or may lead to the total reallocation of these funds back to the funding source.

shared vs. secret evaluation the organizational decision about letting employees see their periodic assessments and work appraisals; under some special circumstances, secret evaluations may be necessary, but generally sharing the results of an evaluation will be far more useful and productive for the organization and the employee.

sheriff the chief law enforcement officer for a county, usually an elected official, having very general law enforcement and civil administrative duties, including crime control, courtroom security, jail operations, service of civil papers, and many other duties.

shift or shift-work the assigned work hours for an employee within an organization that operates for extended work days (more than eight hours per working day) or continuously (24/7). Shifts may be either fixed or rotating.

silent system in American corrections, inspired by Quaker (Society of Friends) values favoring silent introspection, penitentiaries were created where incarcerated offenders were to reside and work in silence. Also known as the Pennsylvania system, it proved to be far more punitive than rehabilitative.

situational leadership/situational management an approach to leading that applies contingency theory to decision-making; advocating decisions and decision-making procedures that are highly flexible and adaptive to changing situations.

skills of leaders related to traits of leaders, the personal attributes and talents associated with successful leadership; in the 1950s many books and articles on leadership attempted to identify specific traits and skills that successful leaders had in common with one another. Most authorities agree that strong communication skills, technical skills, human relations skills, including the virtues of empathy, tolerance of ambiguity, and the ability to work within a team, and conceptual skills are essential leadership skills.

social networks and networking the practice of extending social or professional relationships among a web of individuals or organizations, also used to refer to complex sets of relationships between members of various social systems, from interpersonal to international organizations. The rise of computer technologies to support such expansive networks makes them into a managerial tool.

socialization in employment and training practice, the processes of adapting an individual to a new social group, organization, career, or other social activity; differing therefore from the political meaning of introducing governmental supervision, control, or ownership.

sociological jurisprudence an approach to the study and application of the law promoted by Roscoe Pound, which employed empirical sociological studies and social theories to help resolve legal issues and formulate laws.

span of control the number of individuals routinely supervised by a supervisor.

special agent-in-charge in many of the federal investigative agencies, the title of the investigative official having supervisory authority, usually over an entire office or a specific major investigation.

special distribution in accounting practice, an allocation of funds or resources under special or extraordinary circumstances; e.g.: providing officials supplemental funds when reassigning them to high-expenditure assignments, or providing officials specialized equipment to undertake duties not normally part of their job description.

spoils system a pejorative label assigned to any non-merit based system of governmental patronage appointment; first associated with the practice of President Andrew Jackson appointing only his political allies to government positions, but existing long before Jackson employed it.

standard operating procedures (SOPs) routine organizational practices, often set down as a set of rules to be followed under normal circumstances. SOPs can be overruled under unusual conditions when authorized by a supervisor or manager.

stenography/stenographer a system of shorthand writing, done by an administrative employee (the stenographer), usually in the courts (see also **court recorder**), whose duties involve either taking dictation or faithfully transcribing or recording testimony, motions, instructions, and other spoken words in a hearing or trial.

straight line change a model for change that assumes a steady rate over a fixed or projected period of time.

straight-line depreciation in accounting practice, the assessment of the declining value of an item spread out over a period of time, normally the expected life-time of a facility or a major piece of equipment. It is calculated by taking the purchase price of an asset, subtracting by the likely salvage value, and dividing by the anticipated number of years the asset reasonably can be expected to remain in service.

subscription in accounting practice, a voluntary or semi-voluntary contribution for a specified purpose; the agency collects funds to be transferred to another entity on behalf of the employee; e.g.: one's health insurance premiums or union dues are collected by the agency and transferred to the insurance company or union. Donations for special purposes also can be done by subscription, such as the federal tax check-off for funding political campaigns.

sufficing meeting the immediate needs or requirements of an action or a decision; being sufficient or equal to performing a specified task; to be enough for, but not necessarily the best or most efficient solution.

sunk cost in accounting practice, those funds historically invested in equipment, facilities, training, or practices that cannot be recovered, even if these are abandoned in favor of substitutes.

sunshine laws a general term for a variety of laws and regulations that make the practices, meeting, and records of public agencies open to public inspection.

supervision the practice of oversight over subordinate workers and the functions for which they are responsible.

supervisor an administrator or manager having subordinates reporting to him or her, these individuals under the direction of the supervisor and routinely evaluated by him or her.

supplemental appropriation in accounting practice, an allocation of additional funds outside of the normal budgetary-planning cycle. The agency is given more money for new operations or to fund operations that have become more costly; e.g.: in a period of rapidly rising fuel prices, an agency may be given additional funds to buy fuel.

support staff in the organizational system of Henry Mintzberg, there are five basic parts of the modern organization, and the support staff is one of these; the lower and mid-level clerical and administrative workers who perform duties that are ancillary to the central mission of the agency.

surplus in budgeting, an overabundance of assets, usually funds, that can be reallocated to other organizational needs.

symbolic management coming from Edgar Schein and building upon the Human Relations School assumptions of workplace norms governing the pace and quality of work, as part of the workplace culture, symbolic management refers to using the artifacts, values, and basic underlying assumptions of an organization that a manager can manipulate. Symbolic management includes creating interpretations of events in an organization, and employing the symbols of the organization, such as logos, flags, lapel pins, etc., that can be important to the management of the organization.

symbolic reward a perk or benefit having little monetary value, but providing great pride and satisfaction to the recipient; such as awards for employee of the quarter, plaques and trophies, medals, and other decorations given as commendations.

T-team or tiger team a small work group within a larger organization established to carry out a specified chore or task; this may be a plan, the implementation of a new procedure, the acquisition and application of new technologies, or any similar operation done on behalf of the larger organization; also known as a task force or ad hoc committee.

tactile communication communicating via touch or gesture to augment spoken words; gestures of reassurance, a pat on the back, and similar actions that accompany words, or occasionally take place of them to convey our feelings toward another.

task a discrete chore or duty assigned to a person or unit within the organization.

task analysis part of the planning process, wherein the planner or manager identifies the specific tasks that must be performed by an individual or work group; also used in preparing personnel training plans, work plans, and job descriptions.

task force a small work group within a larger organization established to carry out a specified chore or task; this may be a plan, the implementation of a new procedure, the acquisition and application of new technologies, or any similar operation done one behalf of the larger organization; also known as a "Tiger Team," an ad hoc committee, or T-team.

team a work group, usually temporary in nature, assembled to accomplish a specified task; see also **task force**.

technocratic change one of the varieties of change, driven or brought about by developing technological innovation; modern organizations have to adapt to the application of new technologies and techniques, or fall far behind in productivity or efficiency; imagine a police department today still not using computers and not collecting crime-scene DNA.

techo-structure in the organizational system of Henry Mintzberg, there are five basic parts of the modern organization, and techo-structure is one of these; the specialists in the higher technologies upon which the organization becomes dependent; e.g.: the computer support staff and others who maintain and solve problems related to the complex technologies employed by the agency.

Theory X a philosophy of management associated with the Type A Manager by Douglas McGregor; assuming that workers need to be directed, motivated, and controlled; that they are passive or resistant to organizational needs; will do as little as possible; and are self-centered and indifferent. Hence, the manager must find ways of compelling productive effort from them.

Theory Y a philosophy of management associated with the Type B Manager by Douglas McGregor; assuming that workers can motivate themselves to be productive, so the manager can count on support from the workforce, so that the essential role of the manager is to arrange working conditions and resources so that the workforce can best achieve both their personal goals and the organizational goals.

tonal cue in semantic analysis of spoken language, the tone of voice will reveal aspects of meaning that the words alone do not; such tonal cues will inform the listener of the fuller meaning of the spoken words. Various tonal variations are used, softer or louder annunciation, pace of the speech, and various inflections, to convey added meaning to the words.

training plan an organizational document outlining the specific topics on which members of the organization need to be trained, and scheduling the cycle of training, identifying the sources of trainers, and identifying the locations for training, and equipment or facilities needed to support the training.

traits of leaders personal attributes and personality characteristics associated with successful leadership; in the 1950s many books and articles on leadership attempted to identify specific traits that successful leaders had in common, but only with limited success and often with noteworthy exceptions; e.g.: leaders are tall (but Napoleon was not tall and he was an exceptional leader).

transformational leader a leader and manager who also is an innovator and change agent, with a clear vision of the changes to be attained within the organization.

turnover rate in personnel usage this refers to the percentage of the work-force departing and being replaced in a specified time-frame, usually annually. A high turnover rate often is taken as a measure of low morale or other personnel problems, while a low turnover rate suggests a contented work force.

Type A Manager the authoritarian, order-giver; Type A managers are more likely to decide autocratically and give orders, direct subordinates, and expect compliance to those orders; contrasted with Type B by Douglas McGregor.

Type B Manager the consensus-builder; Type B managers are more likely to make decisions democratically and enter into discussions with co-workers rather than issue orders (reciprocal communication and joint study of the issue).

UCR the Uniform Crime Reports, crime statistics compiled by the Federal Bureau of Investigation from local law enforcement agencies, and published annually as the publication *Crime in the United States*, and also available online at http://www.fbi.gov/publications.htm.

unfreezing and refreezing a model for explaining the process of organizational or social change, developed by Kurt Lewin to explain this social phenomenon; beginning with introducing the conviction that change is needed [the unfreezing], making the desired changes, and then institutionalizing the changed practices, reinforcing them in various ways until they become routine [the re-freezing].

unit of analysis in research methods, that which is being studied, and can refer to individuals, small work groups, or entire organizations.

user fee a charge assessed for using a public service or facility, such as a toll for driving on restricted access highways or a charge to camp in state parks, use public swimming pools, public parking, or to recover the cost of providing special services, such as police escorts for payrolls or security details.

union an association of workers with an occupation (e.g.: correctional officers) or an organization (e.g.: all employees of a specific organization) who unite to seek collective bargaining opportunities with their employers.

union shop by law or negotiation all persons in an organization or an occupation can be required to become members of the union representing that body of workers. This also is referred to as a "closed shop," in contrast to an "open shop," which has a union, but there is no requirement that the workers must join or pay dues to it.

utilitarianism a philosophy that asserts that the value of any thing or an action is determined by its utility (functional value), proposed as an ethical theory by Jeremy Bentham and James Mill, both of whom argued that that all public action and effort should be directed toward providing the greatest happiness for the greatest number of people; part of a rational-choice model for public decision-making.

value-added contribution (VAC) an expenditure for new equipment or training that can add significantly to the productivity of the organization or the work output of the newly trained staff, far beyond the direct cost of the item; i.e.: a new communications system that can make the entire agency more productive and can improve supervision, command, and control.

veterans preference a practice in selecting or promoting civil servants that mandates some form of preference for military service veterans, especially those who may have been disabled in some way as a result of combat injuries.

victim a person harmed or killed by another, or made to suffer from an act or condition imposed upon them by violence, stealth, theft, trick, swindle, or deception.

victimology a relatively new science within criminal justice and criminology that is focused on the identity, roles, relationships, and factors involved in being a victim of a crime, and the responses of the criminal justice system to them.

vital machines a term used by Robert Owen to accentuate the importance of skilled workers at the dawn of the industrial age. By analogy he pointed out that employers gave their valuable new machines a great deal of attention, maintenance, and care, so they ought to do the same for their equally valuable skilled employees.

vocation an occupation or calling for which one is especially suited or qualified; an inclination to undertake a certain kind of work, originally referring to a religious career; but now appropriate to the strong desire to pursue a life-long career in a specific area, such as policing, corrections, the law, juvenile justice, or providing services to victims.

warden the top executive manager in charge of a prison.

witness a person who can provide empirical evidence, such as an accurate account of something seen, heard, or experienced, to the police or prosecutor that is useful in developing a criminal or civil law case; in the law, the person who will testify under oath before a court about their knowledge.

working personality most frequently associated with policing via the contributions of Jerome Skolnick, the concept is that a police officer or other criminal justice official begins to acquire behavioral traits of assertiveness, cynicism, caution, distrust, etc., that he or she does not bring into the occupation but finds adaptive to the work of the organization. Such traits are not part of that officer's personality initially, but may become so over time; or may be put aside when not on the job by those who excel at "not bringing the work home" with them.

workplace harassment any workplace behavior or practice, official or casual, by supervisors, co-workers, or clients that results in the creation of a threatening, uncomfortable, or embarrassing situation for employees, often associated with their sex, race, religion, ethnicity, or other protected attributes.

zero-based budgeting (ZBB) one of the major approaches to agency budgeting, requiring that all expenses be re-justified for each new budgetary period, beginning with a zero base [no allocated funds], adding in for every activity to be undertaken by the agency, done in a priority order. ZBB expenses are therefore allocated to specific, prioritized functions, rather than just continuing activities from the prior budgeting period.

Index

Note: Page numbers in italics indicate boxes, figures, and tables.